Praise for Tim Newark

'Newark's beautifully written and thoroughly researched studies offer new information and penetrating insights on hitherto little-known chapters in the history of American organised crime'
— Robert Rockaway, author of *But He Was Good to His Mother*
'Tim Newark is a remarkably gifted storyteller'
— *The Scotsman*

Praise for Lucky Luciano

'Great detective work here. Tim Newark has uncovered fascinating new angles on the Lucky Luciano story and tells it well'
— John Dickie, author of *Cosa Nostra*
'A must for true-crime fans'
— *News of the World*
'The most balanced biography of a man who often claimed to be a victim, but had little thought for his own victims'
— BBC *History Magazine*

Praise for The Mafia at War

'The Mafia at War is a good example of how proper use of original sources can illuminate the truth and destroy historical myths'
— *Financial Times*
'Tim Newark's admirable study is a meticulous rebuttal of all that is sensationalised and misleading'
— BBC *History Magazine*
'Not only an expose of the Machiavellian behind-the-scenes machinations to ease Italy out of the war but a sobering, and even chilling, study in the realpolitik of war'
— *Sunday Telegraph*
'The victory of [*The Mafia at War*] is the depth the author brings to the subject'
— *New York Post*

Tim Newark is the author of the critically acclaimed *Lucky Luciano: Mafia Murderer and Secret Agent* and *The Mafia at War*. For 17 years editor of *Military Illustrated*, he is also the author of numerous military history volumes, including *Highlander*. He has worked as a TV scriptwriter and historical consultant, resulting in seven TV documentary series for BBC Worldwide and the History Channel, including the thirteen-part TV series *Hitler's Bodyguard*. He contributes political comment pieces to the *Daily Express, Telegraph,* and *Sunday Times*.

EMPIRE OF CRIME

ORGANISED CRIME IN THE BRITISH EMPIRE

TIM NEWARK

PEN & SWORD
HISTORY

First published in Great Britain in 2011 by
MAINSTREAM PUBLISHING company
and reprinted in 2017 by
Pen and Sword History
An imprint of Pen & Sword Books Limited
47 Church Street
Barnsley
South Yorkshire
S70 2AS

ISBN 978 1 52671 304 9

Printed and bound in the UK
by CPI Group (UK) Ltd, Croydon, CR0 4YY

Pen & Sword Books Limited incorporates the imprints of Atlas,
Archaeology, Aviation, Discovery, Family History, Fiction, History,
Maritime, Military, Military Classics, Politics, Select, Transport,
True Crime, Air World, Frontline Publishing, Leo Cooper,
Remember When, Seaforth Publishing, The Praetorian Press, Wharncliffe
Local History, Wharncliffe Transport,
Wharncliffe True Crime and White Owl.

For a complete list of Pen & Sword titles please contact
PEN & SWORD BOOKS LIMITED
47 Church Street, Barnsley, South Yorkshire, S70 2AS, England
E-mail: enquiries@pen-and-sword.co.uk
Website: www.pen-and-sword.co.uk

To all the colonial police officers who put their
lives on the line, doing the right thing

ACKNOWLEDGEMENTS

FOR THEIR HELP in the research of this book, I would like to thank the following individuals and institutions: the staff of the British National Archives, Kew; the British Library, King's Cross, India Office Library & Records, and Newspaper Library, Colindale; Liddel Hart Centre for Military Archives, King's College London; School of Oriental & African Studies, University of London; Federal Bureau of Investigation Records Management Division; James P. Quignel, Harry J. Anslinger Papers, Penn State University; Cliff Le Quelenec, HMS *Belfast* Association; National Malaya & Borneo Veterans Association UK; Mrs Hilary Drummond; Jim Prisk and Keith Lomas, Royal Hong Kong Police Association; Dr K.Y. Lam, curator of the Hong Kong Police Museum; D.S.P. Halal Ismail, curator of the Royal Malaysia Police Museum, Kuala Lumpur; Roderic Knowles, for memories of gold smuggling; Peter Newark, for his extensive crime and police photographic archive; historians Andrew Roberts, Ian Knight and James Morton, for their kind words and suggestions; special thanks to Chris Newark, for his good advice and extensive colonial history library.

CONTENTS

INTRODUCTION

'It is not the man who eats the opium, but the opium that eats the man.'

— Chinese Mandarin maxim

SOMETIMES THE BEST INTENTIONS CAN lead to the worst results. When Great Britain took the moral high ground and agreed to end its lucrative export of opium from Imperial India to China in 1908, it unleashed a century of criminality. Just as America's misguided Prohibition of alcohol made illicit fortunes for the Mafia, so organised crime within the British Empire grew rich on its trade in illegal narcotics in the twentieth century.

Victorian Prime Minister William Ewart Gladstone had predicted this would happen when he argued in Parliament against the abolition of the imperial trade in opium. 'An enormous contraband trade will grow,' he told well-meaning Liberal politicians. 'Does not my honourable Friend see that, supposing he could stop the growth of opium in the whole Indian peninsula, his measure would immensely stimulate the growth of it in China?'

This book is the first to reveal the full extent and variety of organised crime within the British Empire and how gangsters exploited its global trade routes to establish a new age of criminal networks that spanned the world. They even took the liberty of using the very weapons of imperial power – Her Majesty's Royal Navy – to smuggle drugs from continent to continent. HMS *Belfast* – now an iconic museum ship moored in the River Thames – was once packed with Triad narcotics from Hong Kong intended for distribution in America.

Illicit guns were smuggled along ancient trade routes made safe by the British Empire – through the Middle East, across the Persian Gulf, to Afghanistan and India. Most of these weapons were supplied by European arms manufacturers, greedy for profit, who did not care where the guns ended up. Some of the guns were even bought with money given by the Imperial Indian government to border tribes to ensure their loyalty. 'So that we not only supplied the tribesmen with arms of British manufacture,' concluded one cynical veteran of the North-West Frontier, 'but we gave them the money to buy them!'

The imperial prohibition of opium trading caused great tension between the government in London and its colonial governors, who had to deal with the messy outcome of these good intentions. Chinese refugees fleeing civil war in the mainland presented a major problem to Sir Cecil Clementi, Governor of Hong Kong in the 1920s. Faced with a shortfall of opium to meet the needs of thousands of new addicts, he knew that something dramatic had to be done. Rather than seeing the opium trade fall into the hands of criminal smugglers who had no incentive to control the consumption of opium, Sir Cecil took the unconventional initiative of becoming a major dealer himself.

In defiance of the British government's own anti-drugs stance, Sir Cecil organised the purchase of large quantities of opium directly from Persia to dump on his home market and put the smugglers out of business. He even entered into negotiations with other colonies to supply them with much-needed opium, too. It was an extraordinary experiment and Sir Cecil noted with delight the dramatic fall in opium-related crime in his own colony; but the Whitehall bureaucrats couldn't put up with this for long and demanded he cease dealing in the drug.

If Britain had handed a great gift to organised crime, it also took on the burden of pursuing the purveyors of this new evil. Principal among these innovative drugs-busting investigators was Russell Pasha, Commandant of the Cairo Police and founder of the Central Narcotics Intelligence Bureau. Seeing the damage caused by a new wave of opium-derived drugs, especially heroin, on the streets of the Egyptian capital, he set about pulling together evidence of a vast international network, linking East with West. His agents exposed the opium fields guarded by narcotics warlords and tracked down the corrupt pharmaceutical companies in Western Europe who were happy to sell thousands of kilos to ruthless master criminals.

With the coming of the Second World War and its aftermath, political pressures further complicated the world of organised crime within the British Empire. Japan funded its invading armies with profits from criminal enterprises, while anti-colonial movements blurred the line between terrorism, freedom fighting and racketeering. Gangsters aligned themselves with whichever party protected their crooked assets. Sometimes colonial policemen were drawn into the underworld and had doubts about whether they were really on the right side.

'I began to wonder if I was getting a kick out of my business,' said 22-year-old Inspector Drummond of his undercover battle against the Kenyan Mau Mau Rebels. 'I used to tell myself it was a nasty job that had to be done, that after all I was only doing my duty, and that the important thing was I should do it well. But did all of them have to die?'

In Hong Kong, Inspector Wallace agonised over the everyday corruption around him. 'I sometimes feel that it is all rather a bad dream,' he said. 'Even if I leave this colony penniless and in disgrace, at least I shall take my principles with me – and these are more precious to me than anything else.'

The story told in this book for the first time is one of high principles challenged by evil conspiracies, of moral crusaders tested by mobster realities. At the heart of it is an extraordinary global empire seeking a mission for good but derailed by criminal gangs and monstrous illegal profits. *Empire of Crime* is the dark underbelly of our colonial history.

Tim Newark

1

THE UNFORTUNATE MR HARTLEY

IT IS NOT A GOOD idea to take on the British Empire, especially when it has chosen to pursue the righteous path and correct past errors. John Hartley – Englishman, Freemason, Conservative, drug dealer – found himself in just this precarious situation on 6 April 1878.

Standing up in a court in Yokohama, Japan, Mr Hartley faced both Her Britannic Majesty and Motono Morimichi, Superintendent of Japanese Customs. They accused him of smuggling opium into Japan in contravention of the treaty between their two great countries. Hartley argued that the opium was purely for medicinal purposes, but the judge was unimpressed.

'I find that no opium can properly be called medicinal opium unless it contains at least six per cent morphia [morphine]. The evidence shows that the proportion of morphia in it falls far short of the standard.'

The judge admitted that there was some discrepancy between the tests on the sample opium by two different experts, but he felt that was beside the point.

'Not only do I find that the opium in question is not medical opium, I find that it is smoking opium,' he explained. 'The opium used in China for smoking is mostly Indian opium. The flavour of Indian opium, which renders it less palatable a medicine, renders it all the more palatable for smoking, and the absence of morphia, which makes ordinary Indian opium useless as a medicine, is no disadvantage of smoking, if it is not a distinct advantage.'

Hartley was found guilty of smuggling Indian-produced smoking opium into Japan, had his drugs confiscated and was fined $165. But Mr Hartley would not let it rest there. He was aggrieved at being publicly humiliated and losing what he considered his lawful business, thanks to a Japanese boycott of his goods. He demanded an appeal of the judgement. He was a legitimate trader of medical drugs, he insisted, but the judge refused to grant a rehearing of the case.

The following year, Hartley fell ill and blamed the stress caused by the Japanese government continuing to ban his drugs importation business for his poor health. He was losing money and credit and was advised to return home to England. In London, he had sealed samples of his Indian opium tested by the Pharmaceutical Society of Great Britain to prove they were of medical quality. They agreed that the samples contained more than the required amount of morphine.

Triumphantly, with this evidence in his luggage, Hartley took a succession of trains to the Italian port of Brindisi, where he caught a steamer to Alexandria in Egypt and then on to Bombay. Along the way, he continued his correspondence with various experts, building up his body of proof that his opium was high-grade medical Indian opium and not at all destined for some grubby smoking den. After four and a half months' travelling, he arrived back in Yokohama in March 1880.

Tragically for Mr Hartley, Her Majesty's chargé d'affaires was unimpressed by Hartley's tests and the testimonials from several experts. He would not help him contest the Japanese government's decision to boycott his business and claim back some recompense for his lost income. His health now took a further turn for the worse and he feared he was being poisoned by the Japanese government.

After just a week in Japan, he was sent back on the steamer *Malacca* on a voyage that took just under two months. He arrived home to more bad news. His father-in-law and brother-in-law refused to allow him access to his wife and children. His lack of money was the principal barrier, they said, and told him that the process of contesting the court judgement in Japan had unhinged him mentally. But Hartley's sense of injustice went beyond the loss of his family and sanity, and he continued to press on to clear his name.

In 1885, as Hartley was on the way to the Privy Council Office in London for public funds to pursue his case, he was arrested by a court bailiff. He was confined to Surrey County Prison in Wandsworth for two weeks for debt accrued by not paying a food bill for his wife.

In the meantime, Hartley's case had been seized upon by the Anti-

Opium Society and an MP stood up in the House of Commons to denounce Hartley as a drugs smuggler. Pamphlets quoting him as an example of the evil of the opium trade were distributed throughout London from the Egyptian Hall in Mansion House. If that wasn't bad enough for his reputation, stories critical of Hartley were carried across the Atlantic and appeared in US journals.

Further bad news for Mr Hartley came on 24 June 1886. He had asked for the British government to intervene on his behalf but, in response to a question asked in Parliament, the Under-Secretary of State for Foreign Affairs said: 'The case of Mr Hartley is well known to Her Majesty's Government . . . and my predecessor stated that successive Secretaries of State had arrived at the conclusion that Mr Hartley's case was not such as to justify diplomatic interference.'

In 1888, a full ten years after he had first appeared in court in Yokohama, Hartley was morosely wandering around the Bethnal Green Museum in London's East End when he saw a display of Indian medical opium. The samples contained less than the percentage of morphine required by the judge in Japan. Aha, he thought, I was right all along!

In 1890, he was back in Japan, making claims against the Japanese government for illegal acts. He accused them of singling him out for prosecution when German and Dutch merchants were allowed to import similar powdered opium. He claimed that the expert chosen by the Japanese to analyse his opium was in their pay. Above all, he accused the British government of doing nothing to help him in order to please both the Japanese and the Anti-Opium Society.

From Yokohama, he wrote: 'I again beg that the patriotic members of the Community will help me to get out of this country that I may through a member of the Parliamentary Opposition thrash the present government into something like fair play to me and my wife and family, who are robbed.'

But still no one would listen to him and still Hartley would not give up his fight. In July 1897, nearly 20 years after the original case and now living alone in a suburban road in Croydon, he fired off an angry letter to the Prime Minister, the 3rd Marquess of Salisbury.

'My Lord,' he wrote, 'I submit that it is time that our boasted civilisation as a powerful nation should possess the dignity and honour of protecting Englishmen against a Government [of Japan] that is mean enough to boycott him in their Departments of State and Law Courts.'

As an afterthought, he added, 'Sir W. Grantham when QC, MP, wrote me "Why don't you bribe them, Mr Hartley?"'

Well, indeed, it was a very good point. It would have saved him an awful lot of money, not to mention the loss of his family and his sanity – but then again, it wouldn't have been very British . . .

The British Empire made a vast sum of money from the exportation of opium from India to China – and it wasn't for medical use, but intended to feed the habits of millions of addicts. In today's terms, it was as though Colombia was part of an American Empire and New York traders were raking in fortunes from selling cocaine to Europe.

Opium was a popular recreational drug in China in the early nineteenth century. Much of it was obtained from India, where it was swallowed as tablets or drunk as opium-infused water. The Chinese refined its consumption by smoking it, making the high even more intense. When the British East India Company took over trade in India, its members were keen to find a commodity that the Chinese wanted as much as the British wanted their tea. The imbalance in trade between Britain and China because of tea had bothered British merchants for many years, draining English coffers of the silver needed to pay for it. And so they started to trade in small consignments of Bengali-farmed opium sold to Chinese coastal merchants.

As the Chinese demand for opium grew, so did concern at its deleterious effects. The Chinese government of the Qing Dynasty (also known as Ch'ing or Manchu) introduced a succession of bans on its importation, but British merchants got round them by selling their goods to independent middlemen, who smuggled the drug into China. It was too profitable not to. The beneficiaries included Chinese customs officials and bureaucrats, who grew rich on tariffs and kickbacks from the Chinese merchants selling the drug to their population.

Opium was sold at auction in India for four times the amount it cost to grow and process it. Between 1806 and 1809, British traders received seven million silver dollars for opium. At a stroke, it reversed the trade imbalance in tea and made members of the East India Company rich – but this was just the beginning of a narcotics boom. The price of opium was high in China and was enjoyed only by the wealthy classes. At first, this suited the British traders just fine because they didn't want to rock the boat by flooding the Chinese market. But then economic demands pressed them to go further.

The rise of factory-produced cotton, sold from Britain to India, meant that Indian merchants needed to find cash to pay for it, and they turned to opium, encouraging a dramatic growth in its production and a subsequent fall in price. British merchants wanted to increase the amount of opium going into China, but the Chinese only permitted its import through Canton, so that they could control it. In 1833, the British government ended the East India Company's monopoly of trade with China, allowing any Englishman to trade with the Heavenly Kingdom. One of the new companies was Jardine, Matheson & Co.

Dr William Jardine and James Matheson were both Scotsmen who broke away from the East India Company to establish their own immensely lucrative trade in opium and other commodities with China. From their base in Hong Kong, they grew so rich that when James Matheson retired back to Scotland he bought the Isle of Lewis for half a million pounds and built a castle on it. Jardine became an MP and built a magnificent townhouse at 6 Upper Belgrave Street near Buckingham Palace, as well as having his own castle in Perthshire. The multinational corporation known as Jardines still thrives today.

The opium trade rocketed from 18,000 chests to 30,000. One chest of raw opium balls weighed roughly 140 lb. Each chest could sell for £100. In contrast, a policeman in Victorian England might earn £1 a week.

As the opium habit spread among the Chinese middle classes, alarm bells began to ring and the Chinese government feared a breakdown in society, as millions of their formerly productive citizens drifted away from work on opium binges. The Qing Emperor appointed a no-nonsense commissioner, Lin Zexu, to end the trade by closing ports to British ships and seizing opium. British ships were boarded in international waters and their cargo destroyed. The rapidly escalating animosity culminated in the outbreak of the First Opium War in 1839.

In an act of aggression that still angers the Chinese today, British imperial warships backed up the demands of British traders to open up Chinese ports to their goods, including opium. With far superior military technology, the British captured Canton, blew up Chinese ships and humiliated the Chinese Emperor. The subsequent Treaty of Nanking allowed the British to trade in four ports, gave them special privileges and ceded Hong Kong to Queen Victoria. The USA and France soon after concluded similarly beneficial trading treaties with China.

Not everyone in England was impressed by the outcome. *The Times* thundered at the opium trade foisted on the Chinese. Its editorial argued that Britain should wash its hands of the business – 'that we should cease to be mixed up in it, to foster it, or to make it a source of Indian revenue'.

> We owe some moral compensation to China for pillaging her towns and slaughtering her citizens in a quarrel which never could have arisen if we had not been guilty of this national crime.

A young William Ewart Gladstone MP – a future prime minister – had just come back from a trip to Italy with his beloved sister. She was hooked on opium-based laudanum and suffering terribly from her addiction. Furiously, he condemned the opium war in the House of Commons. When an opposition MP boasted of his pride at seeing the British Union flag flying over a burning Canton, Gladstone was scathing.

> We all know the animating effects which have been produced in the minds of British subjects on many critical occasions when that flag has been unfurled in the battlefield. It is because it has always been associated with the cause of justice, with opposition to oppression, with respect for national rights, with honourable commercial enterprise, but now that flag is hoisted to protect an infamous contraband traffic, and if it were never to be hoisted except as it is now hoisted on the coast of China, we should recoil from its sight with horror . . .

The Foreign Secretary, Lord Palmerston, countered this crusading anger by pointing out that Chinese aggression towards British merchants had been motivated not by concern for their people's morality but because of their ballooning trade deficit with Britain.

As China suffered terribly during the civil war of the Taiping Rebellion, Britain continued its lucrative trade in opium. Conflict broke out again between the two countries when Qing officials searched a Hong Kong-registered ship in 1856. The British retaliated by seizing Canton. France joined in and both nations' troops marched on Beijing, burning down the Emperor's Summer Palace. In no position to fight off a modern European army, the Chinese ratified their earlier trade treaty, opened up more ports and paid millions of ounces of silver to Britain and France for their trouble.

Lin Zexu had tried to conduct an anti-opium campaign within China, arresting hundreds of local dealers and destroying their drugs, but in the wake of the Second Opium War, the trade took another leap skywards. Opium imports increased from 58,000 chests in 1859 to 105,000 chests in 1879. To ensure that the money flowed smoothly, the British took over the running of the entire Chinese customs service, putting it under the control of Sir Robert Hart and his staff of 89 Europeans, half of whom were British. As the London *Economist* of 1898 commented: 'The Customs Houses of China are within reach of British shells.'

The British government was becoming addicted to its opium profits. It has been estimated that between one-fifth and one-sixth of the British Indian Exchequer's income came from the business. But still there was a vociferous group that could not accept the legitimacy of the trade.

Sir Wilfrid Lawson's money came from railroads. He was director of the Maryport and Carlisle Railway. Becoming Liberal MP for Carlisle in 1859, he quickly gained a reputation as a vigorous campaigner for temperance. His style was passionate and radical. He had campaigned for the abolition of the House of Lords and disarmament, and it was natural for him to express outrage at Britain's continuing part in the opium trade.

In May 1870, the 41-year-old Lawson stood up in the House of Commons and argued for the motion 'That this House condemns the system by which a large portion of the Indian Revenue is raised from Opium'. At the heart of his argument was the belief that what is morally wrong can never be politically right. He explained that the government of India had changed since the days when it was in the hands of East India Company merchants and that the British government now took a more direct role in the administration of the country.

'Above all,' he said, 'I rejoice to say that the old-spirited foreign policy, which consisted, as far as I could understand it, in bullying the weak and truckling to the strong, is dead – I hope never to revive again.

'The House must understand that this opium, as prepared and sold by the Indian government, is not medical opium; it is not a drug intended for the soothing of men's pains and sufferings.'

Quoting a medical expert, Lawson claimed that the majority of opium smokers 'advance rapidly towards death, after having passed through successive stages of idleness, debauchery, poverty, the ruin of their physical strength, and the complete prostration of their intellectual and moral faculties. Nothing can stop a smoker who has made much progress in the habit.'

Lawson rounded on the assembled MPs and pressed a guilt button that made some nod their heads and others bristle with indignation: 'Slavery was not productive of more misery and death than was the opium traffic, nor were Britons more implicated in the former than in the latter.'

Lawson believed that the British Empire should be a vehicle for spreading goodness in the world, not evil. He feared that the result of the Opium Wars was a growing hatred for the British in the Far East. 'We carried on the war in the most horrible manner,' he said, 'and, among other outrages, perpetrated the greatest piece of vandalism of the present century, in burning and looting the Emperor's Summer Palace.'

Lawson gestured towards the leader of his party, sitting on the front bench. Sir William Ewart Gladstone, now sixty-one years old, had become Prime Minister of Great Britain just two years before and now had the power to enact his earlier beliefs. Lawson reminded the senior politician of his youthful anger at the First Opium War and quoted him directly: 'A war more unjust in its origin, a war more calculated in its progress to cover this country with permanent disgrace, he did not know and had not read of.'

Gladstone sat impassively, staring at the Opposition waving their papers at him, taunting him about his past comments. Lawson was in full flow and described the difficulties now faced by Christian missionaries in China. He read out a letter describing the hostility experienced by Protestant missionaries, one having been chased out of a city in Hunan by a mob, its leader saying, 'You burned our palace; you killed our Emperor; you sell poison to the people; now you come professing to teach us virtue.'

Lawson said that some claimed the opium trade was no worse than selling alcohol at home. 'All I can say is, that two blacks do not make one white.' And there was a major difference between Britain's manufacturers of gin and what was happening in the Far East. 'The government themselves are the dealers in opium; they grow the opium, and sell it to the highest bidder.

'But the real argument is this – the Indian government says it wants the money, and has no other way of getting it.' Looking down at his notes, Lawson quoted a Treasury Minister who had produced a pamphlet on the subject. '"Prevention of the trade is a sacrifice to morality so great," said the Treasury Minister, "that we hardly ought to impose it on our *Hindoo* [*sic*] subjects until we have washed our hands clean by ceasing ourselves to manufacture gin. Until then England surely has no right to force India to be more moral than itself, unless it is prepared to make up to India out of the English taxes the £4,000,000 which this morality would cost."'

Lawson was coming to the end of his speech.

'I am not calling upon the Government immediately to disarrange all their Indian finance. I know it is impossible for them to act at once on any such Resolution; and I am not bringing a railing accusation against any Ministry or against any party. I believe that we have all been guilty.

'We have all suffered this evil to go on too long. It is time to put a stop to such an evil and all I ask this House to declare is that they are ready to sustain Her Majesty's Government in carrying out an Eastern policy more in accordance with the claims of justice, humanity, and national morality.'

It was a bravura performance from Lawson that conveyed exactly the strong sense of moral purpose shared by many senior figures in Victorian Britain. The immense wealth and power brought to their shores by the Industrial Revolution and the British Empire could only be acceptable if it was used for the good of mankind as a whole – not just the benefit of greedy Brits. It was an emotional and philosophical argument that grew stronger through the rest of the century.

But in the crowded chamber of the House of Commons on that May evening, someone had to speak out for the realities of imperial survival and that person was Grant Duff. A 41-year-old Aberdeenshire lawyer by training, he was the Undersecretary for India in Gladstone's government and had full access to the figures.

'The net average amount of our Opium Revenue during the last five years, for which the accounts had been laid before Parliament, was £5,781,890,' Duff told the MPs. 'In the year 1867–8 – the last for which the accounts had been laid before Parliament – it rose to the great total of £7,049,447, after all expenses had been paid. In short, it amounted to between one-fifth and one-sixth of our whole net Revenue.'

The figures raised eyebrows. It was not the sort of sum of money you could easily say 'no' to.

'Unlike most items of national Revenue,' Duff told the House, 'these millions were not the product of a tax upon our own subjects . . . They were a contribution paid chiefly by China, partly by the Indo-Chinese Peninsula and the Eastern Islands, to help us to make India what we desired her to be, and what, if rash hands did not interfere, she might well become – one of the most prosperous portions of the earth's surface.'

To Duff and the architects of the British Empire, it seemed a rather neat transaction that an opium-addicted Chinese middle class should pay for Britain's upkeep of India.

'Was it worth seriously discussing – was it conceivable,' wondered Duff, 'that the British taxpayer – not too lightly burdened already – would allow himself to be mulcted to the tune of some £6,000,000 annually in order that he might pay a benevolence to India? If we were to give up the powerful lever for raising the position of India which this opium Revenue gave us – if we were to give up the better part of our golden dream of improvement and civilisation – would it not be wise to reconsider the whole question of our connection with India?

'To put it plainly, if at one blow the opium Revenue was struck away, the Indian Empire would be on the high road to bankruptcy.'

Duff then explained the machinery of the opium business to the House. The Indian government received three sources of income from it. A small income derived from licences given to retail dealers to sell opium – but comparatively little was consumed in India. It received a much larger income from what was known as the 'Bengal monopoly' and from the tax on the opium exported through Bombay ports. The Bengal monopoly meant that no one was allowed to cultivate opium without a licence. That licence was obtained by agreeing to deliver dried poppy juice at a fixed price to the government factories situated at Patna in the North-West Frontier Province and at Benares in Bengal.

The poppy was a favourite crop among Indian farmers because of the high rate of return it generated for the amount of land used. After the juice was scraped off the poppies, it was sent in jars to a government depot, where it was prepared with infinite care. 'The object being to produce as good a quality as possible,' said Duff, 'for it was upon quality, rather than quantity, that our profits depended. China alone could grow any quantity of opium [but] our object was to produce an opium so good that those who chose to buy from us might, at least, get an excellent article of its kind.'

Once the opium had been processed, it was packed in 140-lb chests and sent to Calcutta, where it was disposed of at monthly sales by auction. 'The profit to the Government,' said Duff, 'consisting of the difference between the price it paid for the crude poppy juice and the price it received for the manufactured article, less all the expenses of manufacture and transport.' Most of the opium sold at Calcutta was bought by native Indian merchants, who took it to China. Further income came from imposing an export tax or 'pass fee' on the produce before it left port.

'We did not invent the system,' explained Duff, 'we inherited it.'

Having heard Lawson's fierce argument against the morality of the opium trade and Duff's economic justification for it, it was now time that the assembled MPs heard from their Prime Minister, William Gladstone – a man who, 30 years earlier, had cursed the evil of the Opium War and had lost his own sister to the pernicious drug.

As Gladstone rose to his feet, Lawson shifted forward in his seat, hoping that the passionate fury of the young man could still inflame the decision-making of the wiser and older politician.

'About the wars which have grown out of questions connected with the opium trade,' said Gladstone solemnly, 'do not let it be supposed for one moment that there now continues that state of things out of which those most unhappy and most discreditable transactions – to say the least – arose 10, 20 or 30 years back. That state of things has totally and absolutely disappeared.'

Once China had accepted the importation of opium and taxed the drug to its own benefit, Gladstone felt the situation had changed.

'From the moment that was done, the question of the growth of opium became wholly detached from all political considerations, and became a matter of fiscal arrangement.'

The Prime Minister said that such a monumental motion to remove the income stream provided by the narcotic would require a thorough Parliamentary inquiry. It would need to discuss the nature of opium and its use, and whether the use of opium was necessarily connected with its abuse.

'If that inquiry be made,' said Gladstone, eliciting the smiles of his closest colleagues, 'I hope my honourable Friend the Member for Carlisle [Lawson] will not be Chairman of the Committee, because, excellent as he is in every other relation, he is merciless in his dealings with that portion of his fellow creatures who are inclined to the greater or lesser use of stimulants, so that he cannot be an altogether impartial judge.'

Gladstone was, in effect, calling Lawson a bit of a party-pooper.

'It is easy to find painful, horrible, heartrending descriptions of the effect produced by an excessive use of opium,' he continued. 'But, on the other hand, there is much evidence to contradict that statement, and to show that, although the use of opium is undoubtedly attended with excess in certain cases, and although that excess is in China what the use of alcohol undoubtedly is in this country – a most fertile source of disgrace, misery, sin and crime – yet they are upon a par, and there is a legitimate and reasonable use of both opium and alcohol.'

As far as Gladstone was concerned, the abuse of opium was no worse than that of gin. 'Undoubtedly my honourable Friend may rely upon his own personal consistency, and I know very well that there is nothing which any man can say against opium that my honourable Friend is not ready to say against alcohol.'

Moving on to the matter of financial dependency on the opium trade, Gladstone argued that it would be hard to replace that 15 per cent of Indian revenue.

'This is a very serious matter as regards the responsibility of this House. Nothing could be more ruinous, and few things could be more discreditable, than for you to pass a vote which, on the one hand, must remain an idle expression of opinion without practical result, [but] if it were acted upon, must simply have the effect of throwing the finances of India into confusion, and greatly compromising the condition, the welfare, and even, possibly, the peace and security of that country.'

And were the British people ready to meet that deficit by digging into their own pockets?

'The other day,' said Gladstone, 'the Chancellor of the Exchequer was so happy as to possess a surplus of something like £6,000,000. If the honourable Member for Carlisle succeeds in carrying this Resolution, is he ready to propose a second, to the effect that the £6,000,000 shall be handed over to the Indian Treasury to supply the first year's deficiency due to the abandonment of the opium Revenue?'

One of Lawson's supporters motioned that he was happy to hand this money over. But Gladstone pointed out the arrogance of changing an entire economy because of their supposed superior morality.

'Until you have proved that this drug is wholly intolerable,' persisted Gladstone, 'and ought to be absolutely proscribed, as productive of unmixed mischief, you have no moral right to deprive a considerable portion of the people of India, who are engaged in the cultivation of it, of what is probably their only means of subsistence.'

And if they did remove government involvement in the trade, what would be the result? 'We cease to impose a transit duty on the opium of the North-West; we cease to exercise what is called the Government monopoly in respect of the opium of the North-East; and what is the effect but an enormous stimulus to the trade?'

Or was Lawson proposing to go further and impose a prohibition on opium cultivation?

'If he is not prepared for prohibition, his case is hopeless,' said Gladstone. 'If he is, he is not much better. By prohibition, you deprive the Government of India of a very large Revenue; you disable it from meeting its engagements; you compel it to impose very heavy taxes upon a country already too much burdened; and you deprive a portion of the people of their means of employment in the raising of this commodity, on which they are very dependent.

'With regard to the opium of the North-west, you will forbid the transit, and you will offer to the smuggler the moderate premium of 600 rupees a chest, or 8s per pound weight, under which an enormous contraband trade will grow. Does not my honourable Friend see that, supposing he could stop the growth of opium in the whole Indian peninsula, his measure would immensely stimulate the growth of it in China?'

With great clarity, Gladstone had predicted what would indeed happen when the Anglo-Indian opium business came to an end. It would unleash organised crime in the region and would allow other countries to step in and fulfil the insatiable desire for narcotics. But, at the time, Gladstone was sure that common sense, as he saw it, would prevail.

'Proposing to himself an end dictated only by benevolence, he has not considered the means by which alone it is possible that end could be attained,' concluded Gladstone. 'Under these circumstances, I am quite sure the House will avoid – as they frequently have to avoid – the snare set by proposing an abstract Resolution of this nature.'

Lawson was disappointed but cannot have been surprised at Gladstone's stance. The Prime Minister was chief executive of the British Empire and no Cumbrian teetotaller was going to derail that magnificent engine of dominion and enrichment.

Lawson got one final word in before his motion went to the vote. Scowling at his front-bench Liberals, he said: 'The argument from the Treasury Bench has been nothing but money, money, money, regardless of morality and Christian duty.'

Lawson's motion was defeated by 151 votes to 47.

Lawson and his supporters may have lost the battle in 1870, but, in the end, they won the war. The unfortunate Mr John Hartley was just one victim among many opium traders, as the zeal of these moral crusaders fired the support of more and more well-meaning Victorian Liberals. In 1874, a group of Quakers in London founded the Society for the Suppression of the Opium Trade. Sympathetic MPs continued to submit resolutions calling for an end to the trade and, in 1891, they finally won a majority in the House of Commons. The following year, Gladstone, Prime Minister once again, was compelled to reverse his support for the opium business by instigating a Royal Commission inquiry into the possibility of prohibiting the production and sale of opium in India.

In India, the local press, both English- and Indian-language newspapers, as well as a group of highly placed Indian government officials, strongly opposed the prohibition of opium. Commission investigators travelled throughout the subcontinent and spoke to 723 witnesses both for and against opium production. The result was a published report that comprised 2,500 pages in seven volumes. Overwhelmingly, the testimonies within the report and Indian public opinion rejected the idea of prohibition. Anti-opium campaigners were furious and accused the inquiry of bias, but its arguments were solid and well reasoned.

Since 1890, the Chinese government had given up trying to stop the wave of opium flooding into its country and had legalised the trade. Opium production within China had already been growing and this just encouraged it further. As a result, the demand for Indian opium dropped. To prohibit it now would be a meaningless sacrifice, concluded the Royal Commission. In addition, the Indian government demonstrated its responsibility by tightly controlling the sale of opium within its own borders, so it was not a problem to its own people, even though that might be counter to its own fiscal interests.

Smoking opium was not popular in India and opium dens were banned. Taking opium pills as a daily medicine was, however, enormously widespread in the subcontinent and Indian popular opinion rejected the concerns of anti-opium campaigners as unwanted western interference. What they objected to most strongly was the importation of alcohol. One Indian official testifying to the Royal Commission suggested 'persuading the people of England to take to opium':

> Opium is amazingly cheap, duty included; it prolongs life after a certain age, and it can be asserted with all the force of truth and seriousness that its substitution in place of alcohol . . . will bring back happiness to thousands of families in Great Britain and Ireland where there is no happiness now.

Despite this robust defence of the Indian opium trade, its days were numbered. At the beginning of the twentieth century, educated English opinion was so strongly against it that when a motion of prohibition was again put before the Liberal Parliament of 1905, this time, without Gladstone at its head, it was passed without the need for a vote.

On 1 January 1908, the British and Chinese governments signed a treaty agreeing to substantially reduce the Indian export of opium to China over the next ten years until it ended completely. In the meantime, in 1906, China had reversed its previous imperial decision to legalise the drug and banned its sale, embarking on a ten-year crusade to eradicate the habit. Bans on the sale and use of opium soon after followed in other leading nations, including the USA.

Regardless of the move to prohibition, there was still an enormous demand for opium in and outside China. As Gladstone – the grand old Victorian prime minister – predicted, the demand was met by a dramatic increase in the illegal supply of opium. As its value rose on the illegal market, drugs smuggling became a worthwhile occupation for organised criminals, and the twentieth century of fabulously rich and powerful narcotics ganglords was born.

If the British Empire had now taken the moral high ground and turned its back on exporting opium, its unparalleled global trade network provided the perfect conduit for an explosion in drugs-related criminal activity. Gangsters needed weapons and gunrunning became a great challenge to the Pax Britannica.

2

THE IMPRESSIVE LT-COL ROOS-KEPPEL

LIEUTENANT-COLONEL SIR GEORGE OLAF ROOS-KEPPEL was a strongly built man of mixed Dutch–Swedish–English blood, with a thick Edwardian moustache. He brooked no nonsense and commanded a significant military force as Chief Commissioner and Agent to the Governor-General, North-West Provinces. Covering the terrain that now borders onto Afghanistan, it was – and still is – one of the toughest regions in the world to police. On the afternoon of 1 March 1911, it was about to get a whole lot tougher.

Hakim Khan, a notorious bandit, had arrived at the village of Tarnab, 25 miles north-east of Peshawar, in what is now called Pakistan, not far from the Afghan border. Hakim was accompanied by at least 30 heavily armed raiders and believed he could pass though this region with impunity. But something happened on that March afternoon between him and the local villagers. Perhaps he had demanded they supply him with young men for his bandit horde, forcing them into service, or perhaps he had taken a liberty with one of the women of the village. Whatever happened, it resulted in the villagers of Tarnab rising up against the bandits.

Armed with British government rifles, axes and spades, they forced Hakim and his bandits to take refuge in a mud-brick tomb compound about a mile outside the village. The bandits made loopholes for their guns in the walls of the tomb to keep the villagers at bay, killing one of them and wounding another. As the anger-fuelled bravery of the villagers began to sap away, they turned to the local imperial police force to help them out.

It was at this point that the 45-year-old Roos-Keppel rode to their rescue. He deployed a force of 200 men of the 82nd Punjabis and 50 troopers of the Guides Cavalry, plus two mountain guns carried by mules. By the time he arrived personally at the surrounded tomb outside Tarnab, it was early evening. Two of the bandits had been killed, but they were keeping up a brisk fire against the cordon of villagers and soldiers. As the light began to fade, it was Roos-Keppel's main task to ensure that none of the bandits escaped into the nearby mountains. This was a golden opportunity to end the criminal reign of Hakim Khan.

'During the night, the cordon was drawn closer and closer,' recalled Roos-Keppel in his report of the action, 'the men taking advantage of the natural cover, which was plentiful, and entrenching themselves in the open spaces. The ground was so favourable that at some points the cordon was within 30 yards of the tomb.'

But Hakim Khan and his bandits were not so easily intimidated. They had dominated the area for years and a few raggedy-arsed villagers and khaki-clad policemen were not going to easily end their rule. Throughout the night they sang songs, fired their guns and boasted of what they would do in the morning. Some of the villagers felt nervous, fearing the wrath of Hakim, but Roos-Keppel kept his nerve and wheeled forward his breech-loaded 10-pounder mountain guns.

> At dawn the guns opened fire from 160 yards, it being, by the nature of the ground, impossible to get a good position at more distant range, owing to the trees surrounding the tomb and the danger to the cordon.

Roos-Keppel had little reason to doubt the effect of his 2.75-inch calibre guns. Their shells pounded the mud-bricks of the tomb, sending up great clouds of dust, and soon made a breach in the surrounding wall. At this point, some of the bandits tried to make a break for it on the west side, but five of them were shot down and killed. Using the distraction created by his comrades, Hakim Khan made a dash from the east side, but he was spotted and killed. The rest of the bandit gang was holed-up in a bastion in one corner of the tomb compound.

> The remainder continued to offer a stubborn resistance and, in order to demolish the bastion in which they had taken

refuge, Lieutenant MacGowan, RA, was forced to bring his guns to a second position within 80 yards of the objective and finally to a third position at 40 yards distance.

Mercilessly, 75 shells smashed down the walls of the bastion. Finally, as the gunfire from within died away, dismounted cavalry, infantry and police edged their way into the ruins of the tomb. Nine bandits were found still alive, but half of them were seriously wounded by shrapnel. 'All were too dazed by the concussion of the shells in an enclosed space to offer any resistance,' noted Roos-Keppel. Twenty others were dead. The survivors owed their luck to part of the roof falling in and shielding them from the exploding shells.

'The destruction of Hakim Khan's gang, which has harried this border for 12 years, will have an excellent effect,' Roos-Keppel told the Secretary to the Government of India, 'and the demonstrations of rejoicing on the part of the inhabitants of this Ilaqa [neighbourhood] are unanimous.' In his report, Roos-Keppel praised the contribution of his officers in responding quickly to the requests of the brave villagers and working together to destroy the gang. The incident even made a small item in *The Times*, although it wrongly reported the final fight was fought in a cave not a tomb.

Roos-Keppel had demonstrated a commendable ruthlessness in snuffing out Hakim Khan, but this did not mean he was a brutal imperialist at war with the local culture – far from it. Throughout his report, he was at pains to recognise the contribution of the local population as unpaid law-enforcers. Ten years earlier, he had demonstrated his mastery of the local language by writing *The Pashto Manual* as a guidebook to colloquial Pashto.

Sir Olaf Caroe, an expert on the Pathans, called Roos-Keppel a 'very fluent speaker of their language, he could turn a proverb, point a moral, quote a poet, make a domestic allusion in perfect timing and in communion with those who heard him – more than any Englishman, he has been claimed as a Pathan among Pathans'. Later, he became a founding member of the Islamia College that evolved into the University of Peshawar.

Descended from a branch of the Dutch Van Keppel family that came over with William of Orange, he was gazetted to the Royal Scots Fusiliers in 1886. He saw action during the Upper Burma War of

1886–7, but then began his long service on the North-West Frontier. Starting as a transport officer, he progressed to the Political Agency of the Khyber and commanded the Khyber Rifles. He never married and frowned at his colleagues for finding wives. 'No need to keep a cow to get your milk,' he said, preferring the company of many passing lovers.

The two distinct sides of Roos-Keppel's character were further illuminated by Caroe, who had met him on a few occasions: 'He loved to mingle sympathy with callousness, pride with an easy familiarity, generosity with [an] ill-humour towards those who displeased him that could be vindictive. He was a man of strong character who stood above all those who surrounded him, a good friend, but a very dangerous enemy.'

The near-biblical destruction he could bring down on his foes was demonstrated on another occasion when Roos-Keppel gave notice to the chieftains and greybeards of an outlaw border tribe that had killed one of his sepoys.

'I gave you the choice between friendship and the sword,' he told them. 'That of these two you might choose one. Your tribe has chosen the sword. Let it be so . . .' He levied a fine of 50 modern rifles and 300 flintlocks, and all the prisoners he had taken from them were dispatched south to India. But worse was to come.

> Your villages which have been destroyed by me and any which
> by God's Kindness may be so destroyed will remain thus in
> ruins, and for the future those villages will not be rebuilt nor
> will their lands be cultivated.

Despite this level of fury, Roos-Keppel did not bring an end to major crime on the North-West Frontier. Two years later, after destroying Hakim Khan, a gang of Pathan outlaws made headlines by stopping a mail train from Peshawar to Calcutta. They shot dead the European driver and guard, plus an Indian fireman. They then advanced through the train carriages, looting the passengers. Unfortunately for them, the outlaws happened to hijack a train containing a small group of British officers and soldiers.

As soon as the bandits walked into the carriage filled with khaki-clad gentlemen, they heard the sound of cocked pistols and unsheathed swords, and the thieves made a hasty retreat, fleeing into the surrounding hills. The British officers commandeered an engine from a goods train and continued their journey undisturbed.

What made Roos-Keppel exceptional was that not only did he have a sound appreciation of crime on a local level, he also saw the bigger picture. Decades of continuous low-intensity conflict along the North-West Frontier between imperial lawmen and bandits had been punctuated by major military conflicts, but this was just one part of a complex system of organised crime that stretched across many countries. The arsenal of weapons employed by Pathan bandits often came from European suppliers, who sent them via Arab arms dealers in the Persian Gulf. From 1908, with the end of British control over the opium trade, this same route would be used in reverse to smuggle narcotics into the Mediterranean and Europe.

For most of the nineteenth century, the British enjoyed an enormous technological superiority in weaponry over their many imperial adversaries. At the Battle of Omdurman in 1898, an Anglo-Egyptian army stopped dead a horde of charging Islamic fundamentalists, twice its number, with an array of rapid-firing Lee-Metford magazine-fed rifles and Maxim machine guns. For only 60 casualties in their own ranks, the Anglo-Egyptian army slaughtered thousands of Sudanese. 'It was a terrible sight,' said a young Winston Churchill in the imperial army, 'for as yet they had not hurt us at all, and it seemed a terrible advantage.'

By the beginning of the twentieth century, the 'terrible advantage' had been eroded by an influx of western arms sold to tribesmen in some of the most volatile parts of the British Empire. None more so than on the North-West Frontier, where combat-experienced Pathan tribesmen gave the British an increasingly hard time with their imported precision-rifled guns. The British retaliated by escalating the arms race with them by devising ever more deadly weaponry, such as armoured cars and bomb-dropping aircraft, on top of the newly improved mountain guns used by Roos-Keppel to such devastating effect against Hakim Khan.

The never-ending conflict on the North-West Frontier was part of the Great Game – the strategic rivalry between the British and Russian Empires – in which the British feared a Russian invasion of India through Afghanistan. The Russians had effectively conquered the Muslim states of Central Asia and it seemed only a matter of time before they would exploit the continuing tribal conflict on the North-West Frontier to grab the Jewel in the Crown from Queen Victoria. But this was a chimera that played better in London clubs as an excuse for increasing arms expenditure in India, because the reality was that Russian influence on the Pathan tribesmen was negligible. The volatility of the region was down to the tribesmen themselves and their hunger for weapons.

The Pathan tribesmen, among them Afridis, Wazirs and Mahsuds, lived on the fringe of the British Empire. As such, they enjoyed none of the benefits of their neighbours to the south, who thrived on the trade and industry of British-controlled India. They lived in a mountainous land of poor agriculture and had to rely on their wits and weaponry to grow rich. For centuries, they had lived primarily as raiders, stealing goods from their neighbours. In the early twentieth century, their one great advantage was their proximity to the imperial frontier, which meant they could benefit from smuggling arms to and from India and then, latterly, illegal drugs. They were one of the largest and most aggressive groups of organised criminals in the world.

The fury of the Pathans was not always directed at outsiders. For most of the time, it was aimed at themselves, as feuding tribes and families competed with each other to dominate the region and gain the most from their criminal activities. 'A rifle to a hill Pathan is literally the breath of life,' noted a British Commissioner in 1901. 'If, for instance, I have a breech-loader and my enemy with whom I am at a blood feud has none, he must get it or go under. There are no two ways about it.' Such a necessity for weaponry meant that the majority of the Pathans remained poor, as any excess income in their community was spent on guns.

The Pathan desire for modern European-manufactured rifles was fed at first by a network of smuggling across the border from India or outright theft from Indian Army depots. 'Coffins had been successfully employed to convey rifles across the frontier under the very eyes of unsuspecting militia patrols,' said one reporter. 'In Calcutta, rifles had been strapped under goods-wagons destined for Peshawar, whence they were secretly carried off by natives on arrival. Ammunition had gone through the Khyber cleverly concealed in bales of merchandise. Bolts had disappeared mysteriously from arms-racks.'

British soldiers sometimes succumbed to selling their rifles to dealers, netting up to £25 for a Martini-Henry. In 1898, a Private Gilchrest of the Royal Scots Fusiliers was sentenced to two years' hard labour for selling a rifle-bolt to an undercover Border Military Policeman. Such were the rewards from the illicit trade that a substantial number of weapons were also imported through the Middle East.

'Some think they are imported from Birmingham or Belgium, and thence find their way via the Persian Gulf to the Indian frontier,' surmised a correspondent in *The Times*. 'Some imagine that they are obtained from the Amir's workshop in Cabul [*sic*]; and some believe they are stolen in India, and sold for fancy prices across the border. Probably from each of these sources the supply is maintained; but, whencesoever they get them, it is certain that the Afridis now possess Martinis in large numbers, and have besides an apparently unlimited stock of ammunition. They have too, a good many Sniders, the bullets of which inflict frightful shattering wounds; and in the recent operations they obtained forty or fifty Lee-Metfords, and made uncommon good use of them.'

As the British tightened up their control on the flow of illicit weapons from within India to the North-West Frontier, so the trade route from the Middle East became more important. In April 1899, George Roos-Keppel, then a captain on Special Duty in the Kurram Valley, told the Secretary of the Government of India that he had bought two carbines, one made in London, the other in Birmingham, from a tribesman who claimed he could supply him with many more. These hadn't come from India, but from the longer route via the Persian Gulf. It was well worth their while. A weapon bought at the port of Muscat in Oman could be sold for many times more by the time it reached the Pathan tribesmen.

As word got back to Europe of the fortunes to be made selling weapons in Muscat for shipment across the Gulf to the North-West Frontier, so Belgian, French and German arms dealers joined the British, who already had a strong presence there. These European gun sellers professed they had no idea where the weapons ended up, only that the Arabs had a bottomless desire for them. Rather than depending on native dhows, the ruthless merchants were helped considerably when the Hamburg-American Packet Company started operating steamers across the Gulf from 1906. Afghan arms caravans awaited the arms shipments on the other side, on the Makran Coast of Persia, present-day Iran.

The influx of wealth into the region saw an inevitable increase in piracy. A British Consul in Basra received a report of a typical incident. Early one morning, a commercial vessel was boarded by two Arabs. 'A watchman was, as usual, on duty on our barge,' wrote the British commander of the SS *Barala*, 'but before he had an opportunity of calling out for assistance two men held him up, one pointing a rifle at his head and the other a dagger, threatening him at the same time that if he dared to shout they would kill him.'

More Arabs boarded the barge and removed a large quantity of cargo. The Briton despaired at the lawlessness of the area, knowing that the local Ottoman Turkish police would do very little about it. It certainly added to the perception that the entire Persian Gulf was riddled with corruption.

By 1907, some 94,000 Martini-Henry rifles had arrived from the Persian Gulf into Afghanistan for sale to Pathan warriors. A year later, it was estimated that a further 30,000 rifles and three million rounds of ammunition were arriving each year. An example of the far-flung network was revealed when a large number of breech-loading rifles, disposed of by the Australian government of New South Wales after the Boer War, ended up on the North-West Frontier with the New South Wales stamp still on them. Not only did such a significant influx of modern weapons threaten security on the North-West Frontier, but, if these arms got into the hands of dissidents within India, it could also fuel a rebellion against British imperial rule within the entire subcontinent.

Through diligent intelligence-gathering, it was Roos-Keppel who reported to the Government of India the exact route taken by some of these arms smugglers from the North-West Frontier. His agent in the Khyber underlined how difficult it was to get these facts.

> As a penalty of 2000 Rupees and the burning of the offender's house has been fixed by the tribe to prevent information concerning the method of the trade reaching the ears of the government, first-hand information is not yet easy to acquire.

But the agent learned of a trip undertaken by a Pathan tribe – the Adam Khel Afridi. They had previously stood aloof from the business of arms smuggling, preferring to manufacture their own weapons, but this trade was being undermined by the superior, cheaper European guns flowing into their realm from across the Middle East. From their richest merchants, they gathered 48,000 rupees and 56 tribesmen set off in September 1908 on the long journey. They travelled in smaller, separate parties, with the money hidden in their clothing. In Karachi, one group was caught changing their silver for gold and were arrested for suspected arms dealing. The rest set sail for the port of Sohar in the Gulf of Oman. They then marched 14 days to Muscat.

'On arrival at Muscat they found themselves in a market which offered free trade in rifles and ammunition at cheap rates,' said the agent.

They selected the rifles, paid for them, had them wrapped in bundles, but they could not take them away. The Muscat traders told the Adam Khel to leave them behind and travel to a point on the opposite shore of the Gulf of Oman outside Persian government control. There, they might have to wait up to three months before they would see their valuable cargo. The Pathan tribesmen must have wondered at the wisdom of this in a region renowned for its lawlessness. But they had little choice. The Muscat traders said the delay was 'rendered necessary by the vigilance of those who sought to hamper the trade'.

The Adam Khel did as they were told and found a spot on the Persian coast where the people lived in caves and sold them camels. After waiting for about a fortnight, several rowing boats appeared, bearing their consignment of guns. The relieved Afridis were impressed by the honest business dealings of the Muscat traders. With the bundles loaded on their camels, the caravan set off in early January for the land route to Kabul.

'The caravan marched for four months,' said the agent, 'encountering many difficulties in the shape of difficult roads and lack of water, but nowhere suffering from attack.' At one stage, they went three days without water, but, eventually, they reached Kabul. The camels were sold in the market and the tribesmen were each given ten rupees to cover their expenses.

Altogether, the Adam Khel expedition brought in about 1,000 rifles and 120 pistols, reported Roos-Keppel. In Muscat, they had bought a

German-made Mauser rifle for 80 rupees. Back home on the North-West Frontier, it sold for 320 rupees. A British-made Martini-Henry rifle was bought for 55 rupees in Muscat and sold for 200 rupees. The cost of importing each weapon was roughly fixed at 20 rupees above the Muscat price. 'The success of the venture has greatly elated the Adam Khel,' concluded the Khyber agent. A similar venture on a larger scale was planned for the following autumn.

Gun smuggling was turning into a gold rush. Something had to be done, and in 1909 the Indian government, spurred by reports such as that received from Roos-Keppel, took military action. The Royal Navy supplied five warships to blockade the Makran Coast, which ran from the Persian Gulf to the Gulf of Oman. Consignments of weapons were seized from native dhows and they interrupted the flow of weapons to the extent that Pathan arms dealers lost considerable sums of money. It resulted in them turning to their traditional methods of raising cash – with an upsurge of raids across the North-West Frontier in 1910.

The naval action created a sense of tension in the Persian Gulf and, when sailors from HMS *Hyacinth* landed at Dubai to search for illicit weapons in December 1910, they were attacked by a gang of locals. Five of the seamen were killed and nine wounded in the clash. A possible explanation for this was shortly after published in *The Times of India*, which said that the Arab press was exacerbating the situation by claiming that the British were so fed up with the illegal arms trade they were going to carve up Persia and then annex Arabia:

> These apprehensions have induced an increasing anti-foreign feeling, which has been intensified by the belief that our measures against the arms traffic are intended to lead to the disarmament of the Arabs, who cling to their rifles as their most cherished possessions.

'The Press demands that renewed attempts shall be made to suppress the Muscat traffic itself,' concluded the article.

Such was the money to be made from selling illicit arms in the Middle East that it attracted some of the most unlikely arms smugglers. Charles MacFarlane was a draper from the Isle of Wight. Owing to ill health and domestic difficulties, he sold his business in November 1911, raising £900. In a pub on the Strand in London, the ex-draper met members of a syndicate that had conceived a plan to sell British guns to the Ottoman Turks. Swept up by tales of the fortunes to be made, MacFarlane invested part of his money with an ex-army officer and the next thing he knew he was sailing on the *Esmerelda* with the amateur arms dealers to a port somewhere west of Tripoli.

On the way, MacFarlane lost £215 gambling with the syndicate. Once in North Africa, the draper, the ex-army officer and his associates travelled 100 miles inland with their cargo of guns to a Turkish fort. Having arrived there and deposited their weapons, they were forcibly recruited into the Ottoman army by a Turkish officer, the deal presumably having gone badly wrong.

The ex-army officer and another member of the syndicate were killed in a subsequent combat. MacFarlane lost touch with the survivors and, alone, broke and suffering from sunstroke, he was put aboard a ship back home by some kindly Arabs. A year later, he was telling his extraordinary story to a bankruptcy court in London. No doubt much of this tale was elaborated to present himself in a sympathetic light, but what it does underline is the extent to which illegal arms dealing had become a widely known get-rich-quick scam in Edwardian England.

By 1911, the Royal Navy patrols in the Persian Gulf had gained the upper hand in their war against the gunrunners. Part of this was thanks to their use of advanced communications technology.

'Wireless telegraphy may be said to have almost doubled the effectiveness of the squadron for its present purpose,' noted a special correspondent for *The Times* embedded with the patrol fleet. 'Very few dhows can escape its vigilance. Every one met with is overhauled and thoroughly searched. If arms are found, they are immediately seized and the dhow taken in tow.' It was painstaking, tedious work. One ship searched 97 dhows before making a single arrest, but it proved to be one of the largest captures recorded – more than 2,000 rifles and piles of ammunition.

For the crew of the smaller boats deployed, it could be a challenging mission, as *The Times* reporter made clear:

It is no child's play for a young officer and a crew of 12 or 14 men to be turned out for a cruise of several weeks' duration, come fair weather or foul, in a small cutter or pinnace, with little or no shelter from the fierce tropical sun or from the sudden squalls which constantly lash those wind-swept waters – and sometimes a Hobson's choice between an ugly sea outside and the dubious refuge of a creek with a party of truculent Afghans on the shore ready to receive them with loaded rifles.

Arnold Keppel was the 8th Earl of Albemarle, a British soldier, and a distant cousin of Roos-Keppel, to whom he dedicated his book, *Gun-Running and the Indian North-West Frontier*. He joined a 1,000-strong expeditionary force that landed on the Makran Coast in April 1911. Consisting of British Indian Army units, including the 104th Wellesley's Rifles, armed with two machine-guns, and the 32nd Mountain Battery, it was led by Colonel Walter Delamain. Their mission was to push through the Marak Gorge, held by tribesmen loyal to the Baluch gunrunning gang leader Mir Barkat, and provoke a confrontation.

'For mile after mile the column forced its way through the deep sand which filled the bed of a shrunken stream,' recalled Arnold Keppel. 'The day was hot and the heat was accentuated by the funnel-like defile into which the sun shone at an almost vertical angle.' The gunrunning bandits had withdrawn before the advancing British. 'Suddenly a muffled shot was heard somewhere ahead, another, then another.'

Scouts located some tribesmen in the gorge hidden behind sangars – piles of stones turned into field fortifications. The vanguard of the 104th Rifles immediately engaged them until the main force arrived, supported by the 32nd Mountain Battery. Under their covering fire, the British Indian units pressed the bandits back.

> Each line was successively carried, while the intermittent 'cough, cough' of the machine-guns followed the retreating force across the open spaces. Each shell from the ten-pounders as it burst on the hillside laid bare a conspicuous round bare patch of blue clay. Many burst right over the sangars.

The fight lasted for almost three hours until midday. By then, three sepoys had been injured, with eight of the 200-strong bandit gang killed and twenty-four wounded. One of their leaders had been especially conspicuous, wearing a red puggaree scarf around his hat, and was shot through both thighs. Their chief, Mir Barkat, was not present, but it was judged that the clash had dented his reputation and reduced his ability to recruit more men.

Back in London, there was some criticism of the measures taken to stop the gun smugglers. 'The cost of the preventive operations in the last two years, exclusive of the operations this season, has been £220,000,' said one critic, speaking to the Central Asian Society. 'It seems bad policy to incur the cost of these endless preventive measures, which must be indefinitely continued . . . I say nothing of the extraordinary position created by the mobilisation of a British squadron to prevent the transit of arms, some of which are still being shipped in the Thames.'

This was the problem – too many Europeans were making too much money out of the business. The Sultan of Oman was willing to stop the trade, but he wanted to be compensated for the £20,000 of annual revenue he would lose. The lack of willingness displayed by the British government in London to grasp this problem and crack down on their own arms manufacturers meant that the army of the Indian government would continue to suffer. 'We shall see our soldiers shot down with rifles some of which were made in England, and exported from England,' said the critic. 'It was in 1897 that the existence of the traffic was revealed, and it was in 1907 that, too late, the first really practical steps were taken to prevent it.'

A further twist to this crooked business was exposed by a colonel who had served on the North-West Frontier. He wondered how the tribesmen found the money to buy all the modern arms flooding into the region. 'They were not a wealthy people,' he said, 'but they must have spent many thousands of pounds upon the purchase of these arms.'

> A great deal of this money came from the Indian Treasury. The subsidies from the Indian Exchequer [used to buy the compliance of the tribesmen] were almost invariably laid out in the strengthening of their military position – so that we not

> only supplied the tribesmen with arms of British manufacture,
> but we gave them the money to buy them.

Despite the evident hypocrisy of the situation, the direct action of the British Indian government in the Persian Gulf did have some impact on the gun smugglers and made the cost of buying guns from Muscat rise to a price where it became less attractive to the Pathans. Nevertheless, it was a sad reality that the commercial interests of British and European home governments outweighed the security concerns of their colonial governments and those serving on the frontiers of empire. The same clash of interests between home and colonial governors would create even more tension in the world of illicit drugs smuggling.

Lieutenant-Colonel Roos-Keppel maintained his strong police role on the North-West Frontier throughout the First World War. In 1920, the man who had done so much to reveal the international network of gun smuggling retired and journeyed back to London. But away from the bandit gangs and the frontier people he understood so well, he was bored and felt his life was meaningless. Within a year of his retirement, he was dead from a combination of heart trouble and bronchitis. He was just 55 years old. *The Times* claimed the 'strain of 30 years of responsible work in the trying climate of the borderland and amid constant danger had broken down his fine physique'. But those who knew him well believed it was the removal from that harsh terrain that had killed him.

'In the Pathan social and political world,' said Olaf Caroe, 'he detected in some sense the realisation in practice of a way of life that not only appealed to him but touched some inner spring of conviction, even of passion.' His home was with the Pathans of the North-West Frontier and that is where he should have ended his life.

Roos-Keppel's talent for plotting a map of international gun smuggling revealed a new kind of foe faced by the British Empire. Using global trade routes – frequently established and guarded by imperial forces – criminal gangs were now able to transport illicit goods between Asia and Europe with increasing success and escalating profits. Nowhere would this be clearer than in the burgeoning underworld business of narcotics, bringing the hedonistic habits of the Far East to the streets of the imperial homeland.

3

THE TRAGIC MISS CARLETON

ONE AUGUST EVENING IN 1918, William Gibson – a 36-year-old partner in an Australian shipping company – strolled out of the underground station at Baker Street and visited a lady friend in a flat at Portman Mansions. He had just travelled back from Chinatown, at the time located in Limehouse in the heart of London's dockland, carrying a little packet containing white powder. In the woman's flat, he 'cooked up' the mixture and injected it into his arm. He told her it helped him get over his alcoholism. The next morning, Gibson was found dead in his bed. He had choked on his own vomit. A post-mortem discovered that he had been poisoned by an overdose of morphine derived from opium. A jury returned a verdict of 'death from misadventure'.

Later that same month, a Chinese man was sentenced to one month's imprisonment with hard labour and recommended for expulsion from the country as an undesirable for managing a notorious opium den in London's East End.

These were relatively minor affairs, but four months later the link between dangerous drugs and London's Chinatown would explode into the public's consciousness with a headlining case. It was the end point of an illicit drugs network that stretched all the way back to Britain's imperial possessions in the Far East.

Twenty-two-year-old Miss Billie Carleton was a successful West End actress when she attended the Victory Ball at the Albert Hall on 27 November 1918. It celebrated the end of the First World War and was an attempt to bring a little piece of glamour back to wartime London. In the early hours, she returned to her apartment in Savoy Court Mansions, buzzing with excitement about moving to Paris or

America, possibly starring in movies. A few hours later, she died in bed from cocaine poisoning. The tragic case became a popular sensation when she was linked to drug-fuelled Dover Street orgies, where the actress was said to have smoked opium and sniffed cocaine. In just a few months, she had apparently spent over £4,000 on these drugs.

Described in the press as a 'frail beauty' and 'delicate', an 'actress of charm and intelligence', Carleton – whose real name was Florence Leonora Stewart – had appeared the day before her fatal overdose in two performances of *Freedom of the Seas*, a light-hearted play at the Haymarket Theatre. At some point that day, she had ordered by telephone a little gold box, which arrived at her apartment containing white powder, 'like sugar', said her maid.

Billie's friend Reggie de Veulle had designed her dress for the Victory Ball and accompanied her for the evening. In the lavatory at the ball, a friend bumped into the dressmaker and he said, 'I am going to take a "sniff" of cocaine.' At the inquest following Carleton's death, it was revealed that de Veulle and Carleton regularly visited a flat in Notting Hill Gate, where they bought heroin and cocaine from an Egyptian man. Another witness went further:

> One night Miss Carleton asked me to take her down to Chinatown. It was about 1 or 2 in the morning when we started. We returned about 6 o'clock. When she got back she was very ill. I went down smoking opium with Miss Carleton. It cost between £5 and £10, and she and I shared.

'Once Miss Carleton came into my dressing room very heavily "doped" at the Prince of Wales's,' said a fellow actress. 'I said "What's the meaning of this? You promised me not to take that stuff!" She said "If you knew how difficult it is to resist when it is brought to me." I asked who brought it and she replied "Reggie de Veulle."'

Mr and Mrs de Veulle lived in Dover Street and Reggie's wife was jealous of his close friendship with the West End starlet. The day after the inquest into Carleton's death was adjourned, Ada Song Ping You was arrested. A 28-year-old Scotswoman married to a Chinese man living in Limehouse, she was charged with preparing opium for smoking at the Dover Street address. When police raided her home, they found two revolvers and all the paraphernalia needed for smoking opium.

On being sentenced to prison with hard labour for five months, Ada admitted to preparing opium at de Veulle's Dover Street flat one night in September 1918. After dinner, around 10 p.m., de Veulle's half-dozen guests moved to the drawing room, where they placed cushions and pillows on the floor. Taking off their clothes, the men put on pyjamas and the women wore chiffon nightgowns. They then sat in a circle while Ada prepared opium for them. Using a little paraffin lamp, she heated pellets of opium. Extracting portions of the opium with a hypodermic needle, she placed them in the bowl of a pipe for the guests to hand round and smoke. Billie Carleton turned up late at the party, coming straight from her performance at the theatre, and disrobed to join the rest.

When Reggie de Veulle's maid was asked to give evidence at the inquest, he had threatened her. 'If you give me away,' he told her, 'I will see your baby starving, and I will get your separation allowance stopped.' When the maid was asked about the amount of money that Billie Carleton gave de Veulle, she was clear: 'He received a lot of money. I thought it was for her dresses. I used to get £2 or £3 from time to time from Miss Carleton for Mr de Veulle in bank notes . . . The £2 was given to me for shopping. I have been to Notting Hill Gate to get cocaine.'

Finally, 38-year-old Reggie de Veulle took to the stand. He had had to leave his Dover Street flat because of being hounded by the press, who then followed him from one hotel to another. He admitted taking a little cocaine himself but denied supplying it to Carleton. Point-blank he denied all the accusations by the string of witnesses, claiming on one occasion that he and Billie had jokingly pretended to take drugs, using white face powder, just to alarm one of their actress friends.

When the inquest was resumed in January 1919, the coroner summed up the case, saying that Billie Carleton had died from an overdose of cocaine administered by herself, that she had had no intention of committing suicide and that the drug was supplied to her by de Veulle. As a consequence, de Veulle was culpable of manslaughter and was arrested on the spot in court. At the subsequent trial, de Veulle was acquitted of manslaughter but was found guilty of conspiring with

Ada Song Ping You to procure cocaine.

In de Veulle's defence, his lawyer said he doubted 'whether people accustomed to taking drugs thought they were doing anything very grave, because it was only since the war that cocaine and opium had been prohibited drugs. Until then drug-taking was not a crime. It might have been a moral sin, but it was not a crime.'

The lawyer was referring to a regulation in the Defence of the Realm Act that forbade the possession of opium and cocaine. Passed in May 1916, it came in response to increased drug abuse by soldiers, who bought the substances from prostitutes and street dealers. The authorities feared it would lead to the deteriorating health of the army. Opium was also being obtained from doctors by men hoping to 'dope' themselves in order to fail medical examinations for the army. A year later, the prohibition was extended to civilians.

Sentencing de Veulle to eight months in prison, the judge concluded: 'Traffic in the deadly drug is a most pernicious thing. It leads to sordid, depraved, and disgusting practices. There is evidence in this case that, following the practice of this habit are disease, depravity, crime, insanity, despair and death.'

A month after the trial, a sapper in the Royal Engineers was charged with attempting to administer cocaine by way of a woman's beer in a Westminster pub. The sapper said he had bought the cocaine by mistake in German East Africa. Discovering what it was, when he came back to England, he claimed he had shown the bottle to the woman in question, saying that if she 'knew any friends of Billie Carleton, they could do some business'. The sapper was sentenced to three months' imprisonment with hard labour.

The tragic Billie Carleton became the prototype of the thrill-seeking celebrity drugs casualty that would be typical of the twentieth century. But there was another kind of victim, one that drew attention because of its proximity to the Great War.

Ex-officer Eric Goodwin was found dead in a London townhouse in Hallam Street, near Portman Square, in January 1922. He had died from an overdose of heroin, as a result of an addiction to narcotics first acquired on the Western Front.

'He had got the habit after he had been given it following his wounds in France,' his doctor said. 'He acquired the craving for [morphia], and he told me how he used to strive to get it.'

To buy some heroin, Goodwin had contacted a black music hall artist, who took him to the Hallam Street house of another 'coloured' show business friend called Eddie Manning, an infamous dealer. There, said the music hall artist, 'Goodwin asked for a spoon and put it in some white powder, to which he added water. He then put a match under the spoon and when it was hot inserted some of the liquid into his arm with a hypodermic syringe.'

It was around midnight and he seemed OK, asking only for a glass of milk, said the music hall artist. But then he began breathing heavily. The next morning Goodwin appeared to be sleeping but was in fact dead.

'The War brought about a change,' concluded Sir Malcolm Delevingne, the British government's expert on dangerous drugs and author of the Defence of the Realm Act regulation covering them. 'The controls that were instituted over international trade threw light on the extent and nature of the traffic in the drugs. The stress and strains of war led to a spread of drug-taking both among the troops and among the civilian populations, which caused serious apprehensions.'

Having for so long considered the problem of drug-taking as something that only happened abroad – afflicting far-flung peoples, principally the Chinese – the addiction was now coming home to haunt the streets of the imperial capital. The trade routes that had comfortably carried it across exotic seas to foreign markets were now being used to bring it back to England. Having made its possession illegal, it was up to the police to discover exactly who was bringing this poison onto their shores.

Won Tip first sailed into Liverpool around 1897, working as a fireman on a steamer ship, keeping the boiler loaded with coal. It was a tough, horrible job and, as soon as he could, he jumped ship and settled in England. From 1904, he served in a shop selling groceries to the Chinese immigrant population in Birkenhead on the west bank of the River Mersey, opposite the city of Liverpool. He was 32 years old, ambitious and hard-working, and he soon took over the management of the shop, plus a boarding house nearby.

Won Tip specialised in recruiting Chinese crewmen for Liverpool shipping companies, putting them up at his boarding house, and so successful was he at this business that he opened up a second lodging house for Chinese sailors. Selling his grocery store in 1916, he concentrated on this far more lucrative side of his business. Or so it seemed . . .

Won Tip's Chinese wife died in 1899, but he had an eye for the ladies and fathered at least one illegitimate child. He married an English woman with a child from a previous relationship. When she died, Won Tip adopted the boy as his own and sent him to a private school. He then married another English woman and together they had three children.

Whether it was the influence of alcohol or the necessity of handling tough people in a rough community, in 1907 Won Tip started to fall out with the law. On several occasions, he was arrested for threatening behaviour and grievous bodily harm, but on almost all occasions he was discharged. In 1915, he was convicted for helping his wife give false information on one of their boarding houses. Facing three months' hard labour and a recommendation for deportation, he appealed against the conviction and had it quashed. Just two months later, he was arrested for threatening to kill someone, but again got off. He appeared to have a surprising ability to avoid punishment.

Up to 1915, Won Tip had told the authorities he came from China, but, with the threat of deportation hanging over him, he changed his family history, saying he came from Hong Kong, thereby qualifying as a British subject.

As with many Chinese living in England, he had made a lucrative sideline out of processing opium for his fellow Asian smokers. Until the Defence of the Realm Act in 1916, this had not been illegal and was carried on quite openly in the Chinese quarter of Liverpool, as well as in London.

Won Tip had built three furnaces in the basement of his boarding house and kept two Chinese men busy producing opium in small six-ounce copper tins that could be hermetically sealed – the purpose being that they could be thrown into the sea and later retrieved.

It was at this stage that Chief Inspector H. Burgess of the Liverpool City Police became involved.

'Although it was no offence to prepare opium or smoke it in this country [up to 1916],' explained Burgess, 'it was, however, a very serious matter in some foreign countries, principally the United States of America, China and in many of our Dominions, but owing to it not being an offence here, Chinamen flocked from everywhere to Liverpool, which became the centre of this trade, and it was from here they exported this drug all over the world.'

The prepared opium was concealed in the small copper pots produced by Won Tip and smuggled aboard ships. When the ships approached a foreign port, the Chinese smugglers threw the sealed pots into the sea and had them collected by accomplices in rowing boats, who fished them out of the water. The owners of the shipping companies could be fined as much as £10,000 if the illicit trade was discovered and did everything they could to prevent the traffic, but more often than not they failed.

Come 1916, Burgess sent a report to the Home Office recommending the deportation of these traffickers as non-desirable aliens. The government acted promptly and in May of that year issued deportation orders against prominent Chinese smugglers. Won Tip managed to avoid the initial purge by pulling down his Birkenhead furnaces, but he carried on trading more surreptitiously. Later in the year, however, he was served with a deportation order and conveyed to Walton Prison.

Having accumulated some considerable wealth over the years, Won Tip hired a top Liverpool lawyer to put his case in the High Court. The lawyer argued successfully that there was no proof to rebut Won Tip's claims that he was born in Hong Kong and so was a British subject. The deportation order was withdrawn and Won Tip went back to his business.

Burgess was frustrated and pursued the line of inquiry to the Governor of Hong Kong, who studied the documents produced by Won Tip. He declared that they were false and that he was not born in the colony. But this process had taken three years; the Home Office felt too much time had passed since his appearance in the High Court to issue a fresh deportation order. Besides, Won Tip, it appeared, had turned over a new leaf. He was even informing the authorities about drug dealers in his community.

Burgess was not so easily convinced, saying he was betraying 'persons in opposition to him with a view of getting them out of his way'.

'Since that time,' wrote the Liverpool Chief Inspector, 'his general conduct has been good. Although the police have suspected him of running and financing gaming houses and opium dens, we have not been able to obtain any evidence against him.' In 1925, he was informed that the untouchable Won Tip and his family had suddenly left for China.

It was with great satisfaction, then, that Burgess received news two years later that Won Tip was in actual fact living on the Continent in Antwerp and was up to his old business. On the surface, he was engaged in supplying Chinese crewmen to the Liverpool shipping firm Branch Line, but secretly he was running an opium den in a Chinese restaurant in the Belgian port and trafficking drugs back to Britain.

On 8 April 1927, information was received by the Metropolitan Police Special Branch in London that a large quantity of opium had been smuggled on board the SS *Cedar Branch* by its Chinese crew. It was originally destined for Leith, the port of Edinburgh in Scotland, but word had got through that there was a shortage of opium in London and the illicit cargo was to be dropped off on the way. When the police arrived to search the ship in the London docks, they were disappointed to find nothing on board of any interest.

Shortly afterwards, 11 Chinese drug traffickers were expelled from Antwerp. The information about them had come from Won Tip and a fellow Cantonese restaurateur who had, most helpfully, been assisting a Special Branch officer based in Belgium. 'Both are well known to me,' said the officer, 'and during the last nine months of the period I was stationed at Brussels gave me considerable assistance in dealing with the smuggling of narcotics to Great Britain and the smuggling of narcotics and arms to India and the Far East.'

Won Tip had placed himself at the centre of the international trade in illicit drugs and guns that spanned the British Empire. But in order to survive in this bitterly contested market, he had returned to playing his old games, knocking out the criminal competition in Antwerp and providing misinformation to the police.

'For some time after his arrival in Antwerp,' continued the gullible Special Branch officer, 'Won Tip was the subject of observation and enquiry by the Belgian Police but no evidence could be then obtained that he was either allowing his premises to be used for opium smoking or was engaged in the traffic of narcotics.'

Burgess knew better, but the slippery Won Tip was no longer in his jurisdiction. In 1929, Won was finally sentenced to a month's imprisonment in Antwerp for smoking opium – the tip of his personal iceberg. But, at last, he was behind bars.

Won Tip managed to keep to the shadows for most of his criminal career, whereas the most infamous Chinese drugs dealer of this period was attracted to the glare of West End glamour in Jazz Age London. Brilliant Chang was born in Canton to a well-off merchant family and arrived in Britain as a student in 1913.

As early as 1917, Chang was caught up in a drugs raid in Birmingham, but he then moved to London and opened a fashionable restaurant in Regent Street. From there, he started selling drugs to London's smart young set, including young actresses like Billie Carleton. Cocaine, heroin and opium were the favourites.

Whenever he took a fancy to one of these attractive women dining in his restaurant, he had a waiter pass them a printed note, which read:

> Please do not regard this as a liberty that I write to you, as I am really unable to resist the temptation after having seen you so many times. I should extremely like to know you better, and should be glad if you would do me the honour of meeting me one evening where we could have a little dinner and a quiet chat together.

More often than not this approach worked, and he could also supply the girls with the drugs of their choice.

The death of Billie Carleton had brought unwelcome attention to the narcotics business, but what really did for Chang was his association with the cocaine-overdose death of Freda Kempton, a nightclub dancer, in 1922. He had dated her the night before her death and given her £5.

Chang was questioned at the coroner's court, but there was insufficient evidence to prosecute him for supplying her with the fatal dose. The jury decided that the poor woman had committed suicide while temporarily insane. 'When the jury returned the verdict,' noted a *News of the World* reporter, 'Chang smiled broadly and quickly left the court. As he passed out, several well-dressed girls patted his shoulder, while one ran her fingers through his hair.'

The blatant sex appeal of Chang and his association with beautiful white women added a charge to the whole affair and ensured his titillating activities remained in the headlines. It was bad news for him. After several police raids, he was eventually forced to sell his restaurant and relocate his drug-dealing business to Limehouse, but even this didn't save him.

A sharp-eyed detective noted that the dilapidated shack Chang rented under a railway arch in Limehouse Causeway was regularly attended by glamorous women stepping out of expensive cars. Put on trial in April 1924, Brilliant Chang was sentenced to 14 months' imprisonment followed by deportation. 'It is you and men like you who are corrupting the womanhood of this country,' said the judge.

After his time in gaol, Chang was supposed to return to Hong Kong, but rumour had it that, like Won Tip, he had simply moved his operation to the Continent, running drugs and prostitutes in Paris.

With the demise of Brilliant Chang, the London East End drugs business continued in the hands of Chinese and non-Chinese who had been operating, more quietly, alongside him. One of these was the Jamaican-born jazz drummer Eddie Manning. His first conviction was for shooting a man in London's West End. The fight broke out in Cambridge Circus when a pimp insulted Manning's girl by throwing a lighted cigar in her face. He retaliated by chasing the pimp and shooting him, along with two other men. He was sentenced to 16 months.

When Manning came out, he went back to his business of running prostitutes, illegal gambling parties and dope orgies. It was in Manning's rented house in Hallam Street that army officer Eric Goodwin took the overdose of heroin that killed him.

Manning continued to deal in opium throughout the 1920s, eventually ending his life in Parkhurst prison, where he died from syphilis.

Despite the presence of other nationalities in the London drugs trade, it was the involvement of the Chinese that lodged in the minds of the public. The scandalous details of Billie Carleton's death were added to by lurid journalistic descriptions of nights spent in the East End's Chinatown. In 1919, George R. Sims visited an opium den in Poplar called the Ladies' Paradise.

> There is a certain fascination about opium-smoking when you see it done in the suggestive mystery of a Chinese lodging-house, with a dull red fire, in the front of which may be a black cat, and a gas stove on which is an earthenware basin, which is filled with the thick, sticky stuff which looks to the uninitiated like black treacle.

It didn't hinder the sales of newspapers when it was explained that many of the young women visiting such dens had most of their clothes removed by the proprietor. This was to ensure they didn't leave before spending all their money.

'Today there are hundreds of Englishwomen in the grip of the opium fiend,' warned Sims. 'The habit once acquired is rarely shaken off. Taken at first to relieve pain or produce pleasure, it soon ceases to be a luxurious indulgence and becomes a necessity. Under its influence, willpower is gradually lost, and moral degradation is the inevitable result.'

This sensationalism had broad appeal and crossed the Atlantic. In *White Slavery*, published in Chicago, its author portrayed an even more vivid nightmare. He warned that young women were being seduced by Chinese men, who showed them round Chinatown, took them into a shop, gave them beautiful silk dresses and then offered them a cup of tea.

'You know the rest,' he wrote. 'The tea is drugged, the girl goes to sleep and wakes up hours later in some cavern way down in the earth, and there she stays, the Slave of the Chinamen until death takes her. And her body is buried in a hole among the endless tunnels of subterranean Chinatown.'

Such melodramatic accounts gave birth to a new genre of pulp fiction. The most famous of these titillating tales were the Dr Fu Manchu thrillers, written by Sax Rohmer, in which the Chinese master criminal runs his empire of vice from London's Limehouse. His evil appearance is described in *The Mystery of Dr Fu Manchu*, published in 1913:

> Imagine a person, tall, lean and feline, high-shouldered, with a brow like Shakespeare and a face like Satan . . . one giant intellect, with all the resources of science past and present . . .

Imagine that awful being, and you have a mental picture of Dr
Fu Manchu, the yellow peril incarnate in one man.

The best-selling books were turned into a series of popular movies
that further fostered the character of the sinister Chinese man as arch
villain.

Curiously, in contrast, in China it was the imperial Briton who was
being demonised. Having brought an end to its opium trade from 1908
onwards, the British might have hoped that their reputation would
improve, but far from it. As they helped the Chinese enforce their
prohibition of smoking opium, they were accused of criminal
corruption.

A major scandal erupted in May 1910 in the port of Weihaiwei – a
British colony since 1898 – in Shandong province in eastern China.
The British governors were accused of shaking down middle-class
Chinese householders. For every opium pipe needle they found, they
charged the owner $5. For every opium pipe bowl, they imposed a fine
of $50. And for a whole pipe, it was a draconian $100. To some Chinese,
this looked like a shameless money-spinner.

'That the British authorities secretly "plant opium" is clear from the
following fact,' complained one. 'There is a wealthy gentleman named
Wang residing in Weihaiwei. The British authorities under cover of
searching for opium took Wang's women folk, tied them up in a yard,
forcibly stripped off all their clothes and wantonly insulted them. No
proof however was forthcoming but subsequently a useless piece of
iron wire was discovered under a wall and this it was insisted was an
opium needle: so Wang was taken into custody, fined $100, and given
one year's imprisonment with hard labour.'

The combination of sexuality and criminality was a familiar one
established in the pulp fiction of the Yellow Peril, but on the other side
of the world it was being applied to the British. The colonial authorities
were so outraged by this libel that they insisted the national Chinese
newspapers publish an apology and pay a fine. Disappointingly for its
liberal sponsors, the British prohibition of opium was not working as
well as they had wished.

As for the Chinese government, they were frustrated by their own
failures to ban the production and smoking of the drug. In September
1910, the Chinese Emperor sent a decree to his provincial governors

censuring them. He accused them of being too quick to prevent its importation but slow to suppress its consumption. He had sent out his own army of secret agents to monitor their progress.

> They show that even in the suppression of opium every province has in its report been guilty of varnishing the truth. For instance from Kirin, Heilungchiang, Honan, Shansi, Pukien, Kuangsi, Yunnan and the New Dominions reports were sent us that the cultivation of the poppy in these provinces had entirely ceased, whereas as a matter of fact in no instance was this the case.

The British Foreign Office could only agree. 'Opium is now produced in more than half of the eighteen provinces of China,' said an FO report. 'The comparative cheapness of the Chinese opium, the lighter duties levied upon it, and the increasing care taken in its cultivation are enabling it to compete successfully with the Indian drug, and a time is confidently anticipated by the Chinese when Indian opium will be entirely supplanted by the native drug.'

Having stepped back from its control of the opium trade, British imperial administrators could now see they had handed this monstrous machine to the Chinese, who had no qualms whatsoever about selling it to their own people, as well as transporting it around the world to emerging markets in the West. This new demand had arisen during the Great War – and hit the headlines with the scandalous death of Billie Carleton – and it would be up to the British to clear up the mess. This task would fall to a British imperial warrior who would make it his personal mission to reveal to the world how dangerous drugs were passing from East to West.

4

THE FORMIDABLE RUSSELL PASHA

WHEN THOMAS WENTWORTH RUSSELL – later known as Russell Pasha – joined the Cairo Police in 1912, he thought he should get to know every aspect of his beat. Six foot three inches tall, he did not go unnoticed as he patrolled the streets of the Egyptian capital, but he possessed a natural authority that indicated to anyone thinking of messing with him that they would be biting off more than they could chew.

The Wagh el-Birket district of Cairo was its red-light quarter. It was built on what used to be a lake fringed by Mamluk palaces but had since become an area filled with hotels for foreign visitors who had fallen on hard times. European prostitutes lived in its crumbling buildings. They were women who no longer commanded the high prices they had earned in Marseilles or their European home towns and were using this as a staging post before being passed on to markets in Bombay and the Far East. Any nationality could be bought, apart from British women, who were banned by the British Consul from operating there.

'A stroll through its narrow and crowded lanes reminded one of a zoo,' recalled Assistant-Commandant Russell, 'with its painted harlots sitting like beasts of prey behind the iron grilles of their ground-floor brothels, while a noisy crowd of low-class natives, interspersed with soldiers in uniform and sight-seeing tourists, made their way along the narrow lanes.'

The king of the vice business in Wagh el-Birket was a huge Nubian called Ibrahim el-Gharbi, who sat cross-legged on a bench outside his house every evening, dealing with his minions. 'Dressed as a woman and veiled in white,' noted Russell, 'this repulsive pervert sat like a silent, ebony idol, occasionally holding out a bejewelled hand to be kissed by some passing admirer, or giving a silent order to one of his attendant servants.'

El-Gharbi controlled the buying and selling of women throughout Cairo and his influence spread beyond the underworld to Egyptian politics and high society. He could provide anyone with any kind of girl or boy they fancied and made a fortune doing it.

In 1916, with an influx of British and Commonwealth soldiers fighting in the Middle East, it was decided to clean up the red-light district and remove the hordes of freelance male and female prostitutes to make way for government-regulated brothels. An internment camp was set up for those reluctant to give up their living.

When Russell mentioned the pivotal role of El-Gharbi in this trade to Cairo Police Commandant Lewa Harvey Pasha, he was surprised to learn that his boss had never heard of him. Harvey Pasha was a fierce Scotsman who had fought with the 42nd Highlanders at Tel-el-Kebir and had a 'temper like a box of fire-works'. Immediately, he ordered that the vice king of Cairo be arrested and brought before him.

'Half an hour later an officer arrived,' observed Russell, 'leading by the hand what looked like a huge negress, clad in white samite, her golden anklets and bracelets clinking as she minced down the corridor. I followed them into Harvey's office and, for a moment, feared I had imperilled the life of my choleric chief, who blew up like a landmine.'

'What the hell do you mean by bringing this disgusting patchouli-scented sodomite into my presence?' Harvey Pasha bellowed.

The red-faced commandant ordered El-Gharbi stripped of his female finery, handcuffed and sent off straight away to the internment camp. It was a gross humiliation for the Nubian; his servants gave out the pretence that he was absent, looking after business in his home village. He spent a year in captivity and was forced out of the city, dying a few years later.

On reflection, Russell wondered whether his dispatch had been such a good idea, as his role was later taken over by European pimps who were not subject to Egyptian law and kept their women in order with the threat of razors and vitriolic acid. But by then, Russell had more pressing demands – he was to be the first global drugs-busting policeman of the twentieth century.

* * *

Thomas Russell was born at Wollaton Rectory near Nottingham in 1879. The son of a clergyman, he was educated at Haileybury and Trinity College, Cambridge. Early on, Russell had a passion for animals, which began when his father allowed a ferret to pop up from beneath his surplice when he was preaching. 'During the course of his life he had an astonishing variety of pets,' recalled his son-in-law, 'including weasels, a cheetah, desert jerboas, a duck-billed platypus and among these exotic fauna a succession of cats and dogs. I remember that he was on affectionate terms with a rhinoceros in the Cairo zoo.' His last pet was a Senussi-speaking parrot called Koko.

In 1902, Russell joined the Egyptian civil service. At this time, Egypt was not directly part of the British Empire but was being administered for the Egyptian king by a British civil service that looked out for its interests, especially the flow of shipping along that conduit of imperial traffic, the Suez Canal.

As an inspector for the Ministry of the Interior, Russell formed a camel corps that brought law and order to the wild desert frontiers of the Nile Valley. He fought with bandits and smugglers, learning the ways of the Bedouin Arabs.

At the beginning of the century, contraband hashish was the major illicit drug entering Egypt. It came from Greece via Cyrenaican ports and was smuggled across the Western Desert by Arab caravans. Forty years later this same harsh terrain, including the sand dunes south of Siwa and the Qattara Depression salt swamp, would be fought across by troops led by generals Montgomery and Rommel. In those early years, the smugglers had no motorised vehicles to help them and relied purely on their camels. What advantage they did have was in their magazine-fed foreign-supplied rifles. They were able to out-shoot the single-loading Martini carbines carried by the Egyptian Coastguard Camel Corps. Early combats between the two forces resembled blood feuds.

Made up solely of Sudanese tribesmen, the Coastguard Camel Corps came unstuck one day when it clashed with the king of the hashish smugglers, a Tripolitan Arab called Abd el-Ati el-Hussuna. Near a waterhole, west of Dakhla Oasis, one of the Sudanese policemen was shot dead as the Arab caravan made a dash across the Western Desert to Egypt. A relative of the dead man, a sergeant major, made it his duty to avenge this slaughter.

For over a year, the police tracked the elusive Abd el-Ati. When they got word from Greece that he was to take possession of another large consignment of hashish, they sent out scouting patrols to find the tracks of his caravan. Once they picked up his scent, they rushed after him in pursuit, nineteen of them mounted on thoroughbred Sudan camels, each carrying four days' forage and water.

On the third night, the Sudanese police made contact with the rearguard of the Arab caravan and fired shots at them. They had a stark choice – either take on the smugglers or perish, because they did not have enough supplies to return empty-handed. The next day, across blistering hot sands, the camel corps dismounted and advanced in open order against the smugglers. To their relief, they saw that the panicking Arabs had dropped a double-load of bullock skins containing water. Normally, the Arabs would have slit the skins to prevent the police gaining them, but under pressure from the attacking Sudanese they had left them intact.

Abd el-Ati fled into the desert, leaving his followers to their fate. The bandit leader's brother, two cousins and four other Arabs were cornered by the avenging Sudanese sergeant major and his troops and were all shot dead. The only prisoners taken alive were ten camels carrying fifty kilos of hashish and seven Mauser rifles. That night, the police dined on camel steaks cooked over the split wooden saddles of the dead smugglers.

It was these tough Sudanese that Russell rode with, learning colloquial Arabic and everything there was to know about smuggling. In later years, fearing armed clashes with police camel patrols, some smugglers used more cunning methods to get past them. In the Sinai, Syrian camels are known to grow fine silky hair on their humps that is then clipped off in the summer and sold. One alert Sudanese police officer noted that an Arab was too reluctant to sell him the fine wool off his camel's hump. So, having his assistant cover the Arab with a rifle, he investigated the camel to find that slabs of hashish had been fixed to the hump and the long hair glued over it. On other occasions, hashish was stored in tin canisters force-fed to camels and lodged in their stomachs. The unfortunate animals were slaughtered on arrival in Egypt.

Russell learned much from his years in the desert, but if he was to progress he had to tackle crime in the great urban centres. He became an assistant-commandant in the vice-ridden port of Alexandria and was then transferred to Cairo. In 1917, at the age of 38, he took over from Harvey Pasha to become Commandant of the Cairo Police, a position he held for the next three decades. He became known as Russell Pasha – taking up the Ottoman title granted to senior dignitaries such as governors and generals.

Ever keen to take to the streets to learn what was really going on in his precinct, Russell first became aware of a new threat to the security of Cairo during the First World War:

> I did a lot of night prowling in those days and knew by heart my way about the slums where the roughs and the cackling laughter of the hashish dens were by now giving place to the emaciated shadows of heroin addicts slinking about round the offal bins.

Cocaine made its first appearance in Cairo in 1916, followed later by heroin. At first, there was little Russell could do about it, as possession of such drugs only carried a fine of one Egyptian pound or a week's imprisonment. The main source of heroin in Cairo was a respectable chemist, who sold it to a queue of wealthy young Egyptians, their carriages waiting outside. The price of heroin was low, costing a few shillings a shot, and a few contractors even paid their labourers in heroin. It was a wise move as the habit spread over the next decade, ensnaring the poor as well as the rich.

'About 1928 I began to realise that something was happening which was producing a new slum population in Cairo,' reported Russell. 'For the first time we heard of the method of intravenous injection of heroin and soon came across its victims. Within a short time we found a new element in our Bulaq slums.'

The tough labourers who came from the Upper Nile to take up seasonal work usually made up the inhabitants of the Bulaq, but Russell found pale, wrecked figures lying about the lanes, some well educated, even speaking English, blaming heroin addiction for their impoverished condition. They survived by begging or stealing enough money for their next shot, scavenging food from bins outside restaurants and hotels. Soon the corpses started piling up, but they weren't from heroin overdoses. They were from malaria – passed on from one addict to another by sharing a needle infected by a malaria carrier.

Stricter anti-drugs legislation was passed in 1925, raising the fine for possession and trafficking to £E100 or one year in prison. Higher fines meant the price of heroin rose from £E120 to £E300 per kilo – and yet the numbers of addicts was increasing. By the end of the year, fines had rocketed to £E1,000 and five years' imprisonment. Such a profitable market with increased risk meant that it became more and more attractive to organised crime. It alone could provide the investment and the muscle to protect it. Russell wasn't the only one to note the impact of their intervention.

'I have to inform you that the Alexandria Police made a further raid last night on a drug den owned by a Cypriot where a large number of persons, including a blind boy of 15, were captured in the act of sniffing cocaine.' The report came from the Ministry of the Interior in Cairo in November 1928. The information they got from that raid led them to visit a flat owned by a Cypriot.

> The man fired several shots at White Bey and Borai Eff of the Criminal Investigation Department as they were ascending the stairs. The Police were checked for a time but eventually rushed the apartment and seized the Cypriot who had reloaded his pistol.

A large quantity of drugs was discovered, tossed down an air-ventilation shaft.

'In view of the desperate attitude of these Cypriot drug traffickers who have now on three occasions used firearms against the Police,' concluded the report, 'I have authorised the Alexandria Police to carry out their raids armed and, if necessary, to return fire.'

News of the increased level of violence, plus an alarming estimation that put the level of addiction as high as half a million Egyptians out of a population of 14 million, meant that this was a national problem that needed serious attention. The Egyptian Prime Minister turned to Russell Pasha as his senior law-enforcer.

At the beginning of 1929, Russell was appointed head of a new organisation called the Central Narcotics Intelligence Bureau. He was given a budget of £E10,000 and recruited his own specialised staff of investigators. His mission was to root out the major traffickers and make their task so difficult that the price of heroin and cocaine would rise so high as to put it out of reach of the average Egyptian worker.

But who were the big dealers? Where did they come from and how could you get to them? It was a whole new industry that Russell and his investigators had to get to grips with very quickly and its network would eventually span the globe. It was at this point that help came from behind a desk in Whitehall back in London.

Sir Malcolm Delevingne was an unlikely drugs-busting hero. At the age of 61 in 1929, he had led the quiet but diligent life of a civil servant. Taking a First Class Honours in Classics at Trinity College, Oxford, he had worked his way up from private secretary to become the Deputy Permanent Undersecretary of State. The highlight of his life had been attending international conferences on labour regulation in Europe.

It was a largely uneventful career, but behind this calm and controlled exterior was a passion to help people less fortunate than himself. In his private life, he became actively involved in raising money for the Barnardo's charity devoted to orphan children. He also made it his business to become an expert on the new scourge of illicit drugs. Indeed, it was Delevingne who drafted the legislation in 1916 that made cocaine and opium illegal in the UK. When Russell needed help with the bigger picture, he turned to Sir Malcolm.

'I corresponded with him freely,' recalled Russell, 'sending him confidential copies of our seized reports and taking his advice as to the handling of complicated international cases.'

In fact, Delevingne had already been on the case the year before Russell headed his new bureau. Pulling together all the information gathered by British imperial representatives abroad and Special Branch police officers at Scotland Yard, he sent a memorandum full of fascinating facts to the British Residency in Cairo. Just as Russell had learned that Greek merchants were behind the export of hashish to Egypt, so Delevingne revealed that they now had an active involvement in the trade of 'white drugs' in the Mediterranean.

Leonidas T. Melissaratos was actually born in Russia, in Odessa, but married a Greek woman and, most importantly, acquired a Greek passport. As a Russian, however, he was drawn to opportunities in the new town of Harbin, founded in north-east China as an outpost for the Trans-Siberian Express. As civil war raged in Russia and the communists took over, so White Russians fled to Harbin and turned it into a busy cosmopolitan metropolis – fast becoming the biggest Russian settlement outside Russia. The Chinese established their brewing and textile industries there, and citizens of Harbin boasted they got the latest French fashions before anywhere else in the Far East.

From Harbin, Melissaratos made regular visits to Shanghai. From there, in the summer of 1922, he travelled to Greece via France. He also spent some time in the port of Hamburg, Germany. To the casual observer, it could have been that the Russian with a Greek name was simply enjoying a lengthy sojourn abroad, catching up on European culture. In reality, he was putting together an international drugs-trafficking ring.

His business partner was Theodore S. Loverdos, a true Greek from Cephalonia. It was his movements of cash that put more meat on the bone. Before he left Shanghai in spring 1926, he purchased through the Chinese branch of a Belgian bank 14 money drafts for a total of £3,500, quite a substantial amount in those days. Ten of these drafts were cashed in Switzerland and four in Athens.

The profitable set-up began to unravel when Melissaratos was arrested in Hamburg and charged with trafficking narcotics between Germany and China. In the course of his examination, he claimed to be representing an export firm based in New York. Due to insufficient evidence, Melissaratos was acquitted and skipped off out of Weimar Germany to Riga in Latvia and, no doubt, many other countries not documented in his passport.

'According to the depositions made by witnesses in the [Hamburg] case,' noted Delevingne, 'Melissaratos appeared as the real organiser and director of the illicit trade in stupefying drugs. It was also ascertained [from an American witness] that Melissaratos actively devoted himself to the placing of prohibited drugs on the Chinese markets and that these drugs originated from a Swiss factory. The forwarding of these drugs was then effected through the medium of Thomas Cook & Son under the guise of travellers' baggage or indeed of diplomatic baggage and the contents were declared to be powder of alabaster.'

This was all very fascinating, thought Russell, but how did this apply to Egypt? Delevingne delved further. British detectives had pieced together a bigger network in which Melissaratos was just one player. They included a Greek called George Tatayo, a Turk from Crete and an unnamed Egyptian. All based in Germany, their principal business was selling narcotics to France. Tatayo was known to have bought a large consignment of morphia and cocaine produced in a factory in Stuttgart and forwarded it to Basle in Switzerland. Their headquarters were said to be in Cairo.

In the meantime, Theodore Loverdos had married a Russian woman in Shanghai and moved to Athens, where he bought a beautiful house for two million drachmas. Part of this money had come from a deal in which he persuaded an American to invest $10,000 in shipping morphia from Germany to Shanghai. In a further twist, he informed the Shanghai customs officers of the shipment to cover his own involvement in the deal, pocketing at least $4,000 and leaving the poor American without any profit.

Melissaratos and Loverdos thrived for the best part of a decade, but then pushed it too far. Cockily, in December 1927, they dispatched two parcels containing four kilos of heroin from Greece to the Greek Consulate at Alexandria in Egypt. Whether this meant they had a compliant agent within the Greek Consulate, or that they were the unknowing recipients of it, is not known. But the Egyptian customs seized the packets and the embarrassed Greek authorities were forced to imprison Melissaratos and Loverdos for a year.

Russell and the British authorities in Egypt read Delevingne's report with increasing anger. International traffickers saw the Egyptians as a soft touch and were happy to flood their country with drugs. What also came out of this was the role of legitimate Western European manufacturers of narcotics – mainly in Switzerland, Germany and France – who produced drugs intended for medical use from raw opium from Asia, but were happy to see vast amounts of this white powder disappear into the black market.

'It seems to me that the people who make and supply these drugs in Europe, chiefly, I understand, Swiss and German,' said Egypt's supreme judge, 'are the worst scoundrels of all, and that the League of Nations should be urged to further exertions.'

In a letter to the British Consulate-General in Alexandria, the supreme judge suggested an even more controversial course of action.

> I have sometimes wondered whether we ought not to try and get the Egyptians to help from the moral side. Suppose His Excellency would see Sheikh Mustafa El Maraghi the Head of the El Azhar and ask him whether it would not be possible to get his Sheikhs and Mosque preachers to denounce the drug taking habit as destruction to mind and soul and as forbidden by Islam; I think he would probably help and it might create sounder public opinion.

'There is perhaps some risk,' he added, 'of ignorant preachers and malicious newspapers representing the drug traffic as due to the British occupation, but ought we not to run this risk?'

Russell thought not, preferring to make this an international crusade by approaching the League of Nations. The problem was that Egypt was not a member of the League. While Russell awaited the necessary legislation for this, he turned his attention to cracking down on the foreign dealers on home territory. Here, he hit another problem. For centuries, foreign traders had been protected from exploitation by Egyptian rulers by a set of privileges called the Capitulations. This made sense when it was a medieval merchant avoiding some terrible arbitrary punishment from a Turkish governor – but in the modern world, it was being used as a shield by drugs barons who claimed their foreign nationality exempted them from the full strength of Egyptian law.

'Had it not been for the protection that the foreign trafficker derived from [the Capitulations],' said Russell, 'the narcotic problem in Egypt would never have reached the magnitude it did.'

Russell got round this by visiting every major foreign embassy and getting their agreement to allow their nationals to be put on trial in Egyptian courts under the same law facing nationals. As a result, Russell obtained expulsion orders against 334 European traffickers in three years.

As Russell's bureau began to have an impact on the amount of heroin coming into Egypt, there was an incentive for native farmers to grow their own opium, despite a ban on its cultivation imposed in 1926. Clever farmers got round this by hiding patches of opium poppies inside larger fields of six-foot-tall bean plants. It was simply not worth the efforts of Egyptian police to wade through these hundreds of acres of beans, but Russell was one step ahead of them. He instructed the fledgling Egyptian Army Air Force to fly over the fields. That way, they could clearly see the little patches of grey-green opium poppies tipped with pale mauve flowers in a sea of dark-green beans.

Sometimes Russell's campaign revealed tales of desperately poor dealers trying to make their stash of heroin stretch a little bit further. One old woman lived in the Khalifa district near a cemetery housing the ancient tombs of the Mamluks. When the police got a tip-off and raided her house, they found her grinding a substance to a fine powder in a pestle to mix with her heroin, so that the local quarrymen could sniff it up their noses. On closer inspection, the substance turned out to be fragments of human skulls scavenged from the nearby cemetery.

Some villagers outside Cairo were so desperate to break their addiction to heroin that they pretended they had been bitten by dogs infected with rabies. The cure for this was so painful that it removed any desire for them to take heroin. Once word of this miracle cure got out, one enterprising village barber fitted a dead dog's jawbones with a steel spring to mimic the marks of being bitten by a mad dog.

Sweeping up big and smaller dealers, Russell's operation was beginning to slow the white drugs epidemic in Egypt, but he knew that the best way to smash it was to hit the major international traffickers. To do this, he needed to get some leads. His first real break came with the arrest of an Armenian carpet seller called Zakarian. Breaking down under interrogation, Zakarian fingered his chief carrier, who was bringing in large consignments from a factory in Switzerland. Russell dispatched one of his assistants to Basle, who, with the help of the Swiss police, uncovered a link with an even larger factory in France supplying narcotics. An examination of bank drafts between Zakarian and the Swiss factory revealed substantial individual transactions of £16,000 and £26,000. These would be dwarfed by the sums of money going to the French manufacturer.

'I realised that we were up against a vast and rich international organisation of the most formidable nature,' said Russell, 'with the prospect before us of having to fight huge political and financial interests.'

Arriving in France, Russell's agent discovered that the Paris factory had exported 7,500 kilos – or seven and a half tons – of narcotics in the previous four years. The League of Nations had estimated that the annual requirement of all legitimate medical and scientific institutions in the world was 2,000 kilos and that just this one French manufacturer had shifted 4,350 kilos of heroin in a year. Although European laws had been introduced to restrict the movement of dangerous drugs, the legislation had been so tightly worded that similar drugs under different trade names could pass unhindered. Also, as far as the authorities in France were concerned, so long as the narcotics were exported out of their country, they didn't care where they ended up.

The international situation was further complicated by drugs barons using Egypt as a transit point for narcotic shipments elsewhere. One devious plan involved two Japanese and an Armenian setting up the Oriental Products Company in Istanbul. The British Embassy in Turkey tipped off Egyptian customs that the Armenian was arriving in Alexandria by steamer. Customs officers searched his baggage but found nothing. It was only when they turned over his cabin that they found 43 kilos of hashish. The Armenian was arrested. Shortly afterwards, a Japanese gentleman came forward, offering to pay any sum to get his colleague released.

The Japanese was promptly arrested too, but then the Japanese Consul in Alexandria revealed that he was friendly with the arrested man and produced a letter from the Japanese Embassy in Istanbul, clearing their trading company of any wrongdoing. Clearly, this was bigger than just the traffickers involved.

Put on trial, the two managed to argue convincingly that the hashish must have been placed in their cabin during a stopover in Piraeus, Greece, when they had switched cabins. The Egyptian customs officers had inadequately searched both of the accused men and had failed to pick up any further incriminating evidence. The case was dismissed, but that customs were on the right trail was revealed later.

'That the [Oriental Products] Company is engaged in illicit traffic,' said a report, 'has been abundantly proved by the discovery – lucky, I understand – at Port Said of heroin, in cases supposed to contain olive oil and consigned by the Company to the Far East. There is no reason to suppose that the Agents of the Company are less unscrupulous than the Company itself.'

Eventually, Russell Pasha got his chance to stand before the League of Nations in Geneva and put his case in January 1930. Although Egypt was still not a member of the League, the police chief was allowed to present his evidence of an international conspiracy to traffic narcotics and other prohibited drugs into Egypt.

'I was extremely nervous at this my first appearance before the Advisory Committee,' recalled Russell. 'Untrained in Geneva etiquette, I was saved, however, from having to deliver a too personal assault by a subterfuge which served me well on this and other occasions.'

He had sent his written report before his own arrival and this proved shocking enough for the Committee members. They were not expecting him to name companies and individuals involved and they advised him to refer only to Monsieur X or Y. But the report was dynamite and the thoroughness of its research demanded action. The immediate result was that Switzerland tightened up its anti-narcotics legislation and France promised to rein in its own activities. What both nations did not want was to be exposed in another public meeting at Geneva by Russell and his team.

This success put the Central Narcotics Intelligence Bureau on the map and meant it started to receive even more top-quality information about drugs trafficking. What seemed to be happening was that as the spotlight was shone on manufacturers in Western and Central Europe, the major traffickers shifted their operations to Istanbul. Turkey produced a large legitimate crop of high-class opium, its government was not tied in to international conventions on narcotics export and it had a long coast – perfect for smuggling.

Russell returned to Geneva in 1931 to expose the growing role of Turkey in the drugs trade. Its government seemed little inclined to do anything about what it considered legitimate business – until Russell spoke to the American Ambassador to Turkey. He communicated to Mustafa Kemal Ataturk, the Turkish soldier who became the first President of his country, that this was not only a problem that affected the health of the rest of the world but also his own nation, as the narcotics habit was spreading among the officers of his army.

Ataturk shut down three major factories and introduced strict anti-trafficking laws. As a consequence, some of the manufacturers moved far away to foreign concessions in China, while others set up factories in Bulgaria. One of these, near Sofia, churned out 1,500 kilos of heroin in its first two months. Middlemen then smuggled the drug into Germany and France, where it left from Hamburg for markets across the Atlantic, or from Marseilles to reach Egypt and the Far East via the imperial highway of the Suez Canal.

Relentlessly, Russell sent his agents into Bulgaria, where they photographed the factories and got their balance sheets of opium imported and heroin exported. They then presented this material to the League of Nations in Geneva. The Bulgarian government reacted by shutting down the factories and the drugs merchants went on the run again.

On 30 November 1931, an Italian-American stepped off the Simplon Express from Istanbul to Berlin. The German police arrested him and among his papers they found some very interesting names. He was plugged into a vast narcotics-trafficking network that truly spanned the globe, from China and Afghanistan to America. He was called August Del Grazio – known as 'Little Augie' on the streets of New York – and he had some very dangerous friends indeed. Among them top mafioso Charles 'Lucky' Luciano and mobster Jack 'Legs' Diamond. Russell Pasha was fascinated – but so was another emerging drugs-busting agent, the American Harry Anslinger.

Putting together the pieces of this complex jigsaw of international drugs trafficking made Russell feel like an aviator flying above the clouds. 'Occasional gaps in the clouds gave a glimpse now and then,' he wrote, 'but it is only now that the clouds have rolled away and a clear panorama has been spread out before us. Our geographical drug map is clear, the countries of raw material, the manufacturing centres, the railroads and sea routes, the ports of departure and ports of destination, all stand out.'

Russell Pasha had done an outstanding job of exposing the global trade in illicit drugs, but it was another thing to stop the lethal men running it.

5

THE FEARLESS MR ANSLINGER

'AS A YOUNGSTER OF 12, visiting the house of a neighbouring farmer, I heard the screaming of a woman on the second floor,' recalled Harry J. Anslinger. 'I had never heard such cries of pain before. The woman, I learned later, was addicted, like many other women of that period, to morphine.'

As the little boy shrank away from the terrible sound, the woman's husband rushed down the stairs and thrust a piece of paper into Anslinger's hands. It was an order for a package he had to pick up from the local drugstore. Anslinger leapt into a cart and lashed at the horses to get to the store as fast he could before, he believed, the woman died. The druggist handed over the package containing the morphine and the boy got it back to the farm. A little while later a hush settled over the house.

'I never forgot those screams,' said Anslinger. 'Nor did I forget that the morphine she had required was sold to a 12-year-old boy, no questions asked.'

Twenty-six years later, Anslinger was US Commissioner of Narcotics. The first Director of the Federal Bureau of Narcotics, he was charged with enforcing the Harrison Act of 1914 and subsequent legislation that controlled the possession and production of opium and coca-derived drugs in the USA. The seeds of his deep hatred of organised crime were sown on this journey from delivery boy to drugs tsar.

Born in the rural township of Altoona, Pennsylvania, the son of a Swiss barber, Anslinger studied engineering at the state university. He paid for his tuition fees by playing piano in silent movie theatres. His first job was with the Pennsylvania Railroad, working alongside construction crews. Many of them were Italian immigrants and several of those came from Sicily. As Anslinger ate his lunch alongside these tough workers, he took a liking to a rugged Italian called Giovanni. He came from a big family and had big dreams for them in America, planning to make the most of his opportunity in a new land to work hard and provide for them. One day, Anslinger found Giovanni in a ditch, shot several times, with blood pumping out of his body.

Rushing the Italian to hospital, Anslinger learned from his workmates that Giovanni didn't like to be pushed around. Most of them paid tribute money to a squat, powerfully built Sicilian called 'Big Mouth Sam', but Giovanni refused – and was shot as a result. Big Mouth Sam had the reputation of belonging to the Black Hand, a gang running a protection racket in the style of the Mafia.

Fearlessly, the 6 ft, 200 lb Anslinger confronted the Sicilian bully.

'I'm Giovanni's boss and friend,' he told him.

The Sicilian blinked.

'What I got to do with Giovanni? I don't know no Giovanni.'

'If Giovanni dies, I'm going to see to it that you hang,' threatened Anslinger. 'And if he lives and you ever bother him again, or any of my men, or try to shake them down any more, I'll kill you with my own hands.'

Anslinger wasn't kidding. Big Mouth Sam backed off and Giovanni lived.

Although seemingly destined for a career on the railroad, Anslinger was becoming aware of the increasing problem of drug-taking among his own generation. Aside from the farmer's addicted wife, he was profoundly bothered by the news of a talented teenage pool player in his home town who had got hooked on opium and died two years later. His inner sense of justice urged him to get more directly involved in this new plague and if it meant confronting organised crime, he'd already had a taste of that. It was a sentiment that chimed with the concerns of his government.

The US government first came across narcotics as a major problem in its Philippines territory, recently won from the Spanish Empire in its war of 1898. Charles Henry Brent was a missionary Episcopal bishop posted to the Philippines and he was shocked at the level of opium addiction among its population. He initiated a commission to investigate and control opium usage. His recommendations got to the desk of President Theodore Roosevelt and he called for an international conference on the subject of opium, held in Shanghai in 1909.

It was followed by the 1912 International Opium Convention, signed at the Hague – the first dangerous drugs control treaty. Uniting 13 nations, including Great Britain, the US, Germany, France, China and Japan, it called on them to 'control or to cause to be controlled, all persons manufacturing, importing, selling, distributing, and exporting morphine, cocaine, and their respective salts'.

Despite these efforts, the Americans felt the British Empire was to blame for the opium epidemic in the Philippines. They pointed the finger at the smuggling of the drug from their protectorate in North Borneo. At first, the British responded to American concerns by abolishing the farming of opium in North Borneo and assuming direct control of its trafficking. But this failed to halt the smugglers.

After several years of increasing levels of opium coming into their islands – reaching a value worth $1.8 million in 1918 – the Americans had had enough. A statement from the US Secretary of War was addressed to Lord Curzon, the British Foreign Secretary.

'This government has devoted all existing energies to stop this traffic,' said the Americans, 'and is now about to initiate a campaign with swifter patrol vessels and sea planes. Chinese residents of Sandakan are active agents in procuring and selling this drug to Moros. These wholesalers are believed to be the chief source of the practice of introducing opium into the Philippine Islands, a practice designed to corrupt and debauch the residents of this island.'

What is clear in this aggressive statement is that despite the well-meaning efforts of the British to prohibit the sale of opium abroad, the trade was being taken over by Chinese residents within their empire.

'Legitimate trade between the Philippine Islands and British North Borneo is almost infinitesimal,' continued the Americans. 'The 40 or 50 small vessels from the Philippines entering Sandakan harbor each month are almost exclusively dedicated to the nefarious traffic in opium.'

The British Colonial Office forwarded these concerns to the Secretary of the North Borneo Chartered Company (NBCC), charged with running this protectorate, and got a robust reply.

'The [US] Secretary of War is mistaken in the assumption that the

North Borneo Government expected to stop all smuggling,' noted the NBCC. 'The North Borneo Government never indulged in such ambitious hopes; what they expected and what has occurred is considerable diminution of the smuggling, and to that end they have made strenuous exertions.'

Furthermore, said the Secretary of the NBCC, the Philippine government were not innocent victims but complicit in the trade themselves.

'In recent years it has been generally believed in the Territory by the Officers of the North Borneo Government that the revenue cutters employed by the Philippine Government – manned and officered by Philippinos [sic] – were themselves accomplices in these nefarious practices.'

In fact, American boats were observed to have invaded their coastal waters. 'Some natives of Sulu reported that a motor boat manned by Filipinos had chased them near the shore at the entrance of Sandakan Bay,' said the Governor of North Borneo. 'They were afraid and jumped overboard and swam ashore, running into the village. Their boat was not seen again. One witness swore that the motor boat belonged to United States SS *Mindoro*, and others recognised her as belonging to an American revenue cruiser.'

The British were sanguine about these infringements, but they were to be noted as increasing the tension in the area.

'The opium traffic in North Borneo is most carefully supervised and restricted,' insisted the Secretary of the NBCC, 'and its consumption is entirely confined to the Chinese adult population. Any tendency of the habit spreading to the non-Chinese population would be promptly dealt with. There is however no sign of any such tendency, indeed the indigenous native population prefer the intoxicating liquor which they distil from the rice of their own production, and which is much more pernicious than opium consumed in moderate quantities.'

To help reduce the amount of opium consumed by the Chinese population of North Borneo, the British had almost doubled its price per ounce between 1914 and 1919. At the end of the day, however, 'an appreciable amount of opium can be easily carried on the person of the smuggler, and consequently the difficulty of ascertaining whether or not smuggling is taking place is very difficult'.

As far as the British were concerned, they were doing their best.

The Americans were less reassured and continued to view the British Empire with suspicion – a stance that would be taken up by Harry Anslinger.

It was while investigating accidents on the Pennsylvania Railroad that Anslinger developed his detecting techniques, and when his boss was seconded to head the state police, the young man went with him. By 1916, Anslinger was running a department of 2,500 personnel and was tasked with investigating arsons. When the US entered the First World War, he volunteered for officer training but was rejected because of a childhood eye injury. Instead, he served in the Ordnance Department, assisting the Chief of Equipment Inspection. Again, his talents were recognised and in 1918 he was transferred to the diplomatic corps, where his fluent German, learned from his Swiss parents, proved useful.

'It was a time of tensions,' recalled Anslinger. 'Every government – including our own – was eager to obtain every scrap of information possible, especially as the war drew to its close.'

Stationed in the Hague, Anslinger had to go undercover, mixing with politicians and high society to glean any useful intelligence. His greatest coup was to bluff his way into travelling with the staff of the Kaiser, then about to abdicate as leader of the defeated German nation. Pretending to be a concerned German official, Anslinger advised against abdication. 'Had he not done so, the Kaiser might well have stayed on the throne,' speculated Anslinger, 'forestalling any chance for a future Hitler gaining power, or a Second World War erupting.' It was a giant claim, that Anslinger could have stopped a world war! But it revealed the ego and ambition of a gentleman who was keen to take on the big foes of his day.

He served briefly as American Vice-Consul in Hamburg, Germany, and part of his job at the time was to repatriate American sailors. 'Young fellows,' he noted, 'whose faces bore the stamp of the opium smoker, the user of morphine or the new "kick" called heroin. I saw it also on the skeleton faces of men in other countries, seeking visas or other help from us.' Anslinger was witnessing at first hand the great wartime leap in illicit drug use described by Sir Malcolm Delevingne.

Anslinger also had a brush with communist agents endeavouring to slip into America and spark revolution there. He tried to warn his superiors in Washington, but they assured him Communism would collapse within a few years and not to worry about it.

'Decades later, in the world of narcotics,' said Anslinger, 'I met this same Red enemy – with the same ultimate goals. And in some measure, I also met the same puzzling unconcern.' Then it would come from the Chinese, who would use their mastery of drugs trafficking as a political weapon.

Anslinger was positioning himself as a lone ranger, alert to America's future problems before she had even fully considered them herself.

In 1923, Anslinger was shifted to consular work in Venezuela. He hated it, as it had taken him away from the intrigue of Weimar Germany. He had recently married a relative of the Secretary of the Treasury, Andrew W. Mellon, and found the South American climate unfavourable for bringing up a family. Eventually, he was moved to a more congenial posting in Nassau, the Bahamas. As a centre of alcohol smuggling, this was just what he wanted to get his teeth into. Prohibition was in force and rumrunners were using it as a base for bringing illicit liquor into the US.

Yet again, the Americans became frustrated by what they considered to be the lackadaisical attitude of the British imperial authorities on the islands. They felt the British could be doing a lot more to hinder the smugglers and forced a conference on them in London in 1926. This time Anslinger was there to challenge their lack of action. He testified to seeing ships loaded with liquor passing in broad daylight from British-controlled ports in the Bahamas to deliver their cargo to bootleggers in the Florida Keys.

Reluctantly, the local British colonial authorities caved in over this activity – which was not at all illegal in their eyes and no doubt furnished their pockets to some degree. They agreed to take a more vigorous attitude to enforcing Prohibition laws by expecting ships to provide them with a certificate of landing. The US Treasury Department was amazed at Anslinger's success and borrowed the young diplomat to pursue similar agreements with Canada, France and Cuba. Anslinger stayed with the Treasury for the rest of his life.

While dealing with illicit alcohol smuggling, Anslinger was aware of the next big threat to his country.

'Another danger was growing almost unnoticed,' he warned. 'The big organised bootleg gangs were looking to the future when

Prohibition would be out. They would have to find other outlets. One lucrative outlet, even then occupying much of the international underworld of that time, was that of narcotics. Big chemical plants of Europe and Asia already were producing vast quantities of drugs which came into this country by various routes and smuggling techniques.'

In September 1930, President Herbert Hoover invited Anslinger to take charge of the newly formed Federal Bureau of Narcotics (FBN) under the overall control of the Secretary of the Treasury. It was to be an elite crime-busting agency, just like the FBI, and Anslinger couldn't have hoped for a more perfect job. He was only 38 years old.

Within a few weeks of being in office, Harry Anslinger was embarrassed by a senator from South Carolina, who stood up in the Senate, waving a tin of opium. He had bought it only a block away from the Capitol. This prompted the FBN to launch its first major investigation of the narcotics underworld and, in 1930, they found that it was still very much dominated by the Chinese.

There were opium dens in most American cities, and Chinese immigrant gangs – the Tongs – ruthlessly controlled them, alongside prostitution and gambling in their communities. The Tong gangsters made for exotic figures. In New York's Chinatown, it was a little moon-faced henchman who took on his rival mob, the On Leongs:

> He wore the shirt of chain mail [with] which all of the Tong killers of the period protected their precious bodies, he carried two guns and a hatchet, and at times he would fight bravely, squatting on his haunches in the street with both eyes shut, and blazing away at a surrounding circle of On Leongs with an utter disregard of his own safety. He seldom hit what he aimed at, or anything else for that matter, but so long as he could pull the trigger he was dangerous to anyone up, down or sideways within range.

With an eye to self-promoting publicity that would sustain him throughout his career, Anslinger met the senator's challenge and targeted the opium dens along Pennsylvania Avenue. He got a break when he recruited an undercover agent from the On Leongs, but the brave Chinese informer was shot down dead in the street by fellow Tong members when they discovered his betrayal. It was an early lesson in the murky reality of Anslinger's business.

Not wanting to risk any more lives, the FBN chief decided on a simultaneous raid of 30 opium dens. With the assistance of 400 police patrolmen, they swooped on the illicit dens, cleared out their smoking equipment and took the operators to police stations. Hour after hour, the saturation raids went on. Anslinger went with the police and on one occasion was confronted by a well-dressed Chinese man in a business suit.

'Why didn't they cart you off with the others?' Anslinger barked at him.

'I'm the mayor of Chinatown,' he replied in flawless English. He protested against the violence of the raids, but Anslinger cut him short.

'You get these dens out of here,' he told him. 'If you or the Tongs try to open up these joints, I'll raid them night after night. We'll smash them into teakwood pulp.'

The worlds of narcotics and prostitution went hand-in-hand, noted Anslinger, taking up the Yellow Peril menace of the previous decade. Chinese pimps were using drugs to seduce young women, especially white girls, giving them a few puffs of opium. 'I felt simply wonderful,' one 18-year-old woman told an FBN investigator. 'I thought it was great. We ate little bits of Chinese candy. I was dancing with a Chinese boy. We danced a lot.'

The Chinese candy was laced with cantharides, a sexual stimulant, the apartments were kept hot and the girls were encouraged to strip off their clothes. After seeing to their 'guests', when the girls wanted to relax the Chinese pimps gave them pills containing heroin. Soon they were hooked and the 'free' heroin had to be earned through serving more and more clients. The link between drugs and sex outraged middle-class Americans and Anslinger successfully used this to ensure his department was well funded.

Having made some initial inroads into the domestic misuse of drugs, Anslinger knew he had to get a grip on how they were getting into the United States. For help with that, he turned to the research carried out by Russell Pasha in Cairo and Sir Malcolm Delevingne in London. The FBN got in touch with their imperial colleagues and one major route into the East Coast cities was revealed as originating in Canada. This had nothing to do with the Chinese and everything to do with the network of Europeans shifting processed white powder drugs from European manufacturers, part of the geographical drugs map already exposed by the Cairo-based Central Narcotics Intelligence Bureau.

A secret report compiled by the Royal Canadian Mounted Police in Montreal, Quebec, chronicled the activities of a drug smuggler called George Howe, who had spoken to an undercover agent a few years earlier.

'Howe has told Dufresne,' said the report, 'that one Rosenblatt, a heavy narcotic dealer of New York City who has recently visited Montreal, has given Howe some $2,000 with which to purchase narcotics in Europe.'

Howe was born in Belgium to a British father and travelled on a British passport back and forth to Canada. In 1920, he brought with him to Montreal a number of statuettes purchased in Brussels. Nine of the statuettes contained 51 eighth-ounces of morphine sulphate and two figurines five half-ounces of cocaine hydrochloride. They were destined for a millinery store in Quebec run by a 'Madam Howe', but the deal went bad when she was arrested.

Undeterred, Howe continued to travel from Antwerp to Montreal. In August 1922, his luggage was thoroughly searched as he stepped off a transatlantic steamer, but no illicit drugs were found. 'Howe stated on return to Canada at that time,' said a report from the Canadian High Commissioner, 'that he had been in Belgium studying chemistry and art.' In fact, he had just had a major cache of narcotics seized from him by the Belgian police.

Howe was closely connected with Laurent Deleglise, who headed a major smuggling ring in Europe. Back in 1919, Deleglise bribed the superintendent of construction on the Cunard Line to get him access to all shipping. Having secured this route, he tried to bribe his way into Ottawa, but was uncovered and had to leave Canada. Thereafter he used a team of smugglers.

'Deleglise was the brains of the whole affair,' said a Canadian investigator. 'His first policy was to keep each employee of his as far away from the others as possible, making each work independently and as far as possible never meet any other.' This way one arrest would not imperil the whole gang. His carriers would deploy a variety of methods of hiding their shipments:

> The shipper of the drugs would load up one or two trunks full of drugs and send them aboard the ship, taking tickets, he would then miss the boat and the baggage would be held unclaimed. The shipper would then arrive by another route or boat and go to some small town and wire or write for his trunks, omitting to send the keys. The Baggage man would explain the difficulty of opening the trunk to the Customs Officer who would not bother his head and pass it out, or possibly the Customs man was squared, this is not known. It is known that he was either crooked or too lax to open the trunks.

When Deleglise sent narcotics to the US, he had them forwarded by express post to a Japanese store in New York City. This may well have been the distribution centre used by several prominent US mobsters who dealt in narcotics in the 1920s, including Lucky Luciano and his criminal mentor, the millionaire gambler Arnold Rothstein. As Anslinger had predicted, these gangsters had made a fortune out of bootlegging alcohol during Prohibition but were now looking to other high-profit methods of illegal income.

Piecing all this past intelligence together, both Anslinger and Russell Pasha focused their attention on destroying the most recent drugs syndicate and its master criminal, who was based in France. Called Elias Eliopoulos, this super-dealer was an elegant gold-tipped-cane-carrying Greek who moved in elevated business circles and was very much at home on the boulevards of Paris. With money in his pocket from his successful entrepreneurial father, Elie – as he was known to his society friends – was hungry to make his own fortune and was very much taken by a conversation he had had with a fellow Greek, who told him about the money to be made from shipping dope to China. Encouraged, Elie was introduced to Jean Voyatzis, the largest importer of prepared white drugs into the Far East. They met in Tientsin in north-eastern China, one of the cities opened to western traders as a result of the Second Opium War.

Elie struck a deal with Voyatzis in which the latter agreed to supply him with raw opium from China. Elie had this sent to two French pharmaceutical manufacturers – the Comptoir des Alcaloides and the Societe Industrielle de Chimie Organique. The French chemists were delighted to receive the opium at below market cost and reciprocated by providing Elie with processed narcotics that he shipped back to Voyatzis. The French companies acted under government licences that supposedly limited their quotas of dangerous drugs, but, no doubt, this was overcome by the enormous supplementary profits to be made from supplying Elie. Soon, he had struck similar deals with other French chemical companies to provide morphine and heroin.

Sitting at the centre of a magnificently efficient narcotics business, Elie and his brother George, who had joined in the venture, enjoyed enormous profits gushing into their bank accounts. At one time, it was estimated that Elie was receiving from Voyatzis more than $50,000 a month. Bearing in mind that Anslinger was only earning $9,000 a year at the time, it is hardly surprising that social commentators noted Elie splashing his cash on champagne, beautiful women and the finest food in the grandest restaurants in Paris.

Such wealth provided protection too, enabling him to bribe French government officials and police. Indeed, he was helpful enough to tip off French law enforcers about rival drug dealers who made the mistake of selling the goods in their own backyard in France.

When the outrageous role of the French chemical companies was finally revealed by Russell Pasha to the League of Nations in Geneva in 1930, similar factories were simply set up in Turkey and Eastern Europe.

Elie rolled with the shift in operations, putting all his efforts into magnifying his profits by supplying drugs to an increasing network of dealers and smugglers spanning the globe – including America – and that very much concerned Anslinger. Principal among these international dealers was the Italian-American August Del Grazio. A known associate of Lucky Luciano and Legs Diamond, he was their main agent in setting up direct links with Elie's dealers in Europe.

Previously, the two mobsters had tried to strike a drugs deal by themselves when in September 1930 they travelled in luxury on an ocean liner to Weimar Germany. The trip ended in farce when the high-profile Diamond was arrested in Germany and deported very publicly back to New York from Hamburg. He growled at journalists, telling them he was there to visit spa towns to cure his stomach ailments. When one cheeky reporter asked him if he had enjoyed his stay in Germany, he barked, 'I hate it.' Others reported he was there to perform in a German cabaret.

Luciano carried on with their narcotics business in Hamburg more discreetly, but handed it over the following year to Del Grazio, who was entrusted with doing business for him with one of Elie's partners. This would also end badly and it revealed a dimension to the international drugs trade that constantly led to its own demise – dealers liked ripping off other dealers.

The double-cross began with Legs Diamond, who had made a fortune out of hijacking consignments of bootleg booze from rival mobsters. When he extended this to the narcotics trade, he made powerful enemies. Carlos Fernandez Bacula was a former Peruvian diplomat based in Vienna and part of Elie's syndicate. Using his diplomatic passport and its subsequent immunity, he smuggled several consignments of heroin into New York – up to an estimated one and half tons of the drug, worth some $37 million. On his final trip, he was staying in a hotel and distributing 150 kilos of heroin through various agents. One carrier came back bloody and beaten, saying that his 50 kilos had been stolen from him.

A few days later, Legs Diamond knocked on the door of Bacula's hotel room and introduced himself. Famously charming, he sympathised with the Peruvian's losses and offered to use his connections to get it back. Bacula knew Diamond's reputation as a ruthless killer but could see little alternative to accepting the offer. A couple of days later, Diamond returned with 30 kilos, saying he'd had to use the other 20 kilos to pay off his contacts. Diamond then expressed concern at the whole of Bacula's shipment totalling 130 kilos.

'You're bats,' he told him. 'Somebody'll bust in. The safest thing to do is to get it to another place. There's a hotel downtown where I got connections. Nobody would touch it there.'

To reassure Bacula, he told him to have the stash guarded by his own Austrian bodyguard. The next day, having moved the drugs, the bodyguard was found dead in a pool of blood in the hotel room. His wrists had been slashed in an effort to make it look like suicide. The 130 kilos were missing, presumably stolen, Diamond told Bacula. The

Peruvian ex-diplomat hurriedly sailed back to Europe to explain himself to Elie.

Diamond probably thought he'd got away with the crude scam, but Elie was far more sophisticated and bided his time. When New York drugs envoy Del Grazio returned to Europe in 1931, Elie set him up in a double-cross. In Istanbul, Del Grazio took receipt of $10,000 worth of morphine cubes. He asked for them to be packed in crates with machine parts and then sent by train to Hamburg, from where they would be shipped to America. The Turkish manufacturer agreed, but had the morphine cubes secretly removed when they reached the warehouse in Hamburg. He was then going to tell the American gangster they had been stolen en route – just as Bacula had been told by Diamond – a perfect moment of vengeance.

Greed, however, got in the way of the sting and another of Elie's colleagues offered the mislaid $10,000 consignment of morphine cubes to Del Grazio – if only he could pick them up in Hamburg. Del Grazio grew suspicious at the similarity of the two deals, and when he turned up at the German port he was furious to be asked to pay twice for the same consignment of drugs! The story of Elie's revenge that went wrong became a major source of amusement in the underworld. But it also revealed a drugs cartel at war with itself and that made it vulnerable to the narcotics-busting crime agencies run by Harry Anslinger and Russell Pasha.

Shortly after the Elie–Del Grazio morphine farce, an American consul in Turkey alerted Anslinger to the 30 November train trip from Istanbul to Berlin taken by Del Grazio, during which the German police had arrested him.

Fearing his business empire was about to implode, Elie sent word to Russell Pasha in Cairo that he wanted to talk and set the record straight. Interviewed in Athens by an agent of Russell's Central Narcotics Intelligence Bureau and an agent from Anslinger's FBN, the suave king of narcotics poured out all the details of his business but maintained he was being falsely linked to the Del Grazio shipment in Hamburg by the devious Americans. He didn't want to go down for a payback that had gone wrong.

With all the information provided by Elie, Anslinger broke up the American end of his network and many of the smugglers were arrested and imprisoned, including Bacula. Del Grazio, however, escaped major punishment and continued to be a key player in New York narcotics, later becoming involved in murky dealings with the CIA and even plotting to get Lucky Luciano out of jail through a secret deal with the US government.

Elie was also too big to be imprisoned. Having told Anslinger and Russell Pasha all he could about the international drugs trade, he was allowed to retire to Greece with much of his wealth intact. When the Nazis invaded his country, he became a passionate anti-Semite and collaborated with them before setting sail for South America. He even turned up in New York, where he paraded his wealth at Park Avenue parties, before being deported back to Greece, where he ended his life, selling arms to both the Israelis and the Arabs.

Elie's Washington attorney informed Anslinger when he passed away.

'Too bad,' replied the FBN chief.

'You're charitable,' said the lawyer. 'After all the trouble he caused.'

'Not at all,' said Anslinger. 'I simply know where he's going – after this, hell won't be fit to live in.'

Although Anslinger would harbour many suspicions about the complicity of the British Empire in narcotics trading over the next few decades, it had been his close working relationship with imperial drugs-buster Russell Pasha that had helped nail one of the biggest crimelords of the period.

6

THE DARING SIR CECIL

JUST AS PRIME MINISTER GLADSTONE had predicted, the British Empire's well-meaning efforts to prohibit the Indian export trade of opium was causing a dramatic rise in illegal smuggling. From his desk in Whitehall, it was the task of the UK's narcotics expert, Sir Malcolm Delevingne, to clear up the mess.

In January 1927, he sent a letter of warning to Prince Charoon of Siam (now Thailand). The British Empire had been encroaching on this independent ancient kingdom throughout the late nineteenth and early twentieth centuries. It had absorbed its northern Shan provinces into Burma and in 1909, with its Anglo-Siamese Treaty, had taken four predominantly ethnic-Malay southern provinces to make the northern states of Malaya – the Unfederated Malay States. Great Britain considered the territory within its sphere of influence and Delevingne did not hold back in telling the Siamese what to do.

'I hear that the Siamese Government have recently arranged for the importation of 1100 chests of Persian opium into Siam through MA Namazie of Singapore,' said Sir Malcolm. 'This Namazie is a connection and business associate of the notorious Namazie of Hong Kong and was himself concerned in some illegal drug transactions in Indo-China not very long ago.'

Delevingne had heard that the government of the Straits Settlements (including Singapore, Penang and Malacca) was buying Persian opium from Namazie and had warned them not to do so again. The problem was that the Chinese population of the Straits Settlements had not been weaned off its addiction to opium and its colonial government, deprived of high-quality Indian opium, was doing its best to replace the shortfall – or face widespread Chinese discontent. Delevingne was aware of this problem, but was keen to cut out the gangsters that were making money out of the situation. So, if only Siam would step into line too, then they could exclude the undesirable Namazie altogether.

'You may also like to know,' said Sir Malcolm, sounding like a high-level dealer himself, 'that our Consul-General in the Persian Gulf has advised us that there would be no difficulty in making direct contracts with the Persian shippers, and if we could give you any help in the matter, I have no doubt the British Government would be very glad to do so. Perhaps we might have a talk about this when we meet in Geneva.'

Apparently, Sir Malcolm was suggesting trading directly with the Persian opium producers and delivering the goods straight to their imperial Asian partners – anything rather than going through crooked middlemen. Eight months later, however, and Sir Malcolm's friendly little words with Asian foreign ministers seemed not to have had the effect he hoped and a senior figure in the Colonial Office, Mr J.J. Paskin, followed up Delevingne's request with a series of stronger warnings to all colonial governments.

One letter was sent to the British North Borneo Company – which had already had a run-in with the Americans over its Chinese merchants selling opium to the Philippines. Paskin told them: 'You are, of course, aware that most of the Far Eastern Governments (British Colonial and others) which used to get practically the whole of their supplies of opium from India have been compelled to turn to Persia to supplement their restricted supplies of Indian opium. The cumulative effect last year was to create a boom in Persian opium.'

The main subject of the letter – as with Delevingne's – was the king of the black market dealers: M.A. Namazie. Having already pulled off one deal, selling opium to the Strait Settlements, they really didn't want to see any other colonial government trading with the Persian wheeler-dealer.

'You are no doubt familiar with the reputation of various branches of the Namazie family in Persia and elsewhere in connection with the illicit traffic in Persian opium,' explained Paskin, 'large quantities of which find their way into China. The employment by a British Colonial Government of a member of a family with a reputation like this was obviously open to serious criticisms which might be difficult to meet if they should be brought forward at Geneva.'

This was the crux of it. Britain, with its prominent anti-drugs stance taken at the League of Nations, did not want to be embarrassed by its colonial governments making grubby little deals with gangsters like Namazie and his family. It was a matter of international prestige, especially as Britain was taking a lead in telling other nations not to partake in the illicit traffic in opium.

'I do not know whether the Company has bought any opium through this firm,' Paskin warned the British North Borneo Company, 'but in any case, we trust that they will see the desirability of falling into line with instructions given to the Straits Government.'

Not everyone was impressed by this argument. The French colonial government of Indo-China (now Vietnam, Cambodia and Laos) had already struck a deal with Namazie. Sir Edward Cook, who was the British financial adviser to the King of Siam, took exception to the Colonial Office's hectoring stance. He believed this was a situation created by their own short-sighted attempts at prohibition and was not afraid to tell them so.

'India's impulsive gesture, which earned such easy applause at Geneva,' complained Sir Edward Cook, 'has forced Siam to take measures to safeguard her supply, and is making more difficult the task of these governments of opium-smoking countries which are genuinely trying to bring the habit under effective control.'

Cook's no-holds-barred confidential report was dispatched to London in September 1927.

'Illicit opium, mainly of Chinese origin, is pouring into Siam, partly by sea and partly from the north via the Shan States,' said Cook. It was selling far more cheaply than legally obtained opium and was undermining the Siamese government's attempts to ration and register opium smokers and dealers. Indeed, it was subverting the role of Siamese officials, who were being bribed to accept the cheaper illegal opium. In the meantime, the Siamese government was seeking to import replacement opium from Persia, but this was forcing her into the hands of some unsavoury characters.

'Namazie is a freelance and stands outside the ring of Jewish and Armenian dealers,' noted Cook. 'He is a British Indian subject by domicile, but a Persian by race. He has intimate connections with the Persian dealers at Bushire [now Bushehr on the Persian Gulf coast] and can nearly always "get in first".'

Based in Singapore, Namazie was able to manipulate the market and sell opium to those middlemen who had struck deals directly with South-East Asian governments, including that of Siam and the Straits Settlements, leaving him with considerable profits. 'Naturally, it is an advantage to deal direct with Namazie . . . On the one occasion on which Siam purchased Persian opium (1110 chests), Namazie quoted substantially less than did the Jews.'

'Namazie is neither better nor worse than the other dealers,' insisted Cook. 'He differs from them in being (a) in better touch with the Persian trader (b) much less well-educated. To the whole lot of them the idea of being deterred by conscientious scruples from doing a promising piece of business, is unintelligible.'

To boycott Namazie, as London was ordering, would serve no good purpose, argued Sir Edward Cook, 'but would be of the nature of eye-wash'.

'The whole business is a dirty one,' he concluded. 'It was not from choice that Siam bought opium from one of the Singapore dealers. She would have been quite content to continue purchasing from India; the price, it is true, was extremely high, but the supply was assured and the opium is pure.'

Cook felt the price of legally supplied opium was way too high and encouraged smuggling. He had been approached by some British firms, who promised to supply Siam with good quality opium, 'but I must say their names – Ziegler and Shirazee – don't inspire confidence.

'I have been forced to the conclusion that any further step forward in Siam in the direction of opium suppression, as well as any success in dealing with smuggling, will necessitate some reduction in the retail price of licit opium.'

Cook's lengthy and knowledgeable response to the Colonial Office's interference into Asian affairs was passed on to the British Foreign Secretary with a note saying 'worthy of sympathetic attention'. It was a strong rebuttal to Delevingne and the liberal establishment.

The crisis faced by Delevingne in 1927 was stark. He had succeeded in stopping the Indian government from exporting opium throughout South-East Asia, but there were millions of opium addicts, mainly Chinese, who still demanded their daily fix. With Persian growers and dealers happy to step in and undercut colonial attempts to control the price of opium, the illicit trade was growing rapidly, giving greater power to the narcotics crimelords. The governors of the colonies were getting impatient for action and leading the discontent was Sir Cecil Clementi, Governor of Hong Kong.

'If no effective opposition is offered,' said Sir Cecil, 'the position of the opium smuggler will grow daily stronger. The interests concerned to oppose ultimate reduction and the profits of the return to illicit business become progressively more formidable. The Hong Kong market is extremely desirable and annual profits from smuggling were not less than 1,000,000 dollars.'

Unless something was done and done quickly, Hong Kong was in danger of becoming the centre of a world trade in illicit drugs.

'There is still enormous wholesale opium smuggling from South China,' continued the desperate Sir Cecil, 'for which Hong Kong is the natural port of shipment and through which the Colony is brought into disrepute. Such business will be encouraged further by any relaxation or failure of the only effective attack that Hong Kong is in a position to make on any part of the smuggling system.'

The situation was getting worse day by day because of the civil war raging in mainland China between rival warlords in the wake of the collapse of the Qing Dynasty in 1911. Chinese refugees were flooding into Hong Kong, raising the colony's population from 600,000 to 900,000 and quadrupling the consumption of opium.

'Reduction of opium consumption is impossible,' said Sir Cecil Clementi, 'so long as militarists require money, China encourages the production and Hong Kong remains the main shelter for refugees.'

To bolster their war chests, the competing warlords, including the nationalist Kuomintang leader Chiang Kai-shek, who would emerge victorious the following year, were keen to exploit the money-making potential of the opium trade by growing and selling it.

In order to defeat this wave of illegal opium threatening to engulf all British colonies in South-East Asia, there was only one answer Sir Cecil could think of. That was to become a dealer himself – to become the biggest dealer in the region. It was, in fact, an idea that had been mulled over by Delevingne himself, in his correspondence with Prince Charoon of Siam earlier in 1927, when he suggested introducing him to Persian exporters. But the difference between Delevingne and Sir

Cecil was that the Hong Kong Governor wanted to radically increase the amount of opium he imported in order to challenge the illegal smugglers directly. Sir Cecil's daring idea was the result of a life spent in South-East Asia, dealing with the reality of gang life on the streets of British colonies.

Sir Cecil Clementi was born in Cawnpore, India, the son of a colonel, and was educated at St Paul's School and Magdalen College, Oxford, where he studied Classics and Sanskrit. A tall, athletic and handsome man, he easily won the respect of his peers. An outstanding scholar and linguist, he was placed fourth in the civil service exams of 1899 and could choose where he wished to serve. Arriving in Hong Kong, he passed his Chinese language exams with ease and was appointed Assistant Colonial Secretary and Clerk of Council in 1907 at the age of 32.

On top of all this, he was the nephew of Sir Cecil Clementi-Smith, the former Governor of the Straits Settlements, a man who knew more than most about the opium trade and the ruthless gangs associated with it. The young man had accompanied his uncle, who was the chief British delegate, to the International Opium Commission in Shanghai in 1909. During this trip, he learned not only everything about the opium trade, but also that it was his fearless uncle who had dared to challenge the rule of the Triads.

After Sir Cecil Clementi-Smith had retired to England, he received a telegram from a Chinese merchant living in Singapore. The wealthy gentleman invited the former governor to have his portrait painted by any artist he liked – he could draw the money for the commission from his bank account in London. The generous gift was to express the merchant's gratitude at being able to live and carry on his business 'without fear of murder or blackmail' – an immunity which he justly attributed to Sir Cecil Clementi-Smith. The portrait hung in the Royal Academy.

When Clementi-Smith had become Governor of the Straits Settlements in 1887, he had made it his number one priority to tackle the local organised crime syndicates, known as Secret Chinese Societies. How dangerous this could be was revealed in that same year when William A. Pickering, a fluent Mandarin speaker and self-styled 'Protector of the Chinese', took on the Ghee Hok Society – a notorious crime gang.

On 18 July 1887, Pickering was sitting in his office when he was approached by a Chinese carpenter offering him a petition. As Pickering gazed at the paper, the carpenter pulled out an axe and slashed at his forehead. A Chinese assistant tried to intervene but was killed outright. Pickering survived the assassination attempt, and the Ghee Hok Society felt the full weight of government punishment, with all their headmen being banished.

No colonial government could succeed in South-East Asia unless it got a grip on the secret societies that dominated their Chinese communities. In Penang in 1887, it was estimated that these gangs had 92,581 members and they controlled all the illegal activities in the colony, including gambling, extortion and prostitution. Frequently, clashes between rival gangs broke out into violent street fights. Their gambling dens were protected behind armoured doors and located down narrow passages, with trapdoors allowing a quick escape. 'Their organisation is so perfect,' said one report, 'their power for striking a blow against the Government so easy and swift, that in a new country, where the security of life and property is all important, their presence cannot be otherwise than a bane.'

In 1889, the Rajah of Sarawak – descended from Sir James Brooke – feared the growing influence of Ghee Hin Secret Society members in his country and had six of their leaders arrested. After a short trial, the six headmen were put before a firing squad of Sarawak Rangers and executed. A statement in the *Straits Times* proclaimed: 'The Rajah of Sarawak knows from painful experience what evil Chinese secret societies can work . . . The Rajah, on discovering what was brewing, lost not a moment in frustrating their plans. Secret society men know now what awaits them in Sarawak, and if they choose to take the risk they deserve the penalty.'

Interestingly, in 1889, newspaper correspondents were already beginning to use a different title for these secret societies – a name that would later be used to describe Chinese gang members in the British Far East: the Triads.

The power of the Chinese gangs grew undiminished into the twentieth century and in Kuala Lumpur in 1909, when colonial police clashed with them, it resulted in a bloodbath. 'The Chinamen were dressed in red cloth,' said a Singapore reporter. 'On approaching the temple the police were met with a volley of bullets and the fiercest fighting ensued, four Chinese being killed and many wounded. A European inspector and a Sikh constable were severely wounded.'

With the eruption of illicit drugs trading following Britain's opium prohibition, it was natural that these Chinese gangs should dominate the distribution of narcotics in Chinese-populated cities throughout South-East Asia. When the 50-year-old Sir Cecil Clementi became Governor of Hong Kong in 1925, he knew this very well, not only from the advice of his streetwise uncle, but also from his own personal experience on the streets of the colony.

More than anyone else, Sir Cecil knew the danger this posed to Britain's ability to control the rapidly growing Chinese population in their colonies, and for that reason he was willing to go further than any other governor and think the unthinkable.

In defiance of the British government's agreement at the Hague Convention to severely limit the buying and selling of opium within her empire, with the aim of suppressing opium smoking completely, Sir Cecil was a realist. In order to defeat the smugglers and destroy their empire of crime, he wanted to buy large quantities of opium directly from Persia and dump it cheaply on his home market – putting the smugglers out of business at a stroke. To achieve this, the Governor needed to buy 40 chests of opium a month from Persia, in addition to its annual allowance from India of 196 chests. That meant more than doubling the amount of legal opium entering the colony.

While he waited for official permission from London, Sir Cecil embarked on his personal drug-dealing exercise by unleashing more legal opium on the market. Within days, government sales had quadrupled. Initial feedback seemed to justify his gamble.

'Steps taken in Hong Kong have now passed beyond the experimental stage,' reported Sir Cecil to London, 'and the fact that there is no sign of increased consumption to balance the increase in Government sales shows its success, which is further evidenced by the fact accepted in the Colony that the smugglers have had a serious set back. In addition the daily average of opium offenders in jail has fallen from 540 to 361, a very important factor in view of its chronic overcrowding.'

Sir Cecil's policy seemed a miracle cure for crime. To carry on, he needed further supplies of opium and asked permission to import these from Singapore while he awaited an influx of opium from Persia. If he didn't get it, he warned, 'I submit that the domination of the Hong

Kong opium market by smugglers may be expected to produce greater international difficulties than any misrepresentation of the successful attempt to make opium smuggling in this Colony less profitable now being made by this Government.'

Sir Cecil's pre-emptory action caused a sharp intake of breath among the pen-pushers in Whitehall. At a secret Cabinet meeting, the disapproval of His Britannic Majesty's Government was made clear.

'It seems to us to be very regrettable that the Governor should have introduced without previous consultation with his Majesty's Government so serious a departure from its established policy.'

Everyone now turned to Sir Malcolm Delevingne to pick up the gauntlet thrown down by the rogue Governor of Hong Kong.

'The position in the Colony is that the plentiful supply of opium from China has greatly increased the consumption of opium in the Colony,' admitted Delevingne. 'It may be conceded at once that if there was a good prospect of driving the smugglers permanently out of business, the resulting advantages would be so great in the long run as possibly to outweigh the disadvantages.'

But, argued Delevingne, to succeed with this campaign would mean Hong Kong committing itself indefinitely to supplying cheap opium to its consumers. As soon as any attempt was made to reduce the supply of opium in order to suppress the habit, the market would be invaded once again by cheap illicit opium from China. It seemed an unsustainable stance, for Sir Cecil to carry on being the chief supplier of opium to his population – 'the sales of Government opium will rise to an enormous figure' – and with it would come an enormous increase in revenue.

In the old days, this would have been very acceptable – indeed, desirable – but not in the third decade of the twentieth century.

'It is hardly necessary to point out,' said Delevingne, 'the handle this situation will give to the anti-British propagandists and the critics of our policy in the United States, in China, and no doubt also in Japan, which is watching us closely. It is inevitable also that our hands will be weakened at Geneva in the efforts we are making to bring the much bigger problem of the drug traffic under better control.'

Rather than encouraging the Persian opium market, the British government was entering into negotiations with the Persian government to reduce its nation's production – 'almost the whole of which for years past has been sent out to the Far East for smoking purposes, in large part clandestinely to the detriment of Hong Kong as well as other countries'. Persia was the new India, as far as opium importers were concerned.

In the face of this, the British Cabinet made it clear to Sir Cecil that they did not approve of his Hong Kong experiment:

> Unless His Majesty's Government is prepared to abandon all its previous pretensions and in effect to repudiate its obligations under the Hague Convention, we fear that we do not see how the change in policy introduced by the governor of Hong Kong can be approved or his request for permission to purchase large quantities of Persian opium can be sanctioned.

This was a blow to Sir Cecil, but he was certainly not alone in expressing discontent with Britain's policy on restricting the export of Indian opium. Delevingne knew this very well. Earlier in 1927, he had received correspondence from the Governor of the Portuguese colony of Macao, saying 'if they could get no Indian opium and if, as a result of the decision of the Persian Government to restrict the cultivation of opium in Persia, the Persian supplies of opium fall off, Portugal would be forced to start the cultivation of opium in Timor'. Interestingly, it was Sir Cecil who helped out the Governor of Macao by selling him several chests of Hong Kong's own stash of opium, but then this had to be made up with more opium from India or Persia . . .

Colonial Office administrator Mr J.J. Paskin was even forced to mention the word 'loophole', as he tried to negotiate his way through Geneva Opium Agreement rules by suggesting that the forbidden export of Persian opium between colonies might be overcome if the 'Straits Government should happen to have a consignment on the sea which could be diverted to Hong Kong without its being "imported" into the Straits'.

The problem with narcotics – the problem created by well-meaning British imperialists in the first place – was that it slowly but surely drew everyone into its net of criminality, including those doing their very best to control it.

Despite nearly precipitating a rift with London, Sir Cecil Clementi remained Governor of Hong Kong until 1930. He was a modernising ruler, establishing Kai Tak airport, which continued in use until 1998, and ending Chinese female maid servitude, which had often encouraged abuse by employers. He went on to take over as Governor and Commander-in-Chief of the Straits Settlements, including Singapore, a post his influential uncle had held.

Married with three children, Sir Cecil retired from colonial service in 1934 and died in 1947. His obituary in *The Times* described his period as Governor of Hong Kong as 'a great success, especially in regard to the restoration which it brought about of Anglo-Chinese friendship'. No mention was made of his attempt to become the biggest opium dealer in South-East Asia or his clash with his colonial masters.

The factional fighting in China and the influx of Chinese refugees into Hong Kong and other colonies – with a subsequent dramatic increase in the number of opium addicts under British rule – was just the beginning of a major new trend in organised crime in the early twentieth century. Chinese gangsters and their political allies were making the most of the British Empire's loss of control of the opium trade and were fast establishing their own power bases. Nowhere was this more clearly shown than in Shanghai – the most dazzling and most wicked of Far Eastern cities in the 1920s.

7

THE DEADLY INSPECTOR FAIRBAIRN

MAURICE SPRINGFIELD LIKED HUNTING WITH hounds – both for sport and as Assistant Commissioner of Police in Shanghai. He used them to pursue gangs of robbers and, occasionally, other quarry.

'By way of variation from robber hunting,' he recalled, 'I was once asked to try to find the corpse of a murdered Sikh, although 48 hours had already elapsed since the killing.'

Springfield introduced his hound to a pool of blood and followed the scent towards a lagoon used by the Chinese for fishing. 'Then followed what resembled an otter hunt on one of the Norfolk reed-fringed lakes.' His dog plunged into the water and swam back and forth over a particular spot in the lagoon. Springfield called the fire brigade to use grappling hooks, but they failed to find the corpse. Three weeks later, it floated to the surface.

On another occasion, on 15 June 1924, Springfield was without his hounds when he had to confront a gang of armed robbers.

'I had been playing tennis and was driving home,' he remembered, 'when I heard a series of shots.'

As Springfield reversed out of a drive, an exhausted Sikh policeman flung himself against the car and handed Springfield a .45 revolver.

'Sahib, Sahib,' he gasped, 'there they go!'

Springfield held his fire as a 'dear old lady' stood between him and the escaping robbers. He ran after them and shot one dead. A second ran out of ammunition and was grabbed by the testicles by a rickshaw driver. As he yelled with pain, a Chinese woman hurled a pan of boiling water over him. Subdued, the robber was taken into custody by Springfield. He was part of a gang that was on its way to rob a wealthy Chinese merchant when the men were stopped by a policeman.

A gunfight had subsequently broken out. For his fearless part in the arrest, Springfield was later sent a letter of gratitude from the Shanghai Municipal Council.

From the way Springfield liked to record his days in the Shanghai Municipal Police, it might sound all larks and japes. But he was, in fact, a senior figure in the fight against organised crime in one of the wealthiest and most important ports in the Far East in the early twentieth century.

Although not directly part of the British Empire, the International Settlement of Shanghai was headquarters to most of Britain's business in China and, thanks to previous treaties, her citizens enjoyed extraterritorial status, which meant they were not subject to local Chinese laws but the jurisdiction of their own consuls. As far as most Britons in China were concerned, Shanghai was part of the empire and the Shanghai Municipal Police (SMP), run by Englishmen, looked after them.

Springfield, originally born in Tipperary but raised in Norfolk, was 20 years old in 1905 when he joined the Shanghai Police Force. Then, Chinese men still walked around wearing their hair in pigtails, denoting their loyalty to the Qing Dynasty in Peking. Although it seemed immensely picturesque and exotic to the young man, he soon learned that Shanghai's unique blend of 60 nationalities living close together could also be very violent.

'Often there were as many as a dozen armed crimes a day,' he noted. 'At one time there were so many firearms in Shanghai it did not pay anyone to smuggle them in. Shanghai was a focal point for adventurers from all over the world and for soldiers of fortune.'

Springfield worked his way up through several posts, including Registrar of the International Mixed Court, Governor of the Gaols and Assistant Commissioner of Traffic, until he became Anti-Narcotics Deputy Commissioner Uniform Branch. Shanghai played a pivotal role in the transit of illicit drugs around the world and it was up to Springfield to disrupt the flow. Needless to say, he approached the task with his usual enthusiasm.

'The hunting for opium, morphia, heroin and cocaine smugglers and dealers was great fun,' he said, 'and was not confined to regular hours.'

Springfield went on raids with his team of Sikh and Chinese

policemen, but he was careful not to have the addresses of their intended targets written on the sheaf of warrants, as his clerical staff were often in the pay of opium dealers. Not only was he looking for shipments of drugs, but also documents that would give him a glimpse of the bigger picture of trading networks. On the night of 26 February 1924, he got very lucky.

An informer had directed Springfield and his team to a small firm at 51 Canton Road. Rushing through the streets of Shanghai in two cars, they caught the manager of the *hong* in the building. As Springfield questioned him, the Chinese man got increasingly agitated and urinated down his legs. The chief of narcotics demanded the man hand over the keys to his several safes, but he refused. Then one of Springfield's Irish officers, searching the upstairs of the building, shouted out, 'Here it is, sir. He's been sleeping on it.'

The policemen had wrenched off panelling and floorboards and taken apart furniture to discover half a stone of opium in a bed.

At the news, the Chinese manager fainted. With the safes open, they found a small quantity of high-quality Indian opium and several phials of different drugs. Most importantly, they uncovered a treasure trove of documents in English, French and Chinese.

'This case later became famous, with international repercussions,' said the triumphant 39-year-old Springfield. The documents were translated and presented to court. 'I think that copies in the region of 150 were printed and subsequently distributed to the famous Russell Pasha and all Consulates representing countries even remotely connected with the opium and other drugs traffic.'

What came out of this pile of documentation and other high-profile cases was the worldwide reach of narcotics smuggling and how Shanghai was an important staging post in this process. Increasing evidence pointed to the role of Japan in this network. Too late to mollify the unfortunate Mr Hartley, who had been ruined by his supposed involvement in trafficking drugs into Japan, it appeared it was the Japanese who were acting as high-level smugglers into their own country.

This was further confirmed by the case of Howard Montague Fogden Humphrey. A senior businessman in the City of London, Humphrey was convicted of drugs trafficking in 1923 and a letter to his Japanese contact was presented in court as evidence.

'If you will entrust to my care a further £5,000 I will buy stock and come to Shanghai or any other Port with the goods,' wrote Humphrey to the Japanese gentleman. 'I am perfectly sure that we can deliver into any warehouse you wish quite safely and that by my own methods there is no fear of loss or confiscation or discovery.'

Humphrey went to France to buy the processed morphine and cocaine and then had it shipped from Marseilles to China and Japan. It was hidden in barrels of printing ink and tins of food. Sometimes it was packed in tubes inside bars of luxury soap.

'I would like to say that I have a perfect organisation,' boasted Humphrey in his letter. 'I have many friends amongst Customs etc. and I understand the business very thoroughly, in fact I do not believe that there is anyone who has a better control. In addition to this I am known to many of the buyers in Japan.

'We buy, say, 50,000 ounces at 16/- [an] ounce – £40,000,' explained the City businessman to his Japanese counterpart. 'I am sure that we could easily sell this quantity in China at 48/- which would realise £120,000, the expenses to deliver to you safely would be about £1,000 including my Passage, therefore we could make a profit of about £79,000. If the goods were sold at this cheap figure, we might even get as much as 200/- per ounce and then we should of course make very much more.'

In between sealing these global deals, Humphrey led the quiet life of a London commuter, travelling from and to his home in Brighton, arriving at Victoria station at 9.45 a.m. and getting back to his family at 7 p.m. each day. His Basinghall Street company made cutlery.

Humphrey's 'perfect' system broke down only when a ship arriving at Hong Kong was boarded by revenue officers and a Japanese subject was arrested. When they slashed open the upholstery on his shipment of sofas and armchairs, they found 2,400 ounces of morphine and 2,500 ounces of cocaine. It was reckoned that the amount of morphine would make 2,100,000 sellable doses. The documents carried by the Japanese passenger linked him to a Chinese firm in Amoy that had dealings with Humphrey. Once the documents were passed on to London, Humphrey was arrested and sentenced to six months in prison and fined £200.

Dealers like Humphrey revealed the wide range of people involved in early narcotics smuggling. It wasn't only the master criminals like

Elie Eliopoulos. When processed drugs could be bought easily from pharmaceutical manufacturers in Paris and shipped on to the Far East, it attracted the civilised businessman whose only necessary qualifications were discretion, organisation and a good relationship with his bank manager. 'All you have to do,' said Humphrey to his Japanese contact, 'is to wire the credit either here (London) or Paris to Barclays Bank Ltd and I will see to all the rest.'

Outside of Europe, however, when illicit opium came from Persia or some other cultivator and was smuggled into China, it was a much more dangerous affair. Criminal gangs had to provide the muscle to protect their consignments from hijack. When Maurice Springfield had to deal with these gangs in Shanghai, it was less about following a paper trail and more about confronting gunmen.

'In my day the dealers and purveyors to the public were cowards, although cunning,' said the narcotics chief. 'It was the smugglers who could be dangerous. But luckily for us they had never had practice or been trained in the handling of revolvers and automatic pistols and they were bad shots.'

Springfield retired from Shanghai service in 1933, by which time he had risen to be Acting Commissioner. He returned to England and thoroughly enjoyed a life hunting in Norfolk with his beloved hounds. He was fortunate to get out with a few good stories; in the 1930s, events in China took a darker turn, as organised crime was forced to ally itself with increasingly perilous politics. This would demand a much more aggressive response from the SMP.

In the first decades of the twentieth century, Shanghai was a fun city and prided itself on its modernity, with multi-storey buildings rising along the waterfront of the business quarter – the Bund – while flickering neon lights illuminated Nanking Road, its premier shopping street lined with western-style department stores. There was the seedy side too, catering to all tastes, and even here, the British were considered to be in charge.

'Prostitutes of all nationalities flocked into Shanghai from Japan, Siberia and the North, and one part of the Settlement appeared to be peopled almost entirely by Russian women,' noted one report in 1927. 'Men were constantly solicited as they walked through the streets, by women who called from windows. The streets in certain quarters were patrolled by *amahs* [housemaids] accompanied by young girls, for whom the *amahs* solicited custom. In one part of the Nanking Road these could be counted by the score at night. Brothels sprang up in houses next to British billets, and I was asked by a Japanese to introduce him "to the Colonel", as he wanted permission to start a brothel.'

Rickshaw men were subsidised by brothel-keepers and would ask gentlemen whether they wished to visit a Chinese or a Japanese house. Chinese and Japanese restaurants were often used as places of assignation. Sometimes there would be a moral crusade in the city, initiated by do-gooder American Protestants, and raids would be ordered to close down the sinful places, but vice continued to dominate the city streets into the 1930s.

Early pornographic films were screened and one Yorkshire-born British visitor described attending such a cinema at the Bubbling Well end of Nanking Road. 'The entrance hall was like the hall of a large private house and was sumptuously furnished,' he recalled. 'There was a picture being shown at the moment, and when I looked at the screen I got a shock. The picture was horribly lewd, not just ordinarily suggestive, but absolutely as lewd as it is possible to make.

'I could see that there were a few good ladies among the audience, and one of them, a young woman of some continental nationality who spoke English with an accent, came and sat down beside me, first asking my permission with a wide smile, which exposed three or four gold teeth . . . Another picture, even worse than the last one, was put on the screen, after which the young lady moved away to another seat, probably thinking that I was no sport.'

The French Concession – a neighbouring colonial possession with jurisdiction separate to the British-run International Settlement – got a bad reputation for harbouring drug dealers. In July 1926, the manager of a popular pharmacy was arrested and made a statement saying that 7,000 ounces of morphia and heroin had been ordered from Germany through a Japanese agent and the drugs were stored in various premises in the French Concession. The manager was handed over to a Chinese Military Court, found guilty and executed by firing squad.

The French authorities took a different approach from the British and thought it was sensible to license opium dens and receive an income from it. As a result, their territory became a base for Chinese mobsters and earned a reputation for pushing the boundaries of decadence in Shanghai. At its centre was the brash 'Great World' entertainment centre, run by a Chinese gangster with police connections. The Great World offered a variety of pleasures:

> The fifth floor featured girls whose dresses were slit to their armpits, a stuffed whale, story-tellers, balloons, peep shows, masks, a mirror maze, two love-letter booths with scribes who guaranteed results, rubber goods, and a temple filled with ferocious gods and joss sticks.

'As I tried to find my way down again,' continued a curious western visitor to the Great World, 'an open space was pointed out to me where hundreds of Chinese, so I was told, after spending their coppers, had speeded the return to the street below by jumping from the roof. When I guilelessly asked why a protective rail had not been placed around an exit so final, the retort was, "How can you stop a man from killing himself?"'

Throughout Shanghai, arms trafficking was endemic, and in one five-month period in 1926 the SMP arrested 19 Europeans and 26 Chinese dealing in weapons and seized 181 automatic pistols and revolvers and over 17,000 rounds of ammunition. It was the wildly escalating use of guns that encouraged William Fairbairn, a leading Shanghai police officer, to develop new methods of policing. These would anticipate the modern age of SWAT squads.

'These views are the outcome of many years of carefully recorded experience with the Police Force of a semi-Oriental city,' wrote Fairbairn in his gun-techniques book called *Shooting to Live*, 'in which, by reason of local conditions that are unusual and in some respects unique, armed crime flourishes to a degree that we think must be unequalled anywhere else in the world.' And this was at a time when American gangsters were shooting their way to notoriety in US cities.

William Ewart Fairbairn was one of fourteen children, born in Mill End in Hertfordshire in 1885 to a bootmaker. His first two names were taken from those of Gladstone – the opium trade battling, and then defending, prime minister. Fairbairn served six years with the Royal Marines and joined the SMP in 1907 as a constable. Specialising in arms training and unarmed combat, he soon gained a reputation for instructing his policemen in the realities of street fighting. He devised his own blend of Japanese and Chinese martial arts that he called Defendu and published a manual for it in Shanghai in 1915:

> One of the essential principles of this science is to meet an attack quickly and by another form of counter attack; the suddenness of this will, in many cases, so bewilder your opponent that it will be possible to apply a hold from which he will find it impossible to extricate himself. In many cases an opponent's greater strength may be turned to his disadvantage.

Fairbairn also focused his attention on perfecting police gunmanship. The traditional stance of standing side-on to a target with the arm outstretched, pointing the gun to aim, was no good for sudden, chaotic gunfights on Shanghai streets. 'In the great majority of shooting affrays the distance at which firing takes place is not more than four yards,' said Fairbairn. 'If you have to fire, your instinct will be to do so as quickly as possible, and you will probably do it with a bent arm, possibly even from the level of the hip.' It was the police officer's first-hand experience of combat that made him such a good teacher:

> It may be that a bullet whizzes past you and that you will experience the momentary stupefaction which is due to the shock of the explosion at very short range of the shot just fired by your opponent – a very different feeling, we can assure you, from that experienced when you are standing behind or alongside a pistol that is being fired.

The proof of the effectiveness of his innovative gun training – shooting quickly from the hip at the assailant's torso – was demonstrated in figures that showed that out of hundreds of armed encounters over a decade of police service in the SMP, only 42 police officers were killed, as against 260 criminals shot dead.

The sort of close-quarter fighting experienced by Fairbairn and his men was exemplified by one incident in which they cornered a notorious kidnapper in 1928. The kidnapping of wealthy people by criminal gangs had reached epidemic proportions in Shanghai. When news came through of one victim being held in a two-storey house on the outskirts of the city on Chusan Road, Superintendent Fairbairn led his team to the rescue.

Issued with bulletproof vests and shields, armed to the teeth with guns and grenades, this was no ordinary police unit. It was a team of experts called the Special Reserve Unit (SRU). Relieved of having to take care of day-to-day routine duties, they were highly trained in dealing with unusual situations. Yet again, this was Fairbairn's innovation and he intended them to be an elite unit.

'They had to be self contained,' he said, 'and prepared to maintain themselves on the scene of trouble for 48 hours without relief from any other Branch of the Force.' Made up of volunteers consisting of Europeans, Sikhs and Chinese, they travelled to trouble spots in specially designed trucks called 'Black Marias'.

On arriving at the kidnapper's house, the SRU set about its business with relentless efficiency. A cordon was put in place, covering the back and front of the house, with snipers aiming at the roof. An armoured raiding party got ready to storm the building. Led by a plain-clothes Chinese detective who was pretending to be a gang member, they forced open the front door and handcuffed one of the kidnapping gang. Advancing cautiously up the stairs behind their shields, they were met with gunfire. As the SRU returned a hail of bullets, one of the gang members ran to the balcony on the first floor, but was hit by a sniper outside. In the confusion, another gang member was shot in the stomach in the method devised by Fairbairn for close-quarter shooting.

Breaking into the room holding the kidnap victim, the police found a terrified hostage with his feet tied, holding a blanket in front of his face. But the chief kidnapper had gone. He had been seen to jump from the roof of the house to a neighbouring roof – across a gap of 12 feet – while being shot at by one of the snipers. Clearly, this was an extraordinary outlaw.

When word came back from a wounded gang member that this man was in fact Yang Siau May, there was a stunned silence among the SRU. Known as the 'Old Small Cat', Yang was chief of the most prolific kidnap gang in Shanghai, with more than 150 criminals under his direct command. Dealing with this highly dangerous man would demand all the special policing skills Fairbairn had devised.

With night falling, Fairbairn ordered floodlights to illuminate the house hiding Yang. The cordon was tightened, with snipers targeting any escape routes from the roof of the building. The SRU would have to storm the house, but before doing so they lobbed in tear gas. Unfortunately, all this activity had attracted journalists and hundreds of sightseers, and some of the SRU were distracted by having to control the crowd. The owner of the building, bathing in the sudden attention of the local media, said that the police should do all they could to apprehend the chief villain, even if meant burning it down.

Wearing gas masks, a storming party edged into the building, clearing it room by room. As they advanced slowly up the stairs, an officer was shot in the arm by Yang. Crouching down, the police fired back into the fume-filled void. Yang retreated to an attic on the second floor. Fairbairn got plans of the building brought to him from the Public Works Department and saw the attic had two exit windows. Both were floodlit and covered by snipers with telescopic scopes on their rifles.

Holding a megaphone, Fairbairn told Yang that he was cornered with no possibility of escape and that he should throw out his pistol and stand at the window with his hands up. No reply came back from the building. The police hurled in more tear gas. Still no response. They tried to rush the stairs up to the attic, but the first policeman had his hat shot off and they scrambled back down again. It wasn't worth the risk and Fairbairn ordered his unit to use hand grenades to force him out or kill him. When one bounced into the attic, Yang picked it up and threw it back, making the police beat a hasty retreat.

Next, a group of SRU in gas masks and body armour pushed a ladder up against the building, leaning it against the attic window. Throwing in three grenades in quick succession, they sprinted up the ladder and, seeing Yang crouching in a corner, opened fire, catching him with a bullet in the thigh. Not cowed, Yang leapt up and ran at the policemen, shooting one in the face – miraculously, the bullet only grazed the police officer's eyebrow. Tumbling backwards, the assault unit had to think again.

As the siege dragged on into the early morning, Fairbairn ordered a platform to be erected opposite the attic window. When one policeman spotted the wounded Yang, he shot at him. Again this only encouraged the gangster to drag himself towards the window to fire his final shots.

At that point, the police raked the building around him with machine-gun bullets and one caught Yang in the spine, finally killing him. It had been an epic shoot-out. Demonstrating the many talents of Fairbairn's Special Reserve Unit, it had, however, showed the die-hard calibre of gangsters they faced in ever more dangerous situations.

Yang may have been king of the kidnappers in Shanghai, but he was a minor player compared to the suit-wearing top mobsters that ran the city's underworld. Unlike other colonial police forces, that took bribes and looked the other way, the SMP made it their business to investigate the upper echelons of organised crime – but they also got help from intelligence agencies within the British administration. For, as the rip-roaring 1920s turned into the war-torn 1930s, the pure moneymaking of local gangsters was replaced by a need for survival that meant top criminals had to align themselves with political parties.

The clash of the warlords following the demise of the Qing Dynasty had been brought to an end by the triumph of the Kuomintang nationalists in 1928, led by Chiang Kai-shek. But the fighting was far from over, as the nationalists had deadly rivals in the Chinese Communist Party. At first, the communists enjoyed support in the major city centres, but the nationalists ruthlessly broke their influence and forced them into the countryside. This struggle for power was mirrored in the shifting allegiances of the two leading criminal gangs in Shanghai – the Greens and the Reds. They were secret brotherhood societies, identical to the Triads recognised by British colonial governors in South-East Asian Chinese communities.

'Particularly worthy of note is the fact that these societies have been founded in Southern Provinces of China,' said a British Intelligence officer, 'by a people of much the same temperament as the Sicilians – the founders of the notorious Mafia.'

The Green Gang – *Ching Pang* – was said to have originated from traditional boatmen who lost their jobs when steamships took over their trade. The Red Gang – *Hung Pang* – had the core of its supporters in Canton, with affiliated groups around the country. In 1911, both these secret societies had thrown their weight and influence behind the Chinese nationalists and helped Chiang Kai-shek sweep into power.

When Chiang needed to purge Shanghai of communists, the Green Gang helped him. On 12 April 1927, more than 300 left-wingers were eliminated in the city. The gangster militia, wearing white armbands over denim overalls, bearing the title 'worker', launched an early morning raid on union branches. Left-wingers were hunted down and shot or beheaded in the streets. Some were said to have been thrown alive into the furnaces of locomotives.

'It is generally believed that in exchange for assistance rendered to him,' said a British Intelligence report, 'General Chiang promised the Green Party in Shanghai a monopoly of the opium business, and it was not long before the party enjoyed the reputation of a gang of racketeers whose activities were on a par with those of their Chicago counterparts – the Capone gang. Nothing of importance happened in Shanghai in which could not be found the influence of the Green Party, workers organisations and labour unions being completely under its domination.'

For part of the 1920s, before Chiang's purge, the Green Gang had used communists to organise strikes as part of their labour racket. In May 1925, a protest involving Chinese students was broken up by the SMP, with the death of ten students. It resulted in increased tension between the local Chinese and police and was the catalyst for Fairbairn establishing his Special Reserve Unit. Among the young agitators accused of being involved was a 31-year-old communist called Mao Tse-tung, who fled to Canton before he could be arrested.

The Green Gang had had a firm hold on the drugs trade in Shanghai before Chiang 'rewarded' them in 1927. They controlled most of the opium dens and even invented their own drugs, creating pills by mixing heroin with strychnine. When an international ban on the trafficking of heroin reduced the amount flowing into China, they imported more raw opium and manufactured heroin in their own factories, some of which occasionally blew up.

The most dominant figure in the Green Gang was Du Yue-sheng. Born into poverty, with the nickname 'Big Ears', this thin, decadent figure began his criminal career as a bodyguard for a brothel. He then endeared himself to the wife of a leading gangster, who also doubled as a detective in the French Concession Police Force. Under her patronage, he rapidly rose up the ranks of the Green Gang, so that when her husband was arrested, Du stepped into his shoes.

Du acquired a four-storey European-style mansion in the French Concession, which became the headquarters of his criminal empire, embracing brothels, opium dens, gunrunning, gold smuggling and protection rackets. It was Du who threw in his lot with Chiang Kai-shek, directing the gangster militia for the anti-communist Shanghai purge. In return for his political services, Du was awarded the 'Order of the Brilliant Jade' and appointed to the board of the Opium Suppression Bureau in the nationalist-controlled city.

Addicted to the drugs he had dealt in from an early age, Du sometimes seemed wrapped in an opium cloud of pleasure, as he enjoyed the company of his two 15-year-old concubines. But an invitation to his mansion could be a very deadly assignation. On one occasion, Du heard a terrible commotion in his house and shuffled to the top of the stairs. Below, he saw one of his gangsters strangling a stubborn union leader. 'Not here!' he shouted. 'Not in my house!' The mobster quickly bundled the body of the union leader into a sack and drove him to a waste ground to dump him. When the half-dead victim struggled inside his sack, the mobster kicked him into a hastily dug grave and buried him alive.

Sometimes, Du used his dinner table as a place of execution. Three French Concession officials who had failed to please him were treated to a grand feast that featured rare mushrooms. Shortly afterwards, all three died from food poisoning. When a French journalist dared to write up the story of Du's domination of the corrupt French Concession, he wisely took a quick ship home, but even then Du's vengeance caught up with him. The vessel was set on fire and sank in the Indian Ocean, drowning everyone, including the reporter.

Two celebrated young English writers, W.H. Auden and Christopher Isherwood, met Du in Shanghai and recorded their own impression of him.

> To visit Du's flat was to enter a strongly guarded fortress. At least a dozen attendants were posted in the hall, and, when we sat down to talk, there were others who stood in the background behind our chairs. Du himself was tall and thin, with a face that seemed hewn out of stone, a Chinese version of the Sphinx. Peculiarly and inexplicably terrifying were his feet, in their silk socks and smart pointed European boots, emerging from beneath the long silken gown. Perhaps the Sphinx, too, would be even more frightening if it wore a modern top hat.

Du's tentacles spread into the legitimate business world and a 'Who's Who' in Shanghai listed him as president of several major banks and hospitals, as well as being a councillor on the French Municipal Council. He had the head of the police in the French Concession on his payroll to the extent that policemen guarded his mansion. He frequently used the corrupt law enforcers to crack down on his criminal rivals. For his personal bodyguard, he chose White Russians.

When Du tried to extend his influence to the British Shanghai Municipal Police, he was surprised to be turned down. The mobster chief alerted the police force that a consignment of his opium was coming into port and they should steer well clear of it. One brave officer refused to be his lackey. Instead, the Chinese superintendent captured the drugs haul, costing Du thousands of dollars. A little later, the same Chinese officer was shot dead outside his home.

The Red Gang did not have the same influence in Shanghai as the Greens, being a junior member of the larger Cantonese organisation. They were small-time drug dealers, but their separation from the political establishment meant they could occasionally threaten the status quo. In order to balance the influence of the Greens, Chiang Kai-shek established his own gang of supporters called the Blue Shirt Society. Chinese fascists numbering some 3,000, they were placed in various political posts.

In the 1930s, the sinister alliance between Chinese generals, politicians and gangsters was threatened by an even more malevolent crime machine – the encroaching Japanese. Having grabbed German colonies in China during the First World War, the Japanese proceeded to dominate the north of the country. In 1931, they occupied Manchuria and established a puppet state called Manchukuo. To help them plunder wealth from their new possessions, the leading Japanese generals and politicians had their own paramilitary forces recruited from Japan's masters of organised crime, the Yakuza.

Initially, distracted by his fight against the communists, Chiang Kai-shek did little to resist the Japanese advance, but in 1936 the nationalists and communists came together to form a united front against their common enemy. Shortly afterwards, the Japanese embarked on a full-blown invasion of the rest of China. Their well-equipped modern armies swiftly overwhelmed Chinese resistance and captured most of the northern and central regions of the country by

1938, including Shanghai. Japanese rule was ruthless and barbaric, with millions of Chinese civilians slaughtered, raped and mutilated and their property looted.

While the nationalists retreated to the impregnable mountains of Szechuan, the communists were left to fight a guerrilla war against their occupiers. As for the British in the International Settlement, it was a terrible wake-up call to the threat posed by the Japanese to the rest of Asia – and the Shanghai Municipal Police were on the front line.

8

THE MUTILATED INSPECTOR HUTTON

TENSIONS BETWEEN THE JAPANESE AND the Shanghai Municipal Police were already showing in late 1937. On Christmas Day, an inspector was driving a police car when he happened to obstruct a Japanese dispatch rider. A few days later, he was asked to explain his action at Japanese naval headquarters. During the course of the interview, he was struck by a Japanese officer and detained. When a superintendent later called to secure his release, he was also ill-treated by the Japanese. This was bad enough, but what quickly followed was a more serious incident.

On 6 January 1938, Probationary Police Sergeant Turner was on duty at the east barrier on Brenan Road when he objected to the rough treatment being handed out by Japanese sentries to a Chinese civilian. He ordered one of the Japanese police constables at the barrier to reprimand them, but the Japanese PC refused, so Turner said he would report his poor attitude. The Japanese PC then told the soldiers that the Englishman had insulted them. The Japanese soldiers proceeded to assault Turner, beating him so badly that he needed hospital treatment.

When two more Shanghai Municipal Police (SMP) officers turned up, they were threatened with loaded rifles and bayonets. It was only thanks to the intervention of a Japanese sub-inspector of the SMP that the situation did not escalate further.

'I feel sure that you and the responsible military and naval authorities will agree with me that it is most deplorable that members of the Japanese armed forces should be permitted to act in this lawless manner,' wrote a British member of the Shanghai Municipal Council to the Japanese Consul-General. 'And I have the honour to request accordingly that you will endeavour to arrange that a strict enquiry be held into these cases and those found guilty suitably disciplined in order to prevent further disorders.'

It is unlikely that the councillor even received an answer to this demand. So little did the Japanese care, the British Prime Minister, Neville Chamberlain, felt compelled to take a personal interest in the case and instructed His Majesty's Ambassador to Tokyo to demand satisfaction for these assaults in the strongest possible terms – 'stronger than we have used in almost any other incident in the present hostilities'. No such satisfaction having been received, His Majesty's Government was left with the conviction that the Japanese government was utterly careless of the rights and feelings of British subjects.

To pursue these incidents further seemed a fruitless task and some British diplomats suggested dropping their insistence on redress. The Consul-General in Shanghai disagreed.

'I think that that would be a mistake,' he said, 'and that quiet acceptance of rebuffs in the hope of not irritating the Japanese is also mistaken. Even if we are not in a position to exact apologies we can express our resentment in forcible terms and leave the Japanese Government with an uneasy feeling that these unsettled incidents are being added to the bill, which perhaps they may some day have to meet.'

Sadly, there would be many more, far worse incidents added to that bill before it was settled in world war.

Fighting between Chiang Kai-shek's Chinese nationalists and the Japanese had already broken out on the streets of Shanghai outside the International Settlement in the summer of 1937. Thousands of Chinese refugees flooded into the European concessions, while Britons stood on the roofs of buildings watching the plumes of smoke rise around them. The fact that the British wanted to keep conditions as normal as possible is reflected in their concerns about assaults on their policemen.

While the Chinese were being slaughtered in their hundreds of thousands elsewhere in the country, the British knew it was important to keep up their stern appearance. It was all a matter of maintaining respect for the empire and, in some ways, the Japanese appreciated this. They knew that the International Settlement was a money-making machine and they wanted very much for that to continue under their control. The same applied to Japanese gangsters busily taking over the illicit drugs trade. They liked stability. On the one hand, their political masters spoke out against opium smoking, while on the other, Japanese traffickers were rushed off their feet fulfilling the enormous demand.

'Japan's record in the opium and narcotics traffic is not one to be proud of,' said the British Consul-General at Mukden, capital of the Japanese puppet-state of Manchukuo. In the north-east of China, there was a large clandestine trade, occasionally exposed by the discovery of heroin factories or the arrest of careless smugglers. 'Recently a Japanese travelling from Tientsin to Mukden with an ordinary funeral urn aroused the suspicion of the police, who insisted on opening the urn and found, not cremated ashes, but morphine. It is impossible to guess how many urns have previously served this purpose.'

Russell Pasha, the great international drugs-buster, believed there was a more sinister purpose behind the Japanese control of opium and its derivatives.

'Japanese-occupied China soon became,' he declared, 'the only country of the world where the increase of drug addiction was a studied government policy. Year after year at Geneva we had to listen to the specious talk of the Japanese delegate: year after year the American delegation and the Central Narcotics Intelligence Bureau gave chapter and verse, showing the state of things in Manchukuo and China north of the wall, but to no effect. Japan had decided upon heroin addiction as a weapon of aggression and deliberately converted the territories she conquered from China into one huge opium farm and heroin den.'

Japanese criminals and their military masters were deliberately subduing the Chinese population by getting them hooked on illicit drugs. It ensured their occupation could run more smoothly and generated vast profits for the gangsters and generals involved. The blatant use of narcotics to enslave the Chinese was observed by Miner Searle Bates, the American-born professor of history at Nanking University:

> The situation through the occupied areas was one of the open sale of opium in government shops or licensed shops, and the aggressive peddling of heroin. In some cases, there was

attractive advertising of opium; in some cases, Japanese soldiers used opium as payment for prostitutes and for labour engaged on military supply dumps.

Bates estimated the Japanese army was making at least $3 million every month out of the sale of opium to Nanking's 50,000 addicts. When he visited Tokyo in 1939, he asked a senior military figure whether he thought the opium plague might be brought under control.

'No, the general told me that so long as the war continues, there is no hope of anything better because no other source of revenue has been found for the puppet government.'

Chinese peasants were compelled to grow opium and then had to sell it to the Japanese army at a price below the market value. Despite taking over thousands of acres of land for poppy cultivation, the Japanese could still not meet the demand from their millions of new Chinese addicts and had to import opium from abroad, especially from Persia. Venerable Japanese firms Mitsubishi and Mitsui were the principal importers and distributors of narcotics in the Japanese-occupied territories. The Imperial Japanese Navy escorted the narcotics shipments through foreign seas.

An American consul in Manchukuo described the fate of some of the Chinese addicts he saw:

> There lay on an ash heap just behind the narcotic brothels seven naked corpses which had evidently been stripped of their rags by fellow addicts. It is generally stated that this is a daily sight . . . There was offered no other explanation than that these dead met their end through narcotic poisoning.

'One thing, which is quite certain,' added Russell Pasha, 'is that she [Japan] allowed no competition in the trade from the Drugs Barons of Europe.' Their days were over – their imperial networks disrupted. The approaching world war would allow local Japanese and Chinese regimes in Asia to get a grip on the trade and they would not let go. It would complete the shift from western to eastern control of the narcotics underworld.

* * *

As for the British in China, their attempt to maintain a dignified distance from the hellish events around them slowly but surely crumbled, as the invading Japanese moved beyond traditional areas of looting and organised crime to steal their way into other areas of business – such as eggs.

In October 1939, the British Board of Trade received an irate letter from the British Egg Packing and Cold Storage Company in Shanghai. For the previous two years, despite the conflict and the increasing interference of the Japanese, the firm had managed to continue its trade in eggs from China to Britain. But recently the situation had deteriorated.

'The spring of 1939 saw an intensified campaign from a Japanese concern – the Mitsui Bussan Kaisha,' explained the company owner, 'which saw fit under the then prevailing conditions, to establish an egg plant of their own and enter the market, not on a free or competitive basis, but under the protection of their Military and Naval Authorities, and the Chinese representing us in the interior as well as locally were intimidated by them, thus obstructing free purchases and conveyance of our eggs.'

The company managed to obtain enough eggs through other means to fulfil their obligations, but later in the year the company owner visited China to see for himself what was going on and was shocked by the outright theft of his produce.

'On 15 October 1939 our upcountry branch office sent us 41 baskets of eggs, roughly 40,000 eggs, the Bills of Lading were in our name and the cargo was paid for by my firm and even Customs duty was paid. When the steamer docked in Shanghai, Mitsui Bussan officials simply helped themselves to the cargo.'

On another occasion, vans containing hundreds of thousands of eggs were hijacked by the Japanese and redirected to their own cold storage units.

'I feel that the wrong done is unprecedented in the annals of British commerce,' said the egg company owner. 'I feel sure that you are in a position to help us considerably in this respect.'

If only they could have. It was no small matter – the *China Press* headlined it as a major crime against British and American egg traders. The industry was the third-largest export business in China and the newspaper reported that no fewer than 500,000 eggs had been stolen by Japanese 'ostensibly acting under instructions from the Japanese military headquarters'.

When the British authorities investigated, they were told, a year later, that the Japanese military had cancelled all permits issued to foreign egg buyers and would 'now only permit exports of egg produce by military transports to Japan'.

It was merely the tip of an iceberg in which the Japanese military transformed itself into a giant criminal operation.

By late 1938, the Japanese had appointed Chinese collaborators to their Special Municipal Government, which became their instrument for ruling the city of Shanghai. They also ran their own police force in parallel with the Shanghai Municipal Police. The potential for clashes was deliberate.

'Armed crime has grown to alarming proportions,' reported the author of the 'Shanghai Despatch', 'and the division of authority between two police forces both claiming sole jurisdiction has inevitably led to incidents. It became evident moreover that these incidents were not the result of mere accident or misunderstanding but were deliberately provoked by the Special Municipality Police and the other armed organisations operating under Japanese auspices.'

In October 1939, a Chinese constable of the SMP was killed and a Sikh constable wounded on traffic duty by gunmen in plain clothes. Later that month, a more serious 30-minute gun battle broke out early one morning when SMP officers stopped a suspicious-looking motorcycle with no lights or licence. They were then fired on by Chinese aligned to the Japanese regime, shooting from the heavily fortified headquarters of a Kuomintang nationalist association. A Chinese constable was killed during the confrontation.

The fact that Japanese-controlled newspapers made a big matter out of this incident, telling the SMP to withdraw from the International Settlement, revealed how far top Chinese criminals had come to an accommodation with the Japanese. Du Yue-sheng, too closely associated with Chiang Kai-shek, had fled to Hong Kong and then on to Chungking, wartime capital of nationalist China. But those senior members of the Green Gang that stayed behind no doubt came to an agreement with the Japanese occupiers, acting as their eyes and ears on the street, as well as making sure the Japanese rulers got their slice of any illicit action.

The Red Gang, not having grabbed such a large slice of the Shanghai underworld as the Greens, were less at home with the Japanese and subsequently backed acts of defiance, including murdering Japanese officials who got too close to their activities. Out in the countryside, it was difficult to tell whether it was an organised resistance or gangsters who were leading the fight against Japanese occupation. The British Consulate-General in Harbin reported an incident to the British in Shanghai in November 1939, when 1,000 bandits rode into the town of Noho.

'The small Japanese garrison was unable to evict the invaders and many Japanese civilians were hunted down and shot in the streets. The Chinese population was not molested and merchants in the town were assured that nothing was required of them. The exclusively anti-Japanese character of this successful raid caused a panic among the Japanese population.'

This was sheer revenge for the ravages of the Japanese army and was led by Chinese who could be characterised either as bandits or partisans but were really a mixture of both. It was a movement that would grow throughout South-East Asia, as native populations vented their anger on the Japanese invaders.

The true nature of some people's allegiances was hard to fathom. Vladimir Michailovich Kedrolivansky came to Shanghai in 1938 as an employee of the US Treasury Department – that is, he was an agent for Harry J. Anslinger's Federal Bureau of Narcotics. Tasked with finding out more about the drugs trade and how it affected the USA, he operated undercover, but the Russian seemed more interested in forging connections between murky elements of fellow émigrés in Shanghai and the Japanese authorities.

The British SIS – Secret Intelligence Service – began to take an interest in Kedrolivansky and noted his close friendship with a female Russian agent, also an employee of the US Treasury Department, who worked in Hong Kong. The SIS concluded that although they might be funded by the Federal Bureau of Narcotics, they 'appeared to be concerned primarily with White Russian crookery and the Japanese'.

In this part of the world, Harry J. Anslinger was a little out of his depth and once news of this was returned to Washington, the US Treasury Department offered to remove Kedrolivansky from the Far East, as they realised he was an embarrassment to the British – and themselves. 'We availed ourselves of their kind offer,' said a British official.

As the 1940s unfolded, with war in Europe already a reality, a bubble mentality evolved in Shanghai as the Europeans witnessed the events around them, wondering how long it would be before they were drawn into the awful drama. A British Shanghai Intelligence report captured the increasingly desperate mood in the city:

> The rise in the cost of living is not unnaturally reflected in a serious rise in crime, especially armed robberies. A phenomenon which contrasts oddly with the poverty generally prevailing is, however, the flourishing existence of large numbers of gambling dens, at which millions of dollars are said to be spent nightly, a large percentage of which must undoubtedly percolate into the pockets of the local Japanese and puppet authorities.

Several high-profile murders occurred across the city, seemingly related to events elsewhere in the world. A well-known French lawyer was shot dead on the steps of his office. At first, he was thought to be the victim of a clash between Vichy French and supporters of General de Gaulle, but it later emerged that he had fallen out with a criminal faction in the French Concession. In June 1941, the Japanese Special Deputy Commissioner of Shanghai Police was murdered in a surprisingly brazen act.

'Various motives suggested for the crime were vengeance on the part of Western District gambling-den racketeers,' said a secret British report, 'for the part played by him in suppressing their haunts; and vengeance of his own Japanese subordinates in the police for the strong line taken by him against their undisciplined habits. In any case it is clear that Mr Akagi was a moderate and as such liable to incur the resentment of extremist elements.'

He seemed to be a rare example of a Japanese authority figure wanting to introduce some justice back into the city. He didn't last long. As the situation seemed unlikely to get any better, several British officers in the SMP got out while they could. Many of them wanted to help out their motherland, as it stood alone against Nazi Germany. One of these men was the deadly efficient Assistant Commissioner

William Fairbairn. He got out in 1940 and immediately offered his considerable weapon-training skills to British covert forces.

With another ex-SMP colleague, Eric A. Sykes, the 55-year-old Fairbairn trained Commandos and US Rangers in close-quarter combat techniques. Together, they devised the Fairbairn–Sykes fighting knife, used by British Special Forces throughout the Second World War. A double-edged slender dagger, it was designed to easily penetrate the ribcage and cause maximum damage. 'It is essential that the blade have a sharp stabbing point and good cutting edges,' explained Fairbairn, 'because an artery torn through (as against a clean cut) tends to contract and stop bleeding. If a main artery is cleanly severed, the wounded man will quickly lose consciousness and die.' A golden version of this knife is now part of the Commando memorial at Westminster Abbey in London.

A number of the SMP stayed on, despite the deteriorating situation. With the attack on Pearl Harbor in December 1941 and the Japanese blitzkrieg across South-East Asia, overwhelming the armies of colonial rulers, their position became more precarious. They were enemy aliens and completely at the mercy of their Japanese governors. British businessmen and administrators in Shanghai were rounded up and tortured under suspicion of being spies. When Japanese policemen or soldiers were attacked by Chinese partisans, the SMP were suspected of being soft on them and letting them escape.

Chief Inspector William Hutton had been in the SMP since 1924. Born in Perthshire, he ended up marrying one of the many Russian women that thronged the city. He stayed on in Shanghai after Britain and Japan went to war and, along with his colleagues, was interned in November 1942. They were held in the former US Marine barracks on Haiphong Road, which had been turned into a concentration camp.

While there, Hutton was accused, along with another policeman, by a collaborating Sikh guard of trying to smuggle a message out of the camp in a hollow pencil. It appears he may have had nothing to do with the offence, but merely stood by his pal. Both men were hauled off to the headquarters of the Kempeitai – the notorious Japanese military police – and were interrogated for four days. The friend readily admitted his guilt and was released, battered but relatively uninjured. Hutton took a more stubbornly resistant stance and was relentlessly beaten.

When he returned to the camp, a cellmate described his injuries:

> Nose mashed, teeth broken out, most finger joints broken. Testicles and penis smashed. Cut into the inside of his right leg were two words, WAR and HURT. Cut into the inside of his left thigh were four letters, ANNA.

Anna was Hutton's beloved Russian wife. Another witness said the word KILLED was also inscribed into the police officer's flesh, along with an incomplete MURD – all defined clearly by dried blood. The mutilations were not part of his torture; they appear to have been cut by himself into his skin as a way of turning his body into a final testament to what had happened to him.

'When I saw him,' said the witness, 'his eyes were rolling around and around, when open. He appeared to be semi-conscious and then lapsed into unconsciousness alternately. At the end of my inspection the doctor felt his feet and invited me to do the same – they were stone cold.'

Hutton was taken out of the camp to a hospital and died that evening, on 15 August 1943. After the war, two Japanese policemen, both members of the Kempeitai, were arrested for Hutton's murder, but released, as the date for completing war crimes trials had expired. Undeterred, Hutton's elderly father persisted and shamed the British colonial authorities into re-arresting the two murderers, who were finally jailed in Hong Kong. Wartime vengeance, however, came from a surprisingly unconventional resistance elsewhere in Japanese-occupied colonial territories.

As the war progressed, there were three main elements among the Chinese resistance to the Japanese in South-East Asia. Two of them were connected to the dominant Chinese political parties – the nationalists, or Kuomintang (KMT), and the communists. Spin-off parties sprang up throughout the British colonies, especially in Malaya. The third element was organised crime. Several secret reports by the British military authorities draw a fascinating picture of how these gangsters fought against the Japanese, while pursuing their own interests.

'There are numerous but small bandit gangs throughout Malaya,' said a Special Operations Executive (SOE) report. 'They are armed with weapons picked up during the Malayan Campaign or bought from those who did so. The gangs are known variously as Sam Seng Tong or Hong Mun, both generic Chinese terms for the secret Chinese Triad societies whose origins are lost in antiquity but which long ago degenerated in Malaya into criminal gangs specialising in "protection" rackets.'

These Malayan gangs launched hit-and-run raids against the Japanese but also exploited the anarchic wartime situation by looting and robbing the local population. At times they aligned themselves with the left-wing Anti-Japanese Union and Forces – the AJUF – or the Kuomintang, depending on whoever best served their interests at the time. 'They are no political problem but will be difficult to identify as they will almost certainly seek to justify themselves as partisans.'

The British sent agents among the AJUF to discover what was going on. 'Bandits are with Hong Mun (Chinese Secret Society) organisation leader Cheong Shak Ph,' noted one of them. 'Bandit strength, formerly 200, split up into five sections, but present strength 100 ... Pre-war these bandits mostly Jelutong tappers and members of Sam Seng Tong (criminal gangs) now call themselves Overseas Chinese Volunteers, also Chinese Guerrilla Forces, and use both KMT and communist badges according to the areas they enter.'

Left-wingers claimed they saw these gangsters mostly wearing hat badges consisting of a white sun with white rays – the KMT emblem – and they were roaming through the jungle, killing and robbing indiscriminately. To suit their own political purposes, the AJUF advised the British colonial authorities to bring an end to these gangs. The British were very aware of the ruthless political games being played out in the jungle and were not so easily swayed.

Peter Dobree was a 28-year-old dairy farmer in north-east Malaya when the Japanese invaded. He joined the Singapore Volunteer Artillery, but when the British garrison fell, he was forced to flee in a small boat to Sri Lanka. Determined to fight back against the Japanese, he was commissioned into the 3rd Gurkha Rifles and volunteered for behind-the-lines operations in Japanese-occupied Malaya. This brought him to the attention of SOE Force 136 and he was parachuted into northern Malaya in December 1944. By the end of March 1945, he had recruited a band of almost 200 Malay and Chinese villagers.

Leading raids against the Japanese, they took particular delight in killing members of the Kempeitai.

Dobree was aware of the many shades of grey in his unconventional campaign and rejected the black-and-white views of the left-wing AJUF, which wanted the criminal gangs working with the KMT eliminated.

'The whole problem has been under consideration by us and we have sought Dobree's advice,' said a top secret British report of June 1945. 'He is of the opinion that the KMT guerrillas, if lightly armed, well controlled and given tasks such as road blocks, can be usefully employed, but if disowned they will become embittered and likely to be troublesome. He reminded us that they are already armed and have been helpful and cooperative.'

The British proposed that Dobree take over the disparate KMT units – including the gangsters among them – in preparation for the anticipated Allied invasion of Malaya. In the event, the dropping of two nuclear bombs on Japan in August brought the Pacific war to a hasty end. In the meantime, the British were becoming wary of the communist-infiltrated AJUF.

'The main point to be remembered in estimating the danger of supporting AJUF is that the rank and file of the guerrilla forces and union is entirely drawn from the uneducated classes in the country,' said the same report. 'These may have been subjected for years to a spate of propaganda and have no doubt been told that they will all live like princes under a republic.'

While it was estimated that 80 per cent of the guerrillas would be happy to return to their families, the British feared that their officers had a political agenda.

'Whether they will be able to retain any following if they decide to go anti-British after that will depend on how well we have managed by then to regain the confidence and friendship of the general body of Chinese in the country.'

For one British agent, however, who had direct experience with AJUF communists, it was already too late:

> The Communists are anti-British and have a Chinese all ready
> to take over as Governor of Malaya; however they tell the
> Malays that the Malays will govern the country. They want

arms badly and will pretend to be pro-British to gain these ends. An instance has occurred of their asking a Malay to steal arms from me. These arms would be a great menace after the war.

The communists were living off rice taken from Malay peasants. 'They do practically no underground work against the Japanese but take great delight in killing Chinese informers and have put the fear of God into would-be Malay informers.'

He concluded, 'They are a boastful, lying, dirty lot of braggarts and a future menace.'

His prediction was absolutely correct, but that problem would not erupt until later in the decade.

9

THE PRETTY ORPHAN GANGOO

AS WORLD WAR RAGED IN China and South-East Asia, organised crime in other parts of the British Empire carried on much as before – especially when it concerned the sex industry.

Gangoo was a little Indian boy, orphaned within minutes of being born when his mother died in childbirth. His father, a poor farmer from a village in Kangra District, in the very north of India in the shadow of the Himalayas, had passed away months before. A neighbour passed the baby on to a woman whose husband was a Havildar – a native officer of the equivalent rank of sergeant in the British Indian Army. She found a wet nurse for Gangoo and raised him as her own.

'When I was three years old, I lost my first benefactor, who died under the spell of black magic,' Gangoo told a friend in wartime India in 1942.

The Havildar remarried and took his new wife and the child with him to his battalion. He regarded the toddler as a mere encumbrance, one he wished to rid himself of as soon as possible, but Gangoo worked a charm of his own and, as he grew older, he developed into a pretty boy.

'The new bride was plain and I was lovely,' he recalled. 'The Havildar's love for me increased as my looks improved with my years, and his repulsion for his wife too increased proportionately. She attributed it to me, and made one or two attempts to strangle me, but the Havildar came to my rescue each time.'

She beat him regularly with a stick, slapped his face till it was raw, plunged her fingers into his nostrils. But she and the soldier were his only carers in the world and he began to get a perverse pleasure from the beatings.

'I missed her blows even more than the Havildar's kisses,' he said. 'What I did mind most was the soldiers' unwelcome attentions. They were revolting. It was cruel of them to treat me as they did, and I hated them for it, but they could persuade me always by their gifts of sweets and occasional tips. I was ten years old and must have looked superb.'

One day, Gangoo was hanging around the bazaar in Peshawar, the busiest city in the Khyber region, when a well-dressed gentleman started chatting to him. He wondered whether the child had ever been to the cinema. The boy admitted he had not.

'Then you have missed the treat of your life,' said the gentleman. 'It is a sight for the gods.'

Gangoo visited the movies and thoroughly enjoyed the black-and-white adventure. The gentleman returned the boy to his home and they agreed to visit the cinema again. On each occasion, the man did not attempt to molest him and Gangoo was happy with the relationship.

'One day he proposed that I should become an actor. I was pretty enough to take on myself the role of a heroine, he said. That would be something delightful. I agreed to follow him to the ends of the earth if he could help me to get that role.'

The gentleman invited Gangoo to go with him to Lahore, capital of the Punjab. With the Havildar taken ill in hospital and his life at home a purgatory, the boy agreed. The gentleman said they would travel abroad to Hollywood and earn a fortune. They would send his photograph ahead of them to the film producers.

'But how can we go overseas without money?' wondered Gangoo.

'That is the point, my boy,' he said. 'Would you believe me if I tell you, you could have money for the asking. If you seriously set yourself to make it.'

'But I am serious.'

'My good boy, nothing is disgraceful,' he assured him, 'if it ends in bringing us gold and taking us across the seas.'

They held hands and Gangoo swore solemnly to the seductive older man: 'You will find me agreeable to any of your propositions.'

In Lahore, Gangoo was introduced to a gang of teenagers in a similar situation to himself.

'The man who had thus led me astray was no other than the notorious gaol-bird Nusroo,' realised Gangoo. 'He had an organisation of his own whose many-sided activities brought him in plenty of money. He had a ring of beggars and crooks. Some of these posed as blind Brahmins. They were no more blind than you or I.'

Sometimes the beggars functioned as cat burglars at night and brought their treasures back to Nusroo, who sold them on through sub-agents all over India. They called the booty 'dat'. Nusroo also ran gambling dens, brothels and nightclubs, where Lahore's criminals met to spend their money and plan robberies. Hindu priests took his money and informed him of pretty girls who could be corrupted or wealthy donors whose houses might be visited by child burglars. Nusroo's newest scam was to run a girls' school attended by teenage prostitutes.

'He had engaged a number of pretty girls,' explained Gangoo, 'to whom he gave receipt-books to go to rich men's houses and induce them to patronise their girls' school by liberally subscribing towards their funds. They kept half the collection and the rest went to Nusroo, who helped run the school. Another girls' school run by some scoundrels received a substantial grant simply for providing pretty girls to be supplied to scoundrels out of whom Nusroo was able to extract money. He was now in need of a boy who would do the collection, from rich folk. I was to be that boy. I was to have no scruples, if I cared to collect money.'

Fortunately, one day when Gangoo was about to fleece yet another wealthy benefactor, the rich man took a liking to him and offered to remove him from his life of crime.

'It was a tough job taking me out of this vicious circle,' concluded Gangoo, 'but he was a very resourceful man, and saved me from their clutches at last, by paying Nusroo for my release.'

Gangoo was lucky, but many other girls and boys were not and disappeared into India's vast underworld sex business.

Prostitution in India had been rigorously controlled when it came to the British Tommy indulging himself. The 1864 Cantonment Act was devised to protect British soldiers from venereal disease by training a caste of Indian women to be kept captive within the military encampments exclusively for their pleasure. These women were well housed and fed, earning more than prostitutes outside, but were forced to undergo frequent medical examinations.

Too many soldiers, however, continued to wander beyond their cantonments to consort with working women and so a second law was introduced – the 1868 Contagious Diseases Act – which enabled the military to exert control over these 'common prostitutes', demanding they register at police stations and have regular clinical examinations. This included the red-light districts of Indian cities, and allowed the police to raid brothels and prosecute any class of prostitute, up to the mistresses maintained by wealthy native businessmen.

A British government report of 1919 examined the state of the urban sex trade in India and Burma. It estimated there were 15,000 professional prostitutes in Calcutta, another 15,000 in Bombay, 1,000 in Madras, 500 in Rangoon and a good deal many more amateurs, or 'clandestines', as it termed them. Generally, the report declared that 'Prostitution in the East is not viewed in the same light as in Europe, as nothing like the same amount of stigma and shame attaches to it out here.'

There were a number of European prostitutes working in Indian cities and these mostly came from the Balkans or Russia. A small number from Austria and Germany had been repatriated during the First World War as enemy aliens. Many of these were said to have arrived via Cairo and Port Said and may well have been victims of White Slave trafficking before they came to India. A number of Japanese, Chinese and Arab women also served the sex trade in the major cities.

Most of these women worked in brothels where the Madam provided board and lodging in return for half their takings. The police considered the Madams useful 'levers' for controlling order in the brothels. Beyond their walls, there was a less controllable world of sex for sale, for example in the Sonagachi quarter of Calcutta:

> This part of the town is a seething mass of Indian prostitutes. The houses and balconies along Chitpur Road and Beadon Square are thronged with prostitutes sitting outside, and the narrow lanes and gullies at the back of these main thoroughfares form a veritable ant-hill of these 'unfortunates'. A very large number are also to be found in the labyrinths of tortuous narrow gullies and lanes at the back of many of the main thoroughfares and arteries in the very heart of the city. These

> Indian brothels and prostitutes are practically under no police
> control or supervision, and no police action is taken against
> them except on the demand of members of the public who may
> be annoyed by their near neighbourhood.

Trouble often arose when foreign pimps took over the running of
prostitutes and kept all their earnings, but whereas the Foreigner Act
could be used to remove Continental Europeans, it was ineffective
against British and Australian former soldiers who took over parts of
the sex trade. There was also a problem with junior police officers
extorting protection money from brothel keepers. Evidence of
kidnapping and the forcible exploitation of women as sex slaves in
India was non-existent.

Having recorded the state of the sex trade in India and Burma under
the British, the writer of the 1919 government report – a district
superintendent of police in Rangoon – then put forward his own
thoughts on reform. There was one topic that concerned him above all
others: the role of white women. He wanted them banned from the sex
business.

> This is called for more from a political than a moral point of
> view. The European prostitute is known by the Indian as
> 'Mem' and by the Burmans as 'Thakinma', and these are the
> self-same terms that are used in speaking of respectable white
> women in the country. It is of course true that the Indian and
> Burman town dweller know quite well that European
> prostitutes are not of the same class or race as the English
> women in the country, but it is doubtful whether the ignorant
> villager who pays a visit to Rangoon is equally aware of the
> difference.

He continued:

> Be this as it may, the white races are at the present time the
> dominant and governing races of the world and anything that
> would lower them in the sight of the subject races should, I
> think, be carefully guarded against, and I do not think there
> can be any doubt that the sight of European women prostituting

themselves is most damaging to the prestige of the white races.

All that was necessary to preserve respect for the white races, insisted the district superintendent, was to set in motion an executive order of government and a declaration of policy that the presence of these women 'is most objectionable and harmful'.

It was a fascinating insight into the psychology of colonial administrators. The idea of white women consorting with black races had always tormented those imperialists who considered themselves to be morally superior to the people they ruled. In the end, it was not to be the loose morality of some white women that would let down the empire but the failure of white soldiers to hold back the all-conquering Japanese.

In 1941, just before the outbreak of the Second World War in Asia, venereal disease was, yet again, proving a major concern for British military commanders. 'We are very much worried about the high incidence of VD in Malaya,' wrote a lieutenant colonel to the War Office. He feared the rates of infection might be even higher than recorded because many servicemen were trying to cure themselves by buying antibacterial sulphonamides at pharmacists rather than reporting themselves to doctors. He also feared the criminal elements of the sex trade. 'Can anything be done to check the prostitutes, pimps, etc.?'

Among the evidence the lieutenant colonel quoted was an anonymously authored letter describing vice in Singapore:

> One small area alone, paradoxically called by the name of a sweet smelling flower, produced five hundred and six cases [of VD] out of the thousand, while about three hundred and fifty-two men associate their downfall to the cafes and cabarets. One cafe alone, which is still open, has produced seventy-seven cases out of this number. Unlicensed houses are common, especially in the cabaret area, where some are even directly above the cafes themselves so that the ardent alcoholic has but a few steps to travel.

Armoured state executioner from Rewah in central India, c.1900. (Private Collection, Peter Newark's Pictures)

Chinese opium smoker in Limehouse, London, c.1900. (Private Collection, Peter Newark's Pictures)

Opium poppy cultivation before the British Empire's prohibition in 1908. (Private Collection, Peter Newark's Pictures)

King of the Opium Ring' – American pulp fiction portrayal of sinister Chinese gangsters seducing white women in an opium den, c.1910. (Private Collection, Peter Newark's Pictures)

Chinese criminal executed. Some degenerate spectators would gamble on
how far the decapitated head would roll after the beheading.
(Private Collection, Peter Newark's Pictures)

Russell Pasha
mounted on a
fine Arab horse.
Commandant
of Cairo Police,
he served in this
role for three
decades, as well
as spearheading
the international
war against illicit
drugs in the
1930s. (Private
Collection, Peter
Newark's Pictures)

Harry J. Anslinger, pioneering drugs-busting investigator and head of the Federal Bureau of Narcotics from 1930 to 1962. (Author's own collection)

Sudanese trooper in the Egyptian Police Camel Corps, tasked with hunting down Arab hashish caravans. (Private Collection, Peter Newark's Pictures)

Zinc cylinder containing opium hidden in a camel's stomach and recovered when the animal was slaughtered. (Private Collection, Peter Newark's Pictures)

These boarding houses were cheap to rent and the girls claimed they were merely entertaining their male friends with a few beers. It was all very casual, with the intention of avoiding any intervention by the police.

'If one interrogates the men more closely as to how they contacted the women,' noted the anonymous letter writer, 'they will usually tell you that they picked her up in a cafe, rarely that they met her outside the cafe. Others say that they got her address from a boy friend; many, that while they were standing about a boy took them off to a house, and finally, some that they knew the house was a brothel by the cross on the wall, or that they were taken there by rickshaw pullers or taxi-drivers.'

'In fact,' concluded the exasperated report, 'one quickly realises that one of Singapore's foremost industries is prostitution and all that goes with it, and that at the moment this profession must be employing, either full or part time, many thousands of individuals.'

This picture was drawn on the eve of the Japanese invasion of South-East Asia. What followed, as in China, was a sinister takeover by the Japanese military of many avenues of organised crime, including the sex business. Throughout their hastily erected empire, the Japanese forced thousands of young women to work in brothels to service their soldiers. Just one example of this occurred in Western Borneo in 1943.

The Japanese naval garrison commander of Pontianak issued an order that no Japanese serviceman was to have casual relations with Indonesian or Chinese women. Instead, he decreed that official brothels be established. Women who were deemed to have already had sex with Japanese were forced into the barbed wire-surrounded accommodation and were only allowed back out on the streets with special permission. To keep the brothels full, the Naval Police – the Tokei Tai – were allowed to scour the streets and arrest any women they fancied, then have them forcibly examined and imprisoned in the brothels.

The Japanese also established civilian brothels, the profits of which went directly into the pockets of the occupying administrators and their criminal colleagues. Women for these brothels were obtained by the Naval Police by dragging them off the streets. The degrading process that followed was described by a Dutch Intelligence officer after the war:

In their search for women, the Tokei Tai ordered the entire

[native] female staffs of Japanese firms to report to the Tokei Tai Office, undressed some of them entirely and accused them of maintaining relations with Japanese. The ensuing medical examination revealed that several were virgins. It is not known with certainty how many of these unfortunates were forced into brothels. Women did not dare to escape from the brothels as members of their family were then immediately arrested and severely maltreated by the Tokei Tai. In one case it is known that this caused the death of the mother of the girl concerned.

This evidence was gathered from an Indonesian medical officer who was forced to examine the girls recruited by the Naval Police and was presented at war crimes trials.

The Japanese had inflicted tremendous damage on the rulers of the British Empire in the Far East, not only in terms of physical damage and death to so many of their subjects but also in terms of prestige. Despite the great bravery and endurance of their armed forces – and their ultimate victory – the British had been humiliated in a string of defeats and they could no longer command the total respect of the native populations. Their military edge had been eroded and their rule savaged.

As the post-war era began, it would demand a tremendous effort to keep a lid on the competing new powers. Certainly, there was a vigorous tide of Communism spreading throughout South-East Asia, but there was also a resurgence of organised crime that would sorely test the resolve of its colonial masters.

10

THE LUCKY MR LAI

ON 29 MARCH 1946, SOME 1,500 Chinese inhabitants gathered at Sungai Ara on the island of Penang, north-west Malaya. Armed guards were placed on roads leading to the meeting. Their instructions were to keep the local Malays away: this was a Chinese-only gathering. When some of them were later questioned by the suspicious colonial police force, they all told the same story: they were 'visiting relations'. When pressed further, they explained they had been 'worshipping the gods'. This did not exactly explain the fresh pinpricks they all bore on the middle finger of their left hand.

Only later was it finally revealed that these Chinese had all attended a mass initiation ceremony organised by the Ang Bin Hoey (ABH) and Sin Ghee Chin secret societies. When word of this got out, it sent a chill through the colonial police headquarters; these were Triad gangs and it was a massive show of strength.

The dramatic initiation ritual had begun as the sun set. White cockerels were beheaded and their blood collected in a cistern. Each Chinese initiate was asked to remove his coat and sit on the ground, while members of the gang bound strips of white cloth around his head. He was ordered to crawl on hands and knees towards the 'Five Gates', each of which was guarded by two men with swords in their hands.

At the first gate, a sword was placed on the nape of the novice's neck. 'Now you have come to take the oath to join the Ang Bin Hoey,' proclaimed one of the formidable guards. 'You must not talk of this when you return to town.'

The initiate agreed and was ordered to crawl to the second gate. Here, he had to repeat an oath: 'I have honoured my father and mother and must not sin.' At the third gate, he was asked to repeat the promise. At the fourth gate, the middle finger of his left hand was pricked by the swordsman with a burnt needle and a drop of his blood squeezed into a chalice. Into this blood, he dipped his finger and licked it. The guard told him: 'We are all brothers of the same blood. From now on you must behave in accordance with your conscience and never misbehave with your Elder Sister-in-Law.' Presumably, this was not a specific instruction, but a general statement of brotherhood.

Passing on to the fifth gate, through a red cloth curtain, the new gang member crawled to a spot at which he was given a date or banana to eat. From there, he shuffled towards a paper image of the Grave of the Elder Brother – to whom he had to pay homage. After that, he was given a hard-boiled egg to eat and asked to jump over a fire. He was then shown a headless rooster and told that a similar fate awaited him if he ever betrayed the secrets of the Ang Bin Hoey or violated its rules.

After all the apprenctice gangsters had been initiated, they were told they would have to attend another gathering at which they would be confirmed and taught the secret signs and codes of the society. 'Incredible, fantastic, and in parts childish as this ceremony may seem,' said a British Intelligence report, 'it varies but little from the well-attested rituals of other Chinese secret societies.' It also echoed the symbolic initiation ceremonies of other organised crime clans, such as the Sicilian Mafia.

Like the Mafia, the Ang Bin Hoey had their 'soldiers'. These were called 'Tiger-General' or '51'. Each gang had at least five of these fighters or strong-arm men whose job it was to collect protection money or assault the victim if he didn't pay up. Expert in martial arts, they settled disputes with other gangs by fighting and were the hit men for any assassinations. The lowest rank of membership was the '49'. He simply paid his subscription and joined in with bigger gang battles, hoping to catch the eye of his superiors. The use of numbers for ranks was a reference to the numerology of the classic Chinese text *I Ching*, which explained the world through calculations.

The 51s were commanded by the '432' or 'Grass-Sandal', who told them whom to attack and passed their protection money on to the gang treasurer, known as '415' or 'White Fan', who administered each gang. Along with 432, he would arbitrate in disputes between gangs before the fighting started. He, in turn, would pass on a cut of all monies received to the '426' or 'Red Rod' – the district leader. He had the power to punish errant members with fines, beatings or death. He organised the mass initiation ceremonies and could call on reinforcements from other areas. Above all was the 'Master of the Mountain', also known as 'Dragon Head'. He was the chief of the society and his word was law.

The Sungai Ara Triad gathering coincided with a leap in crime throughout Penang in 1946. Armed robbery, murder and extortion were widespread and the Chinese population were too afraid to help the police. Even the Chancellor of the Chinese Consulate, who had originally declined an invitation to attend an Ang Bin Hoey ceremony, was forced to be present after being warned he would otherwise face undesirable consequences.

The Triad gangs were hoping to raise their profile in Malaya in order to compete with the Malayan Communist Party (MCP). It was as much their aim to reassert their control over crime as it was to gain political influence. The communists had come out of the war in a weakened state, with little money in their party funds, thanks in part to the devious actions of double agents, and the Triads saw their opportunity to gain the upper hand in peacetime. During the war, the Ang Bin Hoey had fought alongside the communists against the Japanese but had then broken away from them. They didn't like to be under their control.

Triad roots stemmed back to the secret societies that had conspired to end the rule of the Qing in China and had collaborated with the Kuomintang nationalists. When they established themselves in Singapore and Malaya, aside from controlling every form of racketeering, they continued their anti-authority stance by opposing the colonial government. As a result, they were never recognised as a legitimate civil society by the British, who broke up their city meetings, forcing them to gather in the countryside.

'Today [the Ang Bin Hoey] is openly fighting the MCP,' noted a British Intelligence officer, 'not necessarily for political reasons, although its sympathies, if any, are with the KMT.' The Dragon Head of the ABH was keen to be officially recognised – so he could pursue their political agenda – and had renewed his society's bid for registration with the government. But the British took their time with his application, well aware that the Ang Bin Hoey was, in reality, a criminal organisation:

> Its official objects are threefold; to 'render mutual assistance to its members'; to foster friendly feelings amongst them; and to 'exchange knowledge' and 'promote public welfare'. On the other hand its objects as exemplified by its activities appear to be 'protection' of certain hotels, prostitutes and merchants (either members, or persons paying for this protection), and murder and armed gang robbery directed against non-members and those who have presumably refused to pay for protection.

It was true that the clash between the Ang Bin Hoey and the Malayan communists was nothing to do with differences over international politics but came down to gang law. A former Chinese member of a left-wing anti-Japanese guerrilla force had traded on the reputation of the Ang Bin Hoey by trying to extort money under the Triad name. Such false claims have always been looked down upon by organised criminals, as the fear they invoke is a major asset and must not be diluted by false claimants. If anyone does use their name, they should pay for it – as a criminal franchisee. This pretend communist gangster had failed to gain that permission and was subsequently set up by the ABH, which testified against him in court, seeing him sent down for five years.

The left-wing guerrillas did not appreciate this punishment of their comrade and, in revenge, shot dead three members of the ABH. In a further incident, a firefight broke out and two of the guerrillas were shot, as well. As a direct result of this, the Penang MCP created its own secret organisation called the Black Face Society. Its principal aims were fighting the ABH and combating British imperialism. It was also an attempt to bring back party members who had deserted to the criminal gangs. Black Face members were trained in intelligence, propaganda and the handling of weapons.

This explained the mass initiation ceremony on Penang – the Triad gangs were in a desperate arms race with the communists to get more 'soldiers' and outfight them. Having recruited several hundred members in Penang and the north of Malaya, the Triad gangs seemed to be winning the race and embarked on a crime wave that included piracy, as well as robbery, extortion and murder. In one instance, a prominent owner of several junks was murdered after it was believed he had squealed to the police about his ships being robbed by ABH gangsters.

Local businessmen – called *towkays* – were a favourite target for kidnapping. In January 1947, one of these victims was released by police after a rubber plantation worker had led them to the house where gangsters were holding him. Later that month, the informer was awoken by someone trying to stab him. In the struggle, he managed to break away, running into the darkness, but when he turned round, he saw his house burst into flames. He ran to the nearest police station.

The next morning, the informer and the police arrived at the smoking ruins of his house. Inside were the bodies of his wife, mother, father and two daughters. They had all been slaughtered by the ABH in reprisal for informing on them. But that wasn't the end of it. On a nearby rubber estate, a woman and three children related to the informer were found suffering from cuts and burns. Three of them later died.

Such inhumanity roused the local population and they helped the police and army scour the area for the gangsters involved. Eighteen members of the ABH were subsequently arrested and put under military guard.

Undeterred, the ABH spread out from Penang to terrorise rubber-planting districts across the Malay Peninsula. As they raided villages and robbed Asian shopkeepers, there were fears that European rubber planters and their families were at risk, too. British estate agency firms claimed that rubber plantation workers would leave if the police couldn't provide better protection for them. Malay businessmen got the feeling that the local police wanted to get tougher with the gangsters, but were being prevented by the colonial authorities.

'Given a free hand,' said the *Malay Mail*, published in Kuala Lumpur, 'the police of Malaya would have dealt summarily with such persons under the banishment rules and returned them to the land of their birth.' The *Straits Times* in Singapore accused Whitehall of handcuffing the local police force and demanded more ruthless use of exile against Chinese secret societies. The reluctance was due in part to a bigger political game being played out in post-war Malaya.

The British imperial government was more concerned about the threat posed by communism to their rule. Out of a wish not to alienate the Chinese population in Malaya, it appears they did not seek harsher punishment for the influential secret societies. They certainly devoted much time to investigating their political affiliations, as one secret report revealed:

> In order to improve the standing and influence of the [ABH] Society, the original founders persuaded Chinese of the merchant class not only to join their Society but to hold high office on its committee. Some of these merchants were members too of the Kuomintang and may have been influenced in joining the Ang Bin Hoey by their antagonism to the Communists.

Some intelligence agents referred to the ABH as the strong arm of the Kuomintang, but the author of one secret report warned against this assumption. The Triad network was far more profound in its history and hold on the Chinese population than the Kuomintang. The ABH was certainly not its creature; rather it chose to support whichever party served its own purposes first. When leading members of the ABH were arrested, British Intelligence officers took the opportunity to interrogate them about their wider concerns. One of these captured figures was referred to as the 'Incense Master' or '438' – one of the most senior members of the ABH, concerned with its rituals.

'There are Triad Societies in America, France and Australia,' said the Incense Master. 'Why is it that only the British regard Triad Societies as illegal? Why all this fuss about an enquiry? The matter is simple. If Triad Societies are illegal, banish us to China straight away. If not, permit us to exist openly, and we will tell Government who the bad people in the country are.'

It was an intriguing offer. The ABH might be a ferocious criminal organisation, but as political enemies of the communists they were hard to beat. When the Dragon Head of the ABH was brought in for questioning, he made a similar argument.

'I tell you that if the Triad Brotherhood is not allowed to exist,' he said, 'all the Chinese shopkeepers will be forced to join the Kuomintang. If the Ang Brotherhood is not allowed to exist, why are the Communists? The Ang Brotherhood is far less dangerous than the Third International. In fact, its aims are good, and it will help Government. Not so the Communists.'

These quotes were left hanging in the air in the secret report. The implication was clear. If the British imperial government so wished, the ABH would make devoted allies in their battle against communism. It was noted that in China in August 1946 – after the end of the war against Japan and with civil war breaking out between nationalists and communists – the Kuomintang in Shanghai had revived their branch of the Ang Brotherhood as a key instrument in their battle against the Left. Three months later, branches of the Kuomintang in Malaya received instructions from China to cultivate friendly relations with the ABH.

When the Incense Master was invited to attend a meeting with the Chinese Nationalist Consul in Penang, he took the opportunity to complain to the Kuomintang diplomats about the British police action taken against the ABH.

'The history of the Ang people is a glory to China,' said one of the nationalist diplomats. 'And if they do not break the law of the country, there is nothing to fear.'

It was an ambiguous statement – bearing in mind the brazen gangster nature of the ABH – but the Consul assured the Incense Master that he would do his best to resolve his concerns about the police by talking to the colonial authorities. As far as the ABH were concerned, if their efforts had been appreciated by the British during their war against the Japanese, why could they not strike a similar deal in their struggle against the communists?

British Intelligence officers understood very well the political balancing act needed to ensure useful political allies were kept on board, while they also stood up against organised crime. In Malaya, the latter desire seemed to triumph over the former.

'It is probably politically a good thing that action has been taken in Court,' said one British officer, '[letting] banishment proceedings [go ahead] to discredit the Ang Brotherhood before closer links with the Kuomintang were forged.'

'There is more Triad activity at the present time than there has been for 20 years,' he concluded. 'We are now faced with the additional factor that a Triad Organisation exists openly in China on good terms with the Kuomintang.'

That the British felt they did not need to embrace wholeheartedly the deal proffered by the Triads was down to their own success against the communists in Malaya – a secret operation that had been seeded by the Malay Police Force back in the 1930s before the Second World War.

In the British Empire, the leaders of the Russian Revolution saw a major target for their subversive activities and encouraged undercover agents to create communist cells throughout its territories. In 1931, a French businessman was sent to Singapore on just such a mission. Unfortunately for him, the head of the Straits Settlements Police at that time was an exceptional detective called René Onraet.

Born in Darjeeling to a family of French extraction, Onraet had been educated at Stonyhurst College in Lancashire before joining the Straits Settlements Police as a cadet in 1907. His flawless Chinese meant he could adopt many different guises to infiltrate gangster locations. On one occasion, he investigated an opium den by pretending to be a Chinese drain inspector. At another time, he posed as a rickshaw driver.

'Organised crime in Singapore meant one of three things,' noted Onraet. 'Gang robbery, extortion from the public and the scheming of subversive organisations. All of these activities to a very great extent depended on immigration from China, and all derived their strength from Chinese secret societies.'

Chinese immigrants were vulnerable to being exploited by their own people and it was from this pool of imported labour that the Chinese gangsters gained their strength. Most of the mobsters were from peasant families and were physically strong. Onraet described some of their favourite weapons:

> In later years these fellows took to using homemade bombs
> made from antimony sulphide and potassium chlorate mixed
> in with nails, screws and pieces of plate glass. These bombs
> were thrown into the house, generally at meal times, and the
> noise and smoke, to say nothing of the wounds caused by the
> shrapnel, enabled the gang to get to work among a thoroughly
> cowed household. A much more effective bomb was evolved

in due course; it consisted of two or three sticks of blasting gelatine packed into a cigarette tin fitted with a fuse – shrapnel as before!

Cut-down shotguns were also popular. 'Some of these men were real killers,' said Onraet, 'shooting dead unresisting victims simply to terrorise or make a name for themselves. When cornered, they sometimes shot it out from barricaded rooms or housetops.' As in Shanghai, police assault parties used bulletproof waistcoats and shields when raiding mobster hideouts. One officer nearly drowned at night while wearing one of the heavier models of body armour when he mistook the green surface of a Chinese fishpond for a green field. On another occasion, a policeman wore more home-made protection made out of newspaper stuffed into his uniform by a loving wife.

At an early stage, Onraet learned that much Chinese crime was fuelled by their insatiable appetite for gambling, but he was sometimes shocked as to when it took place:

> When I was in China I was once asked by some friends to go and see the execution of some robbers. The execution ground was on a slope running down to a small stream, and on the other side of the stream was another slope whereon the public gathered. In due course half a dozen men were brought out and made to kneel with their heads to the stream. When their heads were cut off, some rolled a few feet, some more, down the slope. There were among the spectators men taking bets on which head would roll furthest!

Onraet's knowledge-led success against Chinese gangs saw him rapidly promoted to director of the local Criminal Intelligence Department, or Special Branch. It was then that he turned his attention to communist infiltrators, raiding their printing presses and offices, and closing down bomb-making factories.

In 1931, when a suspicious-looking French businessman turned up in Singapore, Onraet ran a series of checks on him. Contacts within the French Sûreté revealed that his company did not exist in Paris, and when detectives staked out his office in Singapore, they observed several known communists visiting him.

A police raid on the offices exposed the true identity of the Frenchman. He was Joseph Ducroux, a renowned communist recruiter. Rifling through his files, they uncovered an international network of communist subversives that included Ho Chi Minh – future leader of the Vietnamese Communist Party – then currently in Hong Kong, and his shadowy accomplice Lai Te.

Lai Te was a man of mystery to even his closest colleagues. No one knew his real name. Bizarrely, when he joined the Malayan Communist Party, he chose a western name, 'Wright', but because of Chinese difficulties pronouncing 'r' this became distorted to 'Lai Te', which was further mangled to 'Loi Teck' or 'Lighter'. Of Vietnamese background, born sometime around 1900, he claimed to have been trained in both Russia and France as a member of the Communist Party. Certainly, he managed to get himself noticed. In Hong Kong, alongside Ho Chi Minh, he was part of a pan-Asian revolutionary movement.

As a result of Onraet's diligence, the communist agents were arrested and an attempt to plant revolution in Singapore was foiled. Onraet received much praise and advanced rapidly to become Inspector-General of the entire Straits Settlements Police Force in 1935. Personally, he was dismayed at the light sentences the communists received; in fact, following the Ducroux affair, Lai Te in particular had been allowed to continue his career within the Malayan Communist Party. But for the moment, Onraet would have to let the mysterious communist carry on with his business as usual.

Rebuilding the shattered remnants of the MCP, Lai Te proved highly effective as an administrator, eventually becoming its secretary-general. Part of his success was down to his very good luck. Whenever a meeting was raided or senior party members banished, Lai Te managed not to be there. It was partly because he was the last man standing on so many occasions that his position of leadership within the MCP was unrivalled.

When Japan invaded China, Lai Te expressed solidarity with his communist allies by organising riots against Malaya's importation of soya beans and other food from Japanese-occupied Manchuria. Despite this open insurrection against the colonial authorities, when Japanese soldiers conquered the colony in 1941, Lai Te realised the only future for the communists was to join with the British imperialists in their underground battle against the common enemy. This decision was to be the making of his small but efficient party.

Trained in guerrilla warfare by the British, the Malayan communists proved to be willing recruits, mastering quickly the skills of living behind enemy lines, setting explosives and ambushing enemy columns. Known first as the Anti-Japanese Union Force (AJUF) and then the Malayan Peoples' Anti-Japanese Army (MPAJA), it had grown to be 7,000 strong by the end of the war. Lai Te, considering himself more of a political manager than a fighter, stayed in Singapore, where his astonishing good luck allowed him to survive the Japanese occupation.

Whenever a communist cell was discovered and its members were ruthlessly eliminated by the Kempeitai, the Japanese military police, Lai Te was somewhere else. In 1942, the entire Central Committee of the MCP was arrested by the Japanese, but Lai Te had been delayed on his way to the meeting and avoided imprisonment. A month later, leaders of the MPAJA met in caves north of Kuala Lumpur to discuss their strategy. Lai Te was supposed to be there, but his car had broken down on the way. When he arrived, the Japanese had shot dead 90 of the communist guerrillas in a ferocious gun battle. Good fortune is always valued by the Chinese and Lai Te ruled the MCP without any opposition.

Not everyone, however, was convinced by the communist leader.

Chin Peng was a young Chinese revolutionary who had risen through the MCP during their years in the jungle. He recalled meeting Lai Te face-to-face for the first time:

> I noted the Secretary-General's strong Vietnamese accent. Lai Te was obviously not Chinese. He didn't look Chinese; he didn't sound Chinese. To me, he looked almost Eurasian. He was dark and quite small in stature – no more than 1.65 metres. He looked ill.

At the end of the war, the communists emerged as heroes to the Chinese population of Malaya and were well placed to forge ahead with their political objectives – the eradication of colonial rule. Young radicals like Chin Peng demanded that Lai Te declare war on the British Empire, but Lai stepped back from open conflict. He preferred the more traditional strategy of labour unrest and protests.

Increasingly frustrated by Lai Te's caution, some of the young Malayan communists began to ask awkward questions. How was it that Lai Te was able to travel around Japanese-occupied Malaya so easily? How come he had avoided so many disastrous meetings when other communists were arrested or killed by the Japanese? How come, in fact, before the war, he had managed to avoid so many of the raids on their party by the British? Why was Lai Te so very lucky?

In October 1946, Lai Te was summoned to a meeting of the Central Committee of the Malayan Communist Party in Kuala Lumpur to explain some irregularities in the funding of the party.

'Lai Te duly appeared on the third day for the start of the main meeting,' recalled Chin Peng. 'He began by asking for the prepared agenda. He read it without obvious reaction. For a while he attempted to justify his political analysis until he realised he was failing to win over his audience. He then abruptly changed tack and insinuated that the comrade who had presided over the drafting of the agenda was involved in a plot.'

The accused party member vehemently protested and the strength of his denial unnerved Lai Te, who changed his approach yet again.

'I'm getting old,' he told his colleagues, 'and you all know I've been unwell for a long time. I would like your permission to take a holiday. Perhaps I could use the time to improve my Chinese language skills.'

Lai Te then suggested that Chin Peng would make a good leader of the party. As Lai Te heaped praise on the young man, Chin Peng felt uncomfortable and jumped to his feet. He suspected Lai Te of distracting attention from his own precarious situation.

'Before I had finished my outburst,' said Chin Peng, 'Lai Te, to the total amazement of everybody, burst into tears. He sat weeping silently at the head of the table, his head cradled in his hands. Through his sobs he repeatedly murmured: "You have misunderstood me . . . you have misunderstood me." If his theatrics had been calculated to win sympathy, they were an instant and stunning success.'

The other party members rounded on Chin Peng and said that their leader should be allowed to rest and go on holiday. But party rumblings continued and, in January 1947, a further meeting was convened in Kuala Lumpur. Lai Te was a meticulous timekeeper and when he failed to turn up, everyone was concerned.

Chin Peng drove with his colleagues to Lai Te's home, looking for signs of an accident along the way. Lai Te's pregnant wife was as surprised as they were when they told her that he had not made the meeting. Fearing something serious might have happened to their party leader, Chin Peng and his comrades began to search the city.

'We were at a loss as to how to begin our investigations,' he recalled. 'We had no contacts in the Special Branch. Furthermore, we could scarcely go up to the local police station and report the clandestine leader of the dreaded CPM as "missing, believed kidnapped by the Special Branch".'

Suspecting there might be something more to this disappearance, Chin Peng and his closest party members decided it might be safer for them to also disappear for the time being. In fact, Lai Te would never turn up; he had vanished, along with a large chunk of MCP funds.

In the wake of this scandal, which rocked the Malayan Communist Party, nuggets of information began to surface that revealed the full extent of Lai Te's deception over two decades. It seems likely that Lai Te's 'luck' had first begun in 1931, as a result of the Ducroux affair. When René Onraet had Ho Chi Minh arrested in Hong Kong, his fellow Vietnamese was pulled in with him. It then appears that the first period of Lai Te's double life was exposed, as he had been working as a secret agent for the French Indo-Chinese authorities.

In 1934, realising the potential for an intelligence coup here, Onraet invited Lai Te to Singapore, where he was allowed to continue his career as a communist. His rise to party prominence was helped considerably by informing on his fellow communists and allowing them to be arrested by Onraet's Special Branch detectives. Right up to the war, the Straits Settlements Police knew exactly what the communists were up to because their agent was running them.

With the Japanese occupation of Malaya, Lai Te changed sides yet again. Using his contacts within British Intelligence as collateral, he sold his services to the Japanese. Running the MCP, he was perfectly placed to tell them all about their guerrilla activities and see their leaders slaughtered every so often. He gave out just enough information not to have the anti-Japanese movement snuffed out, but enough to keep himself useful to the Kempeitai. After the war, he saw no reason why he could not continue to play his highly successful game of deception.

Returning to the British, Lai Te promised to keep a lid on communist insurrection. He told them everything they needed to know about the new generation of revolutionaries, and when he finally departed he wiped out their financial resources. It was for this reason that the Malayan Communist Party was in such a weakened state in 1947 and why the Ang Bin Hoey and its Kuomintang allies were in a far superior position. It also explained why the British thought they had no need to join the dubious anti-communist pact proffered by organised crime.

Having the Communist Party completely under its thumb during this period was a tremendous success for the Singapore Special Branch. But with Lai Te's hasty departure, it meant they were suddenly plunged into darkness. The party then began to be run by real revolutionaries. Any moderates within the party were immediately regarded with suspicion and the more radical wing took over. These were the men who demanded insurrection against the colonial government.

Chin Peng took over the MCP and launched his own investigation into Lai Te, learning about his secret deals with the British and Japanese.

'I also uncovered disturbing information about Lai Te's private life,' he said, 'which, remarkably enough, had remained concealed from the rest of us. Miss Jang, a Hakka from Penang, the woman who had addressed the Central Committee the morning Lai Te went missing in Kuala Lumpur, turned out to be the Secretary-General's fourth wife.

'In Singapore I learned that his first wife, a Vietnamese, was the daughter of a government contractor who had purchased a beachside bungalow in Katong for the family. There was also another beautiful Vietnamese mistress who had lost a hand in an accident. She lived in a flat in the Hill Street area of Singapore, paid for by Lai Te. Our Secretary-General had also provided the capital behind the bar and restaurant she ran in the same district.'

With information such as this, the financial motive for Lai Te's life of deception was becoming clearer. Eventually, his good fortune ran out and he was tracked down in Bangkok by Thai communist comrades of Chin Peng. The plan was to kidnap and bring him back for questioning, but the snatch went wrong.

'One grabbed him in a headlock,' recorded Chin. 'Another lunged for his throat. The man gripping him around the neck applied increased pressure. The struggling form began writhing and contorting. Then he frothed at the mouth, went limp and stopped breathing. At the back of the shop house, the men conveniently discovered some lengths of hessian used for making sacks. They wrapped the body in these and waited for darkness.'

That night, the body of Lai Te was dumped in the waters of Bangkok's Chao Phraya river. Apparently, shortly after the killing, a senior Special Branch officer flew from Singapore to Bangkok to meet Lai Te. He was there to warn their ex-agent that he was being tailed throughout South-East Asia by vengeful communists and his life was in danger. 'Obviously, the British were close to the action,' noted Chin Peng with a smile. 'But not quite close enough.'

Having put aside a secret stash of weapons during their time in the jungle fighting the Japanese, the Malayan Communist Party was prepared – and hungry – for an armed confrontation. Their inspiration was Mao Tse-tung's war in mainland China against the nationalists. In February 1948, Chin Peng attended a communist conference in Calcutta, where the keynote speech was given by a Vietnamese delegate who called for a wave of anti-imperialist campaigns across South-East Asia. Inspired, Chin called up his old MPAJA veterans and that year they struck their first blow against British rule.

Early on the morning of 16 June, a dozen communists surrounded the estate office of a rubber plantation in the district of Perak in northern Malaya. Inside were the 55-year-old manager, John Allison, and his 21-year-old assistant, Ian Christian. The young man had served as a Gurkha officer before joining the rubber business. The communists asked them for their pistols. Christian didn't have one, but Allison had one in his bungalow.

Both men had their hands secured behind their back and were taken to the bungalow, where the gun was found. The manager and his assistant were then marched back to the office, tied to chairs on the verandah and shot in the head and body with a spray of machine-gun bullets. The communists took $1,000 from the office safe, but in order to let the world know that this was not just an ordinary crime, the leader of the execution gang told the chief clerk that their purpose was to kill imperialists: 'We will kill all Europeans.' In fact, their killing spree had started earlier that morning, when they had shot dead another estate manager. On both occasions, the killers escaped by bicycle.

These three deaths were the opening shots in what became known as the Malayan Emergency – a 12-year guerrilla conflict that involved the British committing significant police and military forces to its suppression. It was never called a war, being viewed more as a major policing exercise, and at first the enemy combatants were simply termed 'bandits'. For some, the murders of the three British estate managers were just a continuation of the brutal lawlessness that had been sparked by the revival of the Penang-based Triad gangs in the north of the country. But Chin Peng had been careful to make sure his killers announced that this was a different kind of conflict – one of ideology, not theft.

As for the Ang Bin Hoey, they had been contemptuous of the attempts by the Malayan communists to muscle in on their criminal business and had made clear their support of the Kuomintang. But events had altered significantly in mainland China in 1948 and the nationalists were no longer a force to be reckoned with. By the following year, Mao Tse-tung and his Red Army had decisively defeated the nationalists in their civil war and Chiang Kai-shek and his Kuomintang followers had been forced to flee to the island of Taiwan.

With the establishment of the People's Republic of China, there was a new realism among the Ang Bin Hoey and their Triad cousins: although initially able to outgun the communists, they had lost the political patronage of Chiang Kai-shek's nationalists. From now on, they would have to do business with the communists – and that included the MCP. Chin Peng's followers tried to exploit the impetus created by Mao's victory by telling the Ang Bin Hoey that they too had been persecuted under colonial rule and had no friends in the British. The ABH nodded in sympathy and smuggled arms to the communists – for a fee or a favour – but all the time the Triad gangsters watched the unfolding conflict with guarded interest.

'Some [Triad] members have, in fact, assisted the authorities individually during the Emergency,' noted the Federation of Malay Police, 'by joining the Auxiliary Police and Home Guards and have given information against the Malayan Communist Party. This may be a long-term policy to find favour with the authorities, which they think may pay dividends when the Emergency is ended.'

This may well have been true. The communists might have had the momentum of the age with them, but the Triads knew that the British Empire was far from finished and that their colonial police could prove to be a formidable foe.

11

THE SMART COMMISSIONER YOUNG

'The Malayan Police were a proud and touchy lot of people,' noted Jack Morton, Director of Intelligence at the Malayan Special Branch. 'They did not like being criticised or advised by outsiders.' It was bad news, then, when 45-year-old Arthur Young, Commissioner of Police of the City of London, was seconded to head the Malayan police in 1952 at the height of the Emergency. Another Special Branch officer recalled his arrival on the scene with a detailed description of his crisp appearance.

> Young was tall and burly and there was something about his style and his manner that reminded us of a typical London 'bobby'. He had only recently arrived from London and was dressed in a khaki drill short-sleeved police bush shirt worn in jacket form, starched shorts, khaki drill coloured stockings with dark blue tops, and dark blue shoulder epaulettes with the silver insignia of commissioner of police. He carried a swagger stick under his arm.

Almost immediately, the smartly dressed Young ran into controversy by giving his straight-talking opinions to a local journalist.

'Malaya's tall intelligent new Commissioner of Police intends to do some ruthless house cleaning of the Malayan Police Force,' ran the front-page article in the *Singapore Standard*. 'One of his big assignments is to introduce a substantial contingent of Malayan Chinese policemen. He feels that he should depend on developing local talent instead of perpetually depending on importing outsiders.'

Young was referring to the white colonial ex-Palestinian police force officers who made up a key part of the ranks.

'He feels that he will be helped in his job by the fact that he is only staying a year,' continued the report, 'and therefore does not have to worry too much upon whose toes he is treading in weeding out the inefficient.'

The commissioner's candid comments did not go down at all well with the Secretary of State for the Colonies, who demanded an explanation. The secretary was especially concerned about the reaction of police officers who had previously served under difficult circumstances in Palestine. Young batted this criticism back by denying ever having given such an interview to the local press. He recollected 'a casual conversation on a social occasion with a person who described himself as a correspondent', but said he 'expressed no opinions of the kind reported' and 'the account, of course, completely misrepresents my views'. Well, that wasn't completely true either. But Young remained unapologetic about his comments. His view was that he had been brought in to shake things up and that's what he would do, regardless of local sensitivities.

Young arrived at a tricky time for the colony. Communist guerrillas, led by the highly effective Chin Peng, had gained the initiative in the opening phase of the Emergency. The Chinese veterans of the war against the Japanese struck at isolated rubber plantations and tin mines and slaughtered their white owners and anyone who helped them. Using intimidation to get the support of local villagers, they hoped to transform the countryside into an alien territory for the British before advancing into the towns. Their only problem was that the British had extensive experience in dealing with colonial insurgencies and were ruthless in its application.

Learning from their bitter struggle in the Boer War, the British authorities chose to deny the communists any local support by re-settling many Malay Chinese in fortified government camps. Although initially unpopular, this process of establishing some 500 new villages, guarded and supplied with food by the British, proved to be a success, as the living standards inside the camps were an improvement on the impoverished squatter settlements.

On top of this, the Malayan police was rapidly expanded to a 24,000-strong armed force. The entire emphasis of the British response was to avoid a state of war, hence the choice of 'Emergency' as the title for the conflict. It has also been claimed that this term was chosen because many British businessmen feared that their insurance companies would not pay out on losses incurred during a state of war.

Frustrated by this robust policing strategy, Chin Peng got lucky when Sir Henry Gurney, High Commissioner of Malaya, drove by chance into a communist guerrilla ambush. On the morning of 6 October 1951, Gurney set off for a break in the cool mountain resort of Fraser's Hill, 60 miles north of Kuala Lumpur. The commissioner sat next to his wife in the back of their official government Rolls-Royce, as it wound its way up a mountain road through the jungle. It was escorted in front by a police Land Rover, carrying six officers armed with rifles and carbines, and behind by an armoured police scout car. Unfortunately, the steep muddy road proved too much for the armoured car, which was left trailing far behind.

About halfway up the mountainside, the two vehicles were hit by a communist ambush, comprising 30 to 40 guerrillas. Automatic fire from Bren and Sten guns riddled the Land Rover, bringing it to a halt and blocking the path of the Roll-Royce. All the policemen were wounded. Some returned fire, but by then the majority of the guerrillas had moved on to direct their guns at the Rolls-Royce. In order to draw the shooting away from his wife, Gurney opened the door of the car and stepped out towards his attackers. In that he succeeded, because although the High Commissioner was immediately shot dead, his wife miraculously survived the ambush.

The assassination gained Chin Peng the international headlines he craved, but in the long run it proved to be a mistake, as it pushed the British into appointing a new High Commissioner. General Sir Gerald Templer brought with him a ferocious efficiency to the counter-insurgency campaign and won the nickname the 'Tiger of Malaya'.

'With the arrival of General Templer, an electric change came over the situation,' recalled Jack Morton of the Malayan Special Branch. 'An integrated, streamlined machine was rapidly produced. At the summit there was set up a Department of Operations Committee presided over by the High Commissioner himself and drawing together the armed services, the civil authorities, Intelligence and the police in a united effort. The necessary staff organisations, both Operations and Intelligence, were established and this machine ensured that no resources, military, administrative, economic or scientific, were left untapped. The Operations Committee was a policy-making body directing and co-ordinating fully integrated committees in the States and Settlements. It was the job of these subordinate committees to conduct the war against communism in their areas and to mount the joint operations.'

Part of this new machinery was the appointment of Commissioner Arthur Young. Despite his bluff attitude, Young was a highly talented career policeman. Joining the Portsmouth Borough police at the age of 16 straight from school, he worked his way up through the ranks, embracing new technology and successfully promoting whichever department he headed. He devised 'police pillars' containing a two-way microphone handset, so members of the public could call for assistance. At 31, he became one of the youngest-ever chief constables. In 1941, he was senior assistant chief constable of the Birmingham City police, then the second-largest police force in the UK.

During the war, Young was tasked with setting up a training school for police to administer liberated Axis territory. Given the rank of colonel, he stepped ashore in Sicily in July 1943 as Senior British Police Officer in the Mediterranean Theatre. He ensured that London 'bobbies' patrolled the mean streets of Palermo, countering the resurgent actions of the Mafia. He also restored the carabinieri to full force, knowing that they would be the best weapon in fighting organised crime, as it filled the vacuum left by the collapse of the Fascist state.

Increasingly, Young saw his role as a high-concept thinker and, in 1946, he wrote: 'I hold the view that the police organisation is not a police force but a police service.' It was a view he would take to Malaya.

More promotion followed, as Young became an assistant commissioner of the Metropolitan Police and then, in 1950, Comissioner of the Police of the City of London. As always, he worked hard to improve the pay and conditions of his officers and was rewarded with a high degree of popularity within the ranks. His dedication to improving the quality and performance of police officers meant that he was parachuted into various short-term posts abroad, as Britain dealt with the realities of its declining post-war status. In 1950, he established a blueprint for the police in the Gold Coast, the first British territory in Africa to be granted independence. Then came Malaya.

Regardless of fumbling his first days in Singapore, Young had a great talent for self-publicity and it was his desire to improve the public profile of the police in Malaya that informed much of his strategy for the Emergency. He laid out this vision straight away at a meeting in Johore Bharu early in 1952 and an officer present recorded the reaction of his comrades:

> The main gist of what he said was that he wanted to bring about a change in the outlook of the police and that the police should present themselves as 'friends of the people' in the same way as the police did in Britain. Many of us thought that while this might be suitable for London and we would have a go to support him, the situation we faced in Malaya was quite different from Britain's.

To begin with, the police were being shot at by communist guerrillas – not an everyday occurrence in Piccadilly Circus. The officers present at the meeting considered themselves more in the position of front-line soldiers, and the crimes they faced were politically motivated. 'The overall impression he gave us,' said one Special Branch officer, 'was that he intended to attach importance to restoring police discipline, place more emphasis on conventional police work and change the public image of the police from that of a "force" to a "service".' The same words he had used six years earlier. After delivering a speech lasting 15 minutes, Young left the meeting without inviting any questions. He didn't want any.

Young's approach was to normalise the relationship between the police and civilians. In the early years of the Emergency, the police force had swollen to seven times its normal size and become mainly a paramilitary force, engendering fear in the civilian population. Young split the front-line force into two, with fighting units deployed to combat the guerrillas in villages and jungle, while the rest reverted to peacetime duties. In Operation Service, beginning in December 1952, the Malayan police re-branded themselves as friends of the people. The title 'Force' was dropped, replaced by 'Service'; police officers wore cap badges showing two hands clasped in friendship; and they no longer carried rifles or automatic weapons in city streets, but holstered pistols. Even police headquarters were called 'stations', rather than the traditional 'handcuff houses'.

In reality, Young's public-relations exercise could not and would not change strongly held prejudices among the Malayan Chinese, but it did herald a new efficiency. Behind the scenes, significant changes were made in the police intelligence-gathering departments. Special Branch was separated from the Criminal Investigation Department (CID), giving it an enhanced status and allowing it to pursue political and security matters in its own way, separate from investigating non-Emergency crime.

'It was important that the status and duties of Special Branch as the national Security and Intelligence Organisation should be made crystal clear to all concerned,' said Jack Morton, its Director of Intelligence. 'This was done by giving it a Charter which was promulgated by Director of Operations Instruction to all Heads of Departments and Services. It was laid down that none but the Special Branch should run Secret Agents and that Security Intelligence from any source should be channelled to Special Branch at the appropriate level. Special Branch was also designated the authority for the administration and exploitation of defectors and prisoners.'

Even military intelligence officers were seconded into Special Branch and worked alongside police investigators on operations to subvert the will of the communist guerrillas. One excellent example of this ensnared Kim Soong, a guerrilla commander and committee member of the Communist Party. He had a price on his head and had wanted, for some time, to surrender, but he dared not indicate his change of mind. Always accompanied by two bodyguards, he would have to give them the slip, otherwise they would happily execute him as an imperialist agent.

Kim Soong's opportunity to escape came when he set out with his bodyguards to establish contact with another guerrilla camp. British security forces had put pressure on his food supplies and his followers faced starvation. With good reason, he marched off into the jungle to get help from other communist comrades, accompanied by his bodyguards. At some point, isolated in the midst of the thick undergrowth, Kim turned on his guards and killed them. He then made his way to a British base to give himself up.

'Thanks to an alert Field Intelligence Officer with the local military unit, and good briefing by Special Branch, Kim Soong was immediately identified,' recalled Morton, 'and the importance of his position properly assessed. It being established by the recovery of the corpses of his bodyguard that his camp must still be in ignorance of his defection, authority was immediately given to attack it. Kim Soong showed the way and every man in that camp was duly liquidated.'

By expert use of police intelligence, Kim Soong was turned into a key asset and sent back into the jungle to make contact with other guerrilla camps. 'He was suitably briefed with a good cover story and contact arrangements were made to enable him to furnish secret intelligence,' said Morton. 'He proved very valuable indeed until the time came to bring him out. He later proved to be a first-class interrogator at the Special Interrogation Centre at Special Branch Headquarters.'

It was, however, a constant game of cat and mouse, and not all undercover agents survived to tell the tale. A Special Branch report described the fate of one officer caught on the streets of Singapore:

> MCP terrorists shot and killed a male Hylam ['houseboy'] at 8.45am in one of the busiest roads in the City – Kallang Road – and left pamphlets on his body denouncing him by name as a traitor. This is the first occasion in Singapore upon which such denunciation documents have been used. They were cyclostyled [stencil copied] in large characters.

A few days later, a Chinese detective serving with CID was shot and seriously wounded in Singapore. As he lay on the ground, his handcuffs and revolver were stolen from him. At first, it was thought he might have been punished for his involvement with a Triad gang, but cartridge cases recovered at the scene identified his assailants' guns as the same as those used in the previous murder.

The communists were adept at placing their own agents among the civilian population and one intelligence report described a warning system inside government resettlement camps in Johore:

> MCP supporters inside the camps arrange signals which will warn the bandits of the presence of Security Forces. By day the signal is the display of a red blanket, and the beating of latex buckets. By night the signal is the display of three lighted joss sticks near the perimeter wire. When the Security Forces

have moved away, and the bandits can approach, five joss sticks are displayed.

The communists were aware of their own necessity to control public opinion and a document captured from them in South Perak revealed their concerns about legitimate targets. 'It is strictly prohibited to throw grenades at public gatherings, such as theatres,' said the translation, 'where there is a risk of injuring bystanders and thus damaging the MCP's reputation. But throwing a grenade in such places is justified if prominent British imperialists are present, and targets for grenade-throwing are bus companies, shops, individual traitors, British soldiers, police and other treacherous elements.'

Psychological warfare was deployed against the communists and was run by a department close to the Malayan Special Branch. It used a variety of methods to broadcast propaganda, including loudspeakers linked up to aircraft, films, radio, press and field publicity teams. One dimension of this may well have been the widely publicised recruitment of native headhunters from Sarawak to fight alongside the British. Some 264 Iban trackers served with the Security Forces and they claimed magic charms among their armoury of weapons that could scare off evil spirits, as well as tigers.

One journalist delighted in describing an Iban warrior in pursuit of communist guerrillas. 'What he stressed most strongly,' noted the reporter, 'was his anger at having been prevented by the British officer from securing the head of the dead bandit as a trophy: without it, the whole significance of the pursuit and kill was lost.' Several such stories were planted in the Malayan press.

In June 1952, a memorandum from the Secretary for Defence officially decreed that the term 'bandit' was no longer to be used when referring to communist guerrillas. Instead, 'It is accordingly proposed in future,' said the announcement, 'that the term "communist terrorist" will be the general designation for all members of these [communist] organisations.' It meant the communists were no longer regarded as common law-breakers but had some ideological basis for their violent action.

Commissioner Arthur Young left Malaya in 1953, but almost immediately he was sent to another colonial trouble spot in Africa, where he had to tackle the problems created by the Kenyan Mau Mau insurgency. In the meantime, his police reforms continued to pay dividends in Malaya, as the British began to turn the war in their favour.

Jack Moran was a young lieutenant in the Royal Federation of Malaya Police Force. He was one of the officers split off from the regular police force by Commissioner Young to fight communist guerrillas in the jungle. He very much considered himself on the front-line and resented the lack of appreciation for his team's work back home. He also wanted to dispel the idea that they were up against ill-armed raggedy bandits.

'They are a highly trained and disciplined military force,' he explained. 'Its soldiers – one must call them that – are distributed throughout the Federation of Malaya in regiments, platoons, companies, sections and independent platoons; correctly dressed in an adapted uniform – commanded by officers who receive their orders from the Political Commissars – and in the main extremely well armed with weapons of all the latest patterns.'

At the beginning of the Emergency, Moran recalled there were 15 of these communist regiments operating in the jungles of Malaya. Their camps were organised on military lines, even raising and lowering their flag at dawn and dusk. 'I have seen one of those camps in the jungle. It had every detail from barracks – some married quarters, compound and school – down to a field hospital.'

In addition to the uniformed guerrillas was the Min Yuen, the civilian supporters who provided food, shelter and information. 'No one knows their true identity or who they are until some information given betrays them, and it is certain that the unsuspecting person brushes shoulders with Min Yuen agents every hour of the day.'

The most dangerous dimension of the guerrilla force was its Killer Squads. Eliminations Lists were drawn up in the Communist Party headquarters and then distributed throughout the country. Alongside names of those who actively opposed the party were the names of civilians who had simply refused to give money or food to the communists.

'Very few victims escape the Killer Squads,' said Moran, 'being hounded and finally executed quickly and methodically if it takes days, weeks, months or even years. The Killer Squads usually work in small groups of three or four men, and they show a preference for night operation. They are dressed in black shirts, trousers and rubber-soled shoes – ideal garb for night – and their armament is usually a knife, revolver or hand grenade, sufficient for their deadly purpose. There is no discrimination in the names on the Eliminations List. It can mean a Government official, police officer, soldier, schoolmaster, labourer or even housewife of any nationality.'

Moran believed that the police were woefully under-prepared for their first months of combat against the communists. 'The first police units, hurriedly drawn together, went into action wearing khaki uniforms, making themselves beautiful targets against the green of the jungle,' he noted. They had to exchange their truncheons for carbines and Bren guns. The fighting, however, proved attractive to local Malays, who were keen to have their go at the Chinese communists, and they volunteered for service with the colonial police.

The military level of combat encountered was described by police officer Peter Guest, who kept a journal of clashes with the communist terrorists (CTs). On one occasion, two police armoured cars were ambushed by communist guerrillas. It was meticulously planned. They had dug several shallow trenches at the bend of a road, so any approaching cars would have to slow down. When the first armoured car appeared, the terrorists opened fire, halting it so as to block the road for the second vehicle.

Policemen swung open the rear doors of their vehicles and piled out onto the road, being protected by their armoured cars from most of the ambush fire coming from the trenches. Unfortunately, the communists had also grabbed positions on a bank overlooking the vehicles, so they could fire down at the police gunners.

'As a Bren gunner in the armoured car was busy firing from the seat in the turret,' recalled Guest, 'there was a loud crack and he suddenly jerked back with a startled gasp, letting the Bren gun go. The driver looked across and saw that the gunner was clutching his neck and that his hands were covered in blood, as he had been shot through the neck. He was still alive, although in some distress and bleeding badly. With the gunner incapacitated, the driver went into reverse.'

As a result of this ambush, police armoured vehicles were given extra steel plates to protect drivers from rounds coming from all directions. For Guest, payback time came when his unit received information that the local communists in Perak were about to receive a delivery of food. Guest and his ten-man squad decided to turn the tables on them by organising an ambush of their own.

The encounter took place in an overgrown rubber plantation. The police scouts provoked fire from the ensnared communists, and Guest ran to gain the high ground. Taking up a position on a ridge, a major firefight broke out. Bullets smacked into the rubber trees around them, spraying them with plumes of latex. Guest replaced the magazine in his gun and ordered his policemen to advance. Dashing across open ground, he made for some cover.

'As we headed for the bushes,' he recalled, 'it was a nasty surprise to see two uniformed CTs jump up just in front. The image is clear to this day. They were only 25 yards away, wearing jungle green uniforms with brown *puttees* [canvas leggings], and carrying large packs. As they ran I was struck by their odd gait, a knees-up sort of stride, as though they were picking their feet up over objects on the ground. I raised my carbine and took sight on the middle of the back of the second man. I squeezed two shots and knew both had hit him, as I saw the dust jump from his pack. But to my intense frustration, he just kept running!'

Guest fired a third time and this time his man went down.

Pressing on with their attack, Guest and his men got among the communists. At one point, he was only four yards away from a Chinese guerrilla and clearly saw the red star on his peaked cap. Firing his carbine from his hip, he downed him with three shots. Running out of breath, Guest and his comrades threw themselves on the ground. Guest then unhitched a grenade and threw it into the bush.

'By now the firing had stopped and it seemed ghostly quiet,' said Guest. 'I heard a comment to my right, looked across and there was one of my chaps [observing] a uniformed CT lying face down and unmoving.' Wary that the guerrilla might only be faking death to entrap his men and blow them up as they approached, Guest shouted out at him, telling him not to try any tricks. Slowly, Guest wormed his way towards the communist until his carbine was pointing directly at the CT's head. He could see that the man was wounded, but still alive.

'He was Chinese with a thick mop of black hair and looked as if he was in his early twenties,' remembered Guest, 'which made him about my own age. I also noted that he was very well fed, suggesting he had not been back in the field very long after R&R over the border in Thailand.'

The sound of firing withdrew, signalling that the rest of the communists had had enough. Keeping his prisoner covered, other policemen stripped him of his equipment. Guest then offered him a cigarette. Surprised by this kindness, the prisoner revealed that he was part of an eight-strong unit that had a reputation for being both professional and ruthless.

As Guest and his men left the rubber plantation, he came across the body of the invincible communist he had shot at earlier. He opened up the man's pack, which contained a tight roll of oilcloth.

'When unwound, it had two .300 bullets imbedded in it,' said Guest. 'The same calibre as my M1 carbine. So, my two shots had hit his pack but had been stopped in the rolled oilcloth. He had been killed by a shot through the back of the head.'

Many of the white police officers had not been long out of Britain when they arrived in the jungle of Malaya.

'I was twenty-three, very green, and very scared,' said Roy Follows when he first joined the Malayan police force. Armed with a Bren gun, he was given command of a village police post – a wooden shack reinforced with sandbags. Out in the rainforest around him lurked the communist 10th Regiment. Venturing out on a patrol, he stumbled upon a communist camp by mistake. Fortunately, the guerrillas were away and he picked up some haversacks containing valuable documents.

'While I was rummaging through one of them,' he remembered, 'I came across a small tin containing some sort of powder. Before any of the men could stop me, I had tipped it out on the ground – how was I to know that it was opium!'

Across the border in Thailand, the communists had ample opportunity to buy narcotics and the Triads were more than happy to keep them supplied. Opium was also a good currency for buying weapons.

After eight months of learning on the job, Follows was transferred to a jungle company as a platoon commander. His first task was to bring back the victims of communist attacks. Many of these were Malay rubber workers who refused to pay the monthly subscriptions demanded by the communist gangs that lived in their territory.

'When, on one of these grim sorties,' said Follows, 'I found that the man concerned had been mutilated and killed in the presence of his wife and son, I swore that, one day, I would make the CTs pay for their revolting crimes.'

The opportunity came in August 1953 when Follows and his men intercepted a group of local guerrillas as they patrolled through a palm oil estate. Seeing them first, the police dropped to the ground and crawled towards them until they were just 50 yards away in the jungle undergrowth. At that point, they broke cover and charged them, the Malay policemen shouting, '*Bunoh! Bunoh!*' – 'Kill! Kill!'

Firing several rounds from his carbine, Follows saw a guerrilla fall.

'Coming upon a mortally wounded CT, I bent down to relieve him of his weapon,' he recalled in his diary. 'At that moment a sten-gunner, before I had the chance to stop him, fired a long burst at point-blank range into the man's head. His skull made a horrifying sound as bullets blasted it open. Just like a small explosion, his head burst apart, particles of brain spattered into my face, but I didn't care.'

Moments later, a female guerrilla ran towards one of her dead comrades. Follows fired warning shots in her direction, but she ignored them, grabbing the dead man's weapon. Follows fired at her, wounding her in the arm, but, despite letting out a blood-curdling scream, she carried on running into the jungle and escaped. Follows' tally that day was four dead communists – none captured alive.

'Callously, we flung the bullet-riddled CTs into the armoured car,' said Follows. 'Suddenly, the sight of their blood-soaked bodies filled me with disgust. I turned away and retched.'

Just months earlier a police superintendent had warned him of the conditions he would face. 'Grim. Bloody grim,' he told Follows. 'It's a dirty, dangerous war.'

The Malayan Emergency was a new kind of duty for colonial policemen and the casualty rates told their own story. Up to the end of 1956, 2,890 police officers were killed in action, against British military losses of 518. During the same period, the communists suffered casualties of nearly 12,000, more than half of which had been inflicted by the police, not the army. A shower of bravery awards followed – including 13 George Medals, the second-highest civil medal for valour after the George Cross – making the Malayan police the most decorated police force of their time.

Organised crime was now wrapped up in the political machinations of the Cold War. It was difficult to tell the difference between freedom fighters and opportunist gangsters who attached themselves to guerrilla causes in order to gain political leverage and access to riches generated out of chaos. The confusion of the era would even catch out veteran drugs-investigators such as Harry J. Anslinger, head of the Federal Bureau of Narcotics.

12

THE WRONG-HEADED MR ANSLINGER

AS THE BRITISH EMPIRE BATTLED against Malayan communists, chief US drugs-buster Harry J. Anslinger watched developments in communist China with rising fury. In theory, the communist victory over the nationalists in 1949 should have seen an end to the illicit opium trade that had been run by the Japanese and the nationalists hand-in-hand with the Triads. Certainly, this was what retired imperial drugs investigator Russell Pasha had hoped for.

'Now that the war is finished and victory won,' he wrote in 1949, 'we can leave China to deal with the Japanese poisoners who have deliberately ruined so many of her peasants: their methods will be drastic, but the punishment will fit the crime.'

The Japanese may well have been punished, but, as far as Anslinger was concerned, opium and its derivatives were assets too costly and influential for the communists to ignore. In April 1953, the long-serving head of the Federal Bureau of Narcotics (FBN) stood up in the United Nations and gave full vent to his view that communist China was now a major player in the illicit drugs business and she was doing her best to flood the western world with narcotics.

'Large quantities of heroin are manufactured in communist China, all the way from Tsingtao and Tientsin down to Canton,' he told the UN delegates. 'In one factory alone in western China the capacity is 300 lb per day and all of this is for export.'

'At the time the communists occupied Shensi,' continued Anslinger, 'the district was barren and unproductive, so the communists depended on the cultivation and sale of opium to finance their vast military administration.'

But this was not the only reason why communist China was gearing up its production of narcotics: it was a primary weapon in the Cold War, being fought between East and West, argued Anslinger.

'There can be little doubt of the true purposes of Communist China in the organised sale of narcotics,' he said. 'These purposes include monetary gain, financing political activities in various countries, and sabotage. The Communists have planned well and know a well-trained soldier becomes a liability and a security risk from the moment he first takes a shot of heroin.'

The communist world was in uproar when it heard this accusation, and Russian and Eastern European delegates, as well as the Chinese, threw back their own criticism of US underhand politics. But they weren't the only ones to be outraged by Anslinger's claims – so were the British. A key part of the Chinese communist drugs network was said to be British Hong Kong, from whence shipments of Chinese narcotics went to Malaya, the Philippines, Hawaii and the United States, ending up in California, where it was corrupting a new generation of young Americans.

The FBN estimated that some 670 tons of raw opium was being produced and stored in southern China, with at least four tons of it passing every month through Hong Kong on to the Pacific Rim. British newspapers sympathetic to Anslinger's Cold War stance picked up on these claims. Former British Prime Minister Clement Attlee was criticised for touring communist China in 1954 and being too credulous in believing their statements that drug use had disappeared from the country.

At first, the British government took a cynical approach to Anslinger's accusations. A note from the British Embassy in Washington DC said that 'a good deal of the information in Mr Anslinger's statement was furnished by Nationalist Chinese sources'. The defeated Kuomintang had a very good reason for denying their own trade in illicit drugs and shifting the blame to the Communists. On top of this, British diplomats considered that 'Mr Anslinger is under pressure in Washington and having to fight to keep his job, partly because of his lack of success in combating juvenile delinquency in the US and partly for domestic political reasons.'

It was the height of McCarthyism and Anslinger had to parade his anti-Red credentials as openly as any other senior government figure. British Foreign Office bureaucrats could also recognise the need of a fellow civil servant to justify his taxpayer-funded budget. However, as Anslinger continued to quote examples of Chinese communist drug consignments intercepted in Hong Kong, the embarrassment level became too high for the British to ignore.

Behind the scenes, negotiations resulted in a more conciliatory approach from Anslinger and the FBN. In April 1954, the State Department told the British Embassy in Washington DC that the FBN chief would repeat in the next session of the Narcotics Commission his attacks on the smuggling of narcotics from communist China to the United States, via Hong Kong, but Anslinger would be careful to say nothing derogatory about the government of Hong Kong and declare that they were making diligent efforts to suppress the traffic.

'Nevertheless, in view of the extreme sensitiveness here at present of the China trade question,' said a note from the embassy to the Foreign Office in London, 'there is a danger that anything Anslinger says may be misinterpreted in malevolent quarters as evidence that the Hong Kong authorities are conniving in the traffic. We should make it quite clear that this is not so. State Department suggest that our rebuttals would be strengthened if our member of the commission could give some support to Anslinger.'

A few days later, the British Embassy reported that Anslinger was being very helpful and had shown them the draft of the speech he was intending to make on the illicit narcotics trade in the Far East. The bulk of the speech was a strong attack on the Chinese communists but included a paragraph designed to mollify the British:

> While movements of heroin through Hong Kong, because of its geographical location and commercial shipping activity, continued despite efforts of local police who acted vigorously, there has been a noticeable trend towards bypassing this area whenever possible with shipments to other free countries. [Hong Kong] enforcement officials and the courts have taken a positive attitude to thwart the traffickers.

The British Embassy was so delighted with this statement from Anslinger, and accompanying evidence of Hong Kong judicial efforts, that it advised drawing it to the attention of newspaper editors. What is astonishing, however, is that the British government did not feel confident enough in their own intelligence on the drugs trade to robustly refute it themselves. Weirdly, it appears there was even some evidence that British customs officers in Hong Kong may have connived to supply the FBN with faulty data by saying that they had seized opium from communist Chinese suppliers when in fact it had come from traffickers in Bangkok. All this seems to have been accepted as the price Britain had to pay to be seen as a good Cold War ally of the USA.

In reality, other US government departments had their doubts about Anslinger's claims. In November 1956, the Central Intelligence Agency (CIA) produced its own examination of FBN charges of Chinese communist involvement in the illicit opium trade.

'There is no reliable evidence to indicate that the government of Communist China either officially permits or actively engages in the illicit export of opium or its derivatives to the Free World,' the CIA concluded. 'There is also no reliable evidence of Chinese Communist control over the lucrative opium trade of South-East Asia and adjacent markets.' It couldn't be blunter than that in its rebuke of Anslinger and the FBN.

What emerged instead was a more subtle and complex network. There was evidence that small quantities of raw opium were being produced by tribespeople living in Yunnan Province, under communist rule, who then sold it across the border into Burma. It was suggested that Chinese communists tolerated this trade in order not to alienate the tribesmen. Otherwise they maintained a strict anti-opium policy.

'The principal opium-producing areas in the Far East are in Burma and Laos,' said the CIA. 'The production of opium in these countries, in addition to production in Thailand, is sufficient to supply the great mass markets of Burma, Thailand, and Indochina and to provide a further export potential of the equivalent of 150 metric tons of raw opium a year. This export moves principally through Thailand and to a lesser extent through Burma to markets in Malaya, Hong Kong, and Macao.'

The governments of Burma, Thailand and Laos were said, like China, to tolerate the production of opium by minority tribes in order to keep them content, otherwise any attempts to suppress opium production might provoke violent resistance, as the tribes depended on it as their main cash crop.

The big profits from opium, as always, accrued to the opium traders and corruptible government officials. Burmese farmers earned less than $1.5 million for the 90 tons of Burmese opium sold through Thailand each year. In Bangkok, the same quantity of opium was worth $9.5 million. By the time it arrived in foreign markets, such as Singapore, its value had increased to almost $25 million.

'This large increase in value illustrates the lucrative profits earned by the traders, the middlemen, and the opium runners,' said the CIA, 'as well as the bribed government officials involved in the opium trade. This trade is substantially in the hands of private traders motivated by considerations of profit and not by ideological factors.' So much for Anslinger's Cold War narcotics weapon.

Refineries for processing opium into heroin and morphine were mainly located in Thailand, near the Thai–Burmese border. Other clandestine refineries operated in Macao and Hong Kong. Outside South-East Asia, the traditional suppliers of raw opium, who had dominated the market before the war, remained. In 1955, it was estimated that Malaya received 50 tons of opium from Iran and 12 tons from India, but both these regions consumed more opium than they exported. The CIA noted that 'the North American market appears to be supplied principally with opium from Lebanon and Mexico'– not communist China.

'In view of the extremely limited foreign exchange which Communist China might earn from the production of opium,' declared the CIA, 'appreciable official Chinese Communist participation in such production is unlikely. Trade and refinery processing appear to be in the hands of non-Communists, and Communist China does not appear to have any effective control over individuals engaged in these activities.' This from an American organisation at the very forefront of the Cold War.

Several FBN agents were embarrassed by Anslinger's bluster and one of them later went public, saying, 'It destroyed our credibility and now nobody believes us. There was no evidence for Anslinger's accusations, but that never stopped him.'

That said, it was recognised that other communist groups might well benefit from the opium trade. 'It is reported that Communist groups peripheral to Communist China engage in the trade,' said the CIA. 'Their activity may furnish indications of the possible ways in which the Chinese Communists may be involved.' It was suggested that raids by the South Vietnamese government on opium dens were intended to remove them as a source of funds for agents from North Vietnam. It was also reported that a Japanese Communist Party group sold narcotics to finance their political activities.

The Malayan communists appear not to have profited enormously from the drugs trade, as the majority of opium was not trafficked by them but came by ship into the British colony directly from Iran, both because of already established smuggling links and because Iranian opium was considered to have a higher morphine content than Chinese 'Yunnan' opium. There was, however, a smaller trade from Thailand handled by communist guerrillas that included Burmese drugs alongside the weapons and explosives that were bought from Thai arms dealers.

Although under strict post-imperial government control, more than 5 per cent of India's annual crop of 334 tons of legally farmed opium leaked out via smugglers to Singapore and Malaya. Other cargoes of illicit Indian opium made their way to Hong Kong, the Netherlands and Britain. In the Middle East, Iranian opium continued to be smuggled out of the Persian Gulf via the ports of Bahrain, Dubai, Yemen and Kuwait, showing the resilience of criminal highways stretching back to the beginning of the century.

Far from going soft on drugs traffickers, British colonial authorities throughout Asia continued to demonstrate a detailed understanding of illicit narcotics networks and a willingness to do something about them. In the Persian Gulf, several incidents indicated the vigilance of individual Britons.

Before dawn on 20 October 1952, the chief officer of the British tanker *Silverdale* docked in Kuwait, where he caught a Chinese member of his crew and an Arab hauling up a basket from a small boat tied up to the side of the ship. He tried to arrest them, but after a struggle in which other Arabs joined in, the basket was thrown overboard and picked up by the small boat, which speedily made off. The only man the chief officer managed to hold denied complicity and was released, owing to lack of evidence. It was later reported that as the *Silverdale* was nearing Philadelphia, its captain was forced to radio for help, as his opium-smoking crew was on the point of mutiny. US Treasury agents boarded the ship and uncovered 60 lb of opium. Forty-five members of the crew were questioned, three being charged with conspiring to smuggle opium into the United States.

A few days later, a Kuwait oil company security officer spotted a local boat lying alongside a Norwegian tanker. He boarded the ship with his head watchman and saw two men leaning over the rail, each pulling on a rope. They tried to seize the men, observing as they did so two local boats, each containing about five small sacks. One of the men escaped, while the other explained his presence on board by saying, helpfully, that he was not a smuggler. After failing to catch the two boats, the officer organised a patrol along the coastline, but with no success. Returning to the tanker, he had much better luck, finding under a coil of rope two sacks containing a total of 33 lb of opium. The bars of opium were wrapped in pieces of Persian newspaper. The next day the ship was thoroughly searched, but no more drugs were found. The Arab caught on the ship was imprisoned for 33 days by the Kuwaiti authorities.

'The main centre for drug smuggling in the Persian Gulf States is Kuwait,' said a British Foreign Office report. 'Kuwait is convenient for the persons engaged in this illicit trade because a very large number of tankers leave each year for parts of the world and can be used to convey the drugs to their destinations.' High-level communications with the ruler of Kuwait and the sheikh in charge of oil installations at the port had borne fruit, both of them having 'repeatedly expressed their determination to stamp out this traffic', having 'sought the help of HMG [Her Majesty's Government] in doing so'.

Among the measures to be taken was the establishment of a special unit of the sheikh's security forces to search the oil jetty and its ships, as well as a night patrol to stop local craft approaching moored tankers. A revised Dangerous Drugs Queen's Regulation was introduced to give police officers under HM's jurisdiction the power to search ships and suspicious persons.

From another part of the empire, the Deputy Director of the Singapore Narcotics Bureau was called in to Kuwait to give his advice on their drug-smuggling problem. The sheik even visited London, where he asked for help in training his anti-drugs squad. Subsequently, another officer from the anti-narcotics department of the Singapore government was seconded to Kuwait for a few months to assist his men before going on to Borneo to undertake similar work.

'We hope, therefore, that the activities of the drug-smuggling groups who have used Kuwait in the past will have been checked,' concluded the upbeat report.

'The Royal Afghan Embassy presents its compliments to Her Majesty's Foreign Office,' began a letter sent in April 1957, following up on a request to the UN the previous year. 'This Embassy would like to bring to the notice of Her Majesty's Foreign Office that Afghanistan has put forward her claim to be recognised as an opium exporting country to the twentieth session of the Economic and Social Council of the United Nations.' It was a momentous announcement. Afghanistan, until then a persistent irritant on the fringe of the British Empire – noted more for producing bandits and arms smugglers – wanted to join the big boys of opium production and export.

The CIA had already been alerted to its aspirations in this field. Since early 1955, the Afghan government had been asking the UN for permission to sell 40 tons of opium on the world market. The CIA believed this was an overestimate of what it could produce and was merely being put forward for bargaining purposes. 'It is also believed,' the agency noted darkly, 'that part of Afghan production is exported clandestinely.' It was the very beginning of what would become one of the great narco-states of the late twentieth century.

It was bad news as well for their closest rival in the region, as was made clear in the letter from the Afghan embassy: 'The eleventh session of the United Nations Assembly was also in favour of the Afghan claim to export opium, but in the last session of the Economic and Social Council of the United Nations, due to the disagreement of the Iranian delegation, this case was referred to the Commission of Opium and Narcotics for rediscussion.'

It was hardly surprising that Iran should object to the competition. Having exploited the opportunity provided by the sudden reduction of opium exports from British India, it was earning too much money from selling the product directly to its former colonial markets in South-East Asia, both legally and illegally.

Indeed, Iran turned to the British for help in stalling the UN application of the Afghans. Sir John Russell, a senior diplomat at the British Embassy in Tehran, was coming under pressure to offer his support. He was an old-fashioned imperial figure who was once invited on a hunt by some Persian tribal leaders. He told them he was only a moderate shot but ending up shooting every bird he aimed at, bagging more than his host, who prided himself on his marksmanship. That evening, the tribal chief challenged the diplomat to a bout of stick-dancing, with the intention of breaking his legs. Luckily, a fellow guest intervened to prevent the diplomatic incident.

Russell was a man not easily cowed and he revealed his true feeling on the opium matter in a letter to the Foreign Office in London. 'We fully appreciate the need to go carefully in this matter,' he wrote, 'and not to give any firm assurances about our voting intentions – We also of course realise that there is nothing the United Nations or anybody else can do to stop the Afghans growing the stuff if they want to.'

The reason for his defeatism was explained later in the letter.

'Unfortunately there is no doubt that illicit Afghan opium is now coming in large quantities,' he wrote. 'Khozaimeh Alam, who is a cousin of the Minister of the Interior and occupies himself mainly with running the family's large estates over in Birjand, told me a couple of days ago that if he had been with me in Meshed [Masshad, the second-largest city in Iran, near the Afghan border] he could have taken me to any one of a dozen merchants and helped me buy a ton of the stuff over the counter!'

The Iranian went on to blame the existence of a flourishing black market on his Minister of Health, who, he said, had done nothing effective to provide a substitute for the opium traditionally used by peasants as the one and only medicine to cure all their ills. As opium addiction amongst the working classes sprang almost entirely from this, the Iranian argued that it could not be cured until an adequate rural health service was established.

In the meantime, illicit Afghan-produced opium was making its way into Iran, undercutting its own home-grown opium, destined for more lucrative overseas markets. It was just the beginning of a major new supply of narcotics.

Anslinger and the FBN should have been focusing on this new source, but instead, as late as 1961, a year before his retirement from the FBN, Anslinger was still going on about the communist narcotics menace – even after everyone else had dismissed it. Weirdly, he shut his eyes to the role of the Kuomintang in the drugs trade, saying,

'When Chiang Kai-shek ruled over mainland China, the Nationalist government for several years conducted a campaign against dope that included the suppression of the traffic.' This was, in fact, the golden age of the nationalists' partnership with the Green Gang and Du Yue-sheng.

To prove the continuing threat of Red China and the decadence of the West that made it so easy for them to ply their trade, Anslinger fabricated a story about a meeting in Hong Kong between a high-level Chinese communist and an American airline pilot. The communist proposed a deal to the pilot in which he would fly $250,000 of morphine from Hong Kong to Bangkok and on to the US in return for a one-eighth stake in an opium-processing factory inside Red China.

Over a gin sling, the American pilot considered the offer.

'Sorry,' he said, 'but the fact is I already own two opium dives, a house of prostitution and a gambling pad in Hoboken, New Jersey. I don't have a moment to myself any more.'

'The Communist walked away,' claimed Anslinger, 'shaking his head about the ways of American bourgeoisie capitalists.'

From being a fearless campaigner against early drugs trafficking, Anslinger had been seduced by the patriotic demands of the Cold War and the bureaucratic need to please his government. His wrong-headed campaigns severely downgraded the FBN.

Following his retirement in 1962, after 32 years at the top of his department, the FBN was merged with the Bureau of Drug Abuse Control to form the Bureau of Narcotics and Dangerous Drugs in 1968. Five years later, this was incorporated into the present Drug Enforcement Administration (DEA) – the USA's main weapon against drug lords in the twenty-first century. Anslinger witnessed all these changes. He died from a heart attack in 1975 at the age of 83.

In contrast, imperial drugs warrior Russell Pasha offered more level-headed advice in his retirement. World war had interrupted the far-flung imperial trade routes that brought heroin to Egypt and, as a result, hashish had become more popular on the streets of Cairo and Alexandria.

'All hashish imported [into] Egypt is the result of cultivation in the Lebanon and Syria,' he warned. 'And it is there that the campaign of prevention must begin.'

Russell Pasha also knew that the conflict between Israel and the

Palestinians, which had erupted after the war, meant there were new organised criminal gangs that needed to fund their arms smuggling with drugs deals. It was a trend picked up on by the organisation he had founded in Cairo, the Central Narcotics Intelligence Bureau. In their report of 1948, they warned that 'post-war gangs are better organised, take great security precautions, and rarely hesitate to use firearms if in danger'. In particular, they pointed the finger at Palestinian terrorists, who were alleged to have 'obtained arms from Egypt in exchange for narcotics'.

World war had significantly changed the balance of power around the globe and this profoundly affected the future of the British Empire. Not only had the battlefield successes of the Japanese encouraged communists and nationalist rebels to rise up against the British in South-East Asia, but they had also revealed the weakness of empire in other parts of the world. In the Near East, the British had struggled to contain the Arab–Jewish conflict in Palestine in the 1930s, and during the war extremist elements sought to undermine British control. In Africa, similar pressures built up in their colonies.

At first, as in Malaya, these outbursts of rebellion were viewed purely as matters of law and order and were the responsibility of the colonial police forces. The rebels were regarded as organised criminals, even though they were freedom fighters to their supporters. Thus, the 1940s and 1950s saw periods of intense colonial police activity in both the Near East and Africa in which thousands of policemen took on armed groups of insurgents. Unlike in South-East Asia, illicit narcotics were not a major part of this, but some of the rebels did engage in criminal activities to support their campaigns. On other occasions, gangs of criminals created such a climate of terror that they shook the resolve of their imperial rulers.

13

THE IMPLACABLE MR STERN

AT TEN MINUTES PAST MIDDAY on 22 July 1946, a truck drove up to the basement entrance of the King David Hotel in Jerusalem. Five men dressed as Arabs jumped out of the truck and forced their way through the service entrance. Arab kitchen staff were warned away with guns, as the men unloaded several milk churns, pushing them along the corridor past the British military telephone exchange until they reached a nightclub that lay directly beneath the offices of the Palestine Government Secretariat. They then piled the milk churns against columns in the empty space. Alerted by the noise, a Royal Signals officer confronted the deliverymen but was shot twice in the stomach.

Ten minutes later, the violent deliverymen escaped, clambering back into their truck as British soldiers ran after them, firing shots. At that moment, 100 yards way from the hotel, a small bomb in a box beneath a tree exploded on the road, making everyone duck. A police cordon was immediately raised around the seven-storey hotel – the biggest building in Jerusalem – and a group of officers entered the basement to inspect the strange delivery. Everyone working inside the hotel was advised to open the windows.

At 12.37 p.m., an enormous explosion erupted from the milk churns, ripping off the entire corner of the King David building and completely destroying 25 rooms occupied by the secretariat of the British Palestine Government and the Defence Security Office of British Military Headquarters. Seven floors collapsed on top of one another as though they had been hit from above by a 1,000-lb bomb. People passing by on the streets outside were flung against stone walls like rag dolls. In a small government building opposite the hotel, one British official saw the face of a clerk sitting next to him cut in half by a flying shard of glass.

'A sheet of flame passed my window, followed by clouds of smoke, and we were thrown over,' recalled one British intelligence officer. Another was knocked off his seat, as the wall of his office disintegrated. Amazingly, inside the hotel, a Palestine police officer tasked with investigating the milk churns was blown along the corridor away from the bomb and emerged from the wreckage covered in dust but unhurt. A restaurant-bar directly above the explosion, usually packed at midday, was empty because most of the customers had left as soon as they heard soldiers firing at the truck. Many, many others, however, were not so fortunate.

As the dust settled on the mountain of rubble, bulldozers, drills and cranes were brought in to remove the massive chunks of concrete and masonry. Bodies and parts of bodies were dragged out; the death toll reached 91 men and women killed, with 46 injured. The majority of the dead were Arabs and British working in the hotel. Some people had been torn apart with little left to identify them and it took three weeks to put names to all the remains. Police Sergeant S.W. Mills was given this grim task and recalled the process of identifying the very last corpse:

> After about three weeks, I heard a metallic clink noise from somewhere near the cadaver of a male person, who was the last of the victims left in the mortuary. I discovered a set of keys had dropped from the body which must have been blown into it at the time of the explosion and decomposition now released them from imprisonment. It had a name tag attached and we were able to call at a house in Givat Shaul quarter, where a very pregnant Jewish woman was able to identify the keys as belonging to her husband. They also fitted the locks in several parts of the house. This is how we cleared up the last KD casualty.

The day after the bombing, the British Prime Minister, Clement Attlee, stood up in the House of Commons in London and made a statement. 'Honourable members will have learned with horror of the brutal and murderous crime committed yesterday in Jerusalem,' he said. 'Of all the outrages which have occurred in Palestine, and they have been many and horrible in the last few months, this is the worst.'

But who was it exactly who committed the atrocity?

'The basic cause of the disturbances in Palestine since the Great War,' declared the British General Staff in 1939, 'has been the resentment in the Arabs at the intrusion of the Jews into what they regard as their country. Jewish immigration has been permitted as a result of the Balfour Declaration made in November 1917.' This gave the full backing of His Majesty's Government to the establishment of a national home for the Jewish people.

'The Arabs have never accepted the Balfour Declaration,' continued the British Staff report, 'and in fact claim that Palestine is included in the Arab countries which were promised independent status by the British government in their negotiations with King Hussein of the Hedjaz prior to the Balfour Declaration.' In other words, the Arabs felt double-crossed for their support of the British against the Ottoman Empire during the First World War.

Arab rioting first broke out in 1921 in Jaffa and continued into the 1930s. The rise of the Nazis in Germany in 1933 increased the pace of Jewish immigration until, by 1935, 60,000 Jews had arrived in just one year in Palestine. The situation was exacerbated when it was discovered that some of these Jews had attempted to smuggle in a large consignment of guns to protect themselves from Arab assaults. In 1936, militant Arabs responded by proclaiming a general strike and sparking a series of armed attacks against the British authorities.

Attempting to keep the peace against this lawlessness was the Palestine Police Force. Established in 1922 in direct response to the Arab disturbances of the previous year, it called itself a gendarmerie. Two-thirds of its ranks were filled with British Auxiliary military police, who had been disbanded in Ireland – known as the notorious Black and Tans – as well as former soldiers. 'This original composition,' noted a British general, 'gave the force a military efficiency, combined with a certain ruthlessness of method, which it appears to have maintained throughout its history.'

In 1926, following complaints about the methods deployed by the gendarmerie, it was reorganised into a more regular police force, with Arabs and Jews serving alongside the hardcore of British. Come 1936 and the outbreak of Arab hostilities, the loyalty of some of the Arabs was doubted and there were incidents in which they betrayed their colleagues to the rebels. At one point, the recruitment of Sudanese was considered, but a British major made it clear why it would not work:

> It is possible that the [Sudanese] Begas would be regarded by both Arabs and Jews as inferior or even as Niggers. Their employment might eventually lead to dissatisfaction or unsettled feelings on their return to the Sudan and it would be a grave mistake to run any risk of this.

Instead, it was recommended that Indian ex-soldiers be recruited to fill any gaps, with the first choice being Sikhs.

From 1936 onwards, Arab criminal gangs launched ever more deadly assaults on the Palestine Police Force. 'Their objectives were small police and military parties,' said one report:

> They robbed villages of money and food, recruiting the more hot-headed villagers. They were reasonably well armed with rifles and even one or two light automatics. Their preference was for a long-range ineffective firefight and if attacked with any determination, they quickly retreated, often leaving fairly well-handled rear guards. Once clear, they dispersed rapidly in anticipation of air attack. In many of the gangs, a proportion of the rebels were uniformed, usually khaki shirts and breeches, with perhaps headcloths of a distinctive colour.

On 18 July 1936, four British police officers were patrolling a section of the Jerusalem–Nablus road when they ran into an Arab ambush in the Wadi Harameh, or 'Valley of Thieves'. Halted by a roadblock, they came under intense rifle fire from the hills around them. Their sergeant was hit immediately and died shortly afterwards. The three constables held on to their position despite being heavily outnumbered, but were acutely aware of their ammunition running low.

Eventually, one of them managed to turn round their patrol vehicle and, despite being badly wounded in the process, drove back to their base. For over an hour, the two remaining policemen clung on, as Arab bullets ricocheted around them. When a relief column finally arrived, the two police constables had just ten rounds between them. All three survivors were rewarded with the King's Police Medal (KPM) for Gallantry.

Just six days later, Detective Constable Said Mahmoud was shot three times in a busy marketplace – the third bullet passing through his cheek. In great pain, the policeman returned fire and managed to catch hold of his assailant. In the fight, the Arab escaped, but another policeman shot him dead. With blood pouring from his mouth, Mahmoud refused to go to hospital until he had identified as his attacker the dead man in the mortuary. He, too, received the KPM.

On 9 September 1936, four British police constables rushed to Rosh Pina on the road to Galilee when they heard that a Jewish vehicle had been ambushed. Arriving there in an open pick-up truck, there was no sign of the Jewish-owned car but every indication they had been set up. From the hills around them came fire from a large Arab gang of up to 70 men. With no cover to hide behind, the young policemen had little choice but to kneel in a circle and shoot up at the hills. When their tight circle of bodies was later found, they were surrounded by piles of expended cartridges. They had fought to the very last round. Their funeral in Haifa was said to have been one of the largest seen in Palestine.

The British dealt with the Arab gangs by devising a cordon system in which any contact with rebels triggered a process by which reinforcements were rushed to the area and surrounded the insurgents. They then advanced to the sound of firing, as aircraft flew low over the Arabs, shooting them up with machine guns and dropping bombs. 'Most of the casualties were inflicted by low-flying air attack,' concluded one field analysis.

For three years, Jewish settlers generally held back from large-scale retaliation against the militant Arab gangs. But as rumours began to spread of a settlement being discussed in London, in which the British would agree to the creation of an Arab state of Palestine incorporating a permanent Jewish minority, extremist Jewish organisations hit back with a series of bombings that killed many Arabs.

By early 1939, the British government had settled on the creation of an independent Palestinian state, in which both Arabs and Jews would be represented according to the size of their populations, to be set up ten years' hence. Moderate Arabs gave this proposal their support, but many Jews rejected it, saying it was a betrayal of the idea of settling the land as their National Home – a permanent Jewish state. They also objected to a limit being put on Jewish immigration into the country. Moderate Jews decided on a campaign of non-cooperation and illegal immigration, but the more radical groups opted for direct action against the British.

Jewish rioting, bombings and sabotage grew in intensity. Arab villages were invaded and their houses demolished. Two British detective inspectors investigating a Jewish crime scene were blown up by a landmine placed outside the door of a house.

The majority of these violent incidents were orchestrated by the Irgun Zvai Leumi, or National Military Organisation, dedicated to establishing a Jewish state by force of arms. Rejoicing in its attacks on the British, it issued pamphlets claiming responsibility for ever more outrageous acts. The British authorities responded with the cordon system they had used against the Arab gangs and rounded up hundreds of Jewish extremists or shot them in numerous engagements.

With the outbreak of war against Nazi Germany in September 1939, the majority of the radical Jewish leadership, including the commanders of Irgun, agreed to cease actions against the British authorities in Palestine and give them their support for the duration of the conflict. As a result of this ceasefire, many interned Jewish radicals were released in the summer of 1940. Among them was a die-hard group of extremists who rejected the compromise of their leaders and funded their cause with a string of criminal acts.

'It soon became evident that their policy was to overthrow the Irgun and take its place,' said British secret intelligence in 1941. 'They began by raiding caches of arms belonging to official Zionists and by robbing Jewish banks and burgling the houses of rich Jews. Consistent reports declared that they had made approaches to the Italians, posing as a Jewish Fascist group, with the idea that in the event of an Axis Victory they would emerge as a dominant Jewish party. It was suggested that in return for Axis funds they should supply the enemy with military information.'

With the eclipse of the Italians as a military power in North Africa, the progress of these Jewish extremists took an even more bizarre turn. It had the effect of causing 'the Group to look to Germany for possible support and on 1.8.41, it published a bulletin contrasting the weakness and alleged disunion of the British Forces with the united might and strength of Germany'.

An agent close to the radical group summed up their twisted logic:

> Their attitude has remained consistently anti-British and against the war effort. Their policy of re-insurance with the enemy has been maintained and they carried it to the Germans as to the Italians. Their line is that, after all, a British defeat will not mean the end of Jewry, and sensible Jews who have not associated themselves with the British war effort may well look to remain in a relatively good position in Palestine after a German victory.

The leader of this extremist gang was the 34-year-old Avraham Stern.

Born in Poland, Stern spent his early life as a refugee, fleeing from the Germans during the First World War. He was later separated from his mother while living in Siberia. At the age of 18, he emigrated to Palestine. Studying at Hebrew University in Jerusalem, he was inspired by the idea of creating a Jewish homeland and served with Haganah, a Jewish paramilitary force, when their community was attacked by Arabs. When his local commander established the Irgun Zvai Leumi, he joined them as an officer. For Stern, his relationship with the newly emerging nation was like a love affair, about which he wrote numerous passionate poems. His revolutionary fervour ensured he rose high in the ranks of Irgun.

Throughout the 1930s, as deputy leader of the underground army, Stern organised terrorist assaults on Arabs, including planting bombs aimed at killing civilians.

One policeman remembered meeting him when he was arrested by the British in 1939. 'One night sticks in my mind,' he recalled, 'while I was joint Duty Officer, when four suspected terrorists were left in my keeping while arrangements were made for their detention. One stared back at me in a very hostile manner. His name was Abraham [*sic*] Stern.'

Stern also travelled back and forth to Poland, where he organised routes for illegal immigration into Palestine. With the help of the

Polish government, he planned to train 40,000 young Jews to seize Palestine from the British. When Germany invaded Poland, this plot came to a swift end and Stern was interned, along with the rest of the Irgun leadership in Palestine.

When Irgun came to terms with the British, Stern was furious and split from his comrades, setting up his own small group of extremists, later known as Lehi – Fighters for the Freedom of Israel. Among his 40-strong splinter group of militants was Yitzhak Shamir, the future prime minister of Israel. Stern's uncompromising position against the British put him at odds with both Haganah and the Jewish Agency – the governing authority of Palestinian Jews – who publicly condemned his activities. Without any official support, Stern was forced to fund his group by robbery and the heavily armed gang embarked on a crime spree.

In January 1942, Stern Gang members attacked a Jewish bank official carrying £1,000 through the streets of Tel Aviv. In the shoot-out that followed with the police, two Jewish passers-by were shot dead. One of the three captured gangsters was sentenced to death. In retaliation, Stern and his comrades set a deadly trap.

On 20 January, a small bomb exploded inside the room of a building in Yael Street in Tel Aviv. The incident brought Deputy Superintendent Solomon Schiff and a small party of police officers to the scene. When they entered the building, the Stern Gang detonated a far larger bomb containing gelignite and rivets. Schiff was blown out through a window and killed immediately. Two other police officers later died of their injuries.

The Palestine Police Force was hungry for revenge and within a week four members of the Stern Gang were tracked down and shot dead in a firefight. On 12 February, a house was raided on Mizrachi Street. Tovah Savorai recalled the moment the policemen entered her house.

'At about 9.30 there was a knock at the door, too gentle a tapping to signal the presence of the police,' she said. Tovah and her husband were both members of Lehi and Stern was sheltering with them. When he heard the knock on the door, Stern hid himself in a wardrobe.

'At the door stood the "good" detective, Wilkins, with two men behind him,' remembered Tovah. 'Wilkins was always very polite; too polite, perhaps. He asked me why I hadn't gone to visit my husband,

Moshe, and if I weren't worried about him. I told him that if I had gone to the hospital, I would have been arrested immediately. They searched my room.'

One of the policemen opened the door of the wardrobe. Seeing only clothes, he thrust his hand inside to check further and felt the body of Stern. Triumphantly, he yanked him out.

'At the same time [the policeman] put his right hand into his back pocket and took out his gun. I ran between him and Yair [Stern] and said, "Don't shoot! If you shoot, you shoot me." In my innocence I thought I had saved Yair's life. How wrong I was. They made him sit on the sofa. More detectives appeared, they had handcuffs and used them to bind Yair's hands behind his back. They told me to get dressed and go downstairs. I got into a small car . . . suddenly I heard three shots.'

The official police report said that Stern had tried to escape and was shot dead. Others considered he had been executed by the British – as a result, membership of the Stern Gang more than doubled. Attacks on police stations and policemen continued throughout the war. On 6 November 1944, the Stern Gang raised their international profile considerably with an attack launched on foreign soil against a senior British politician.

Lord Moyne, British Resident Minister in the Middle East, was returning to his residence in Cairo for lunch when two gunmen confronted him. One shot his driver dead, while another fired three shots into his neck, chest and stomach. The two assassins made their escape on bicycles but were chased by a brave member of the minister's staff. He informed a patrol policeman mounted on a motorbike, who overtook the two gunmen at a nearby bridge.

The assassins fired back, but a crowd of locals surged towards them and were on the verge of lynching them when two policemen intervened and arrested them. In prison, the two gunmen happily admitted their guilt, knowing their job was to make the most of the involvement of the Stern Gang in the affair and gain maximum political coverage. Lord Moyne was treated in hospital but died shortly afterwards. The two gunmen were put on trial and hanged.

A massive police crackdown followed and many members of the Stern Gang were arrested in Palestine, but intelligence remained sketchy on their true motives and the British Palestinian authorities turned to the Jewish Agency to get an inside view of the extremists' intentions. The Jewish Agency was playing a difficult game, in that it was resolutely opposed to the violent actions of these renegades but also knew they were popular among their more radical supporters. As a consequence of the spectacular success of the Stern Gang, Irgun was coming under pressure to rejoin the fight against the British.

'Dissension is believed to have occurred in the ranks of the Irgun Zvai Leumi, with the result that some of its leading members, followed by others of less importance, have now resigned,' revealed a Jewish Agency informer in January 1945. 'Most of these dissidents claim that they joined the organisation in the belief that it was composed of a body of idealists, but experience had convinced them that it had degenerated into a gang of racketeers. The threat, however, of reprisals from their brethren among the Yishuv [Jewish settlers] has probably also been a deterring influence.'

Then came an ominous claim.

'It is thought not unlikely that the two organisations' – that is, both Irgun and the Stern Gang – 'may attempt some dramatic coup, particularly if the murderers of Lord Moyne are condemned to death. But it would be an act of desperation and not a sign of renewed strength.'

A month later, a secret intelligence report in MI5 files suggested there might be another dimension to the activities of Jewish terrorists.

'The Stern Group,' it said, 'would seem to be receiving support from the French, whose activities against law and order in Palestine have increasingly required our attention. We already know from "Top Secret" sources that French officials in the Levant have been clandestinely selling arms to the Haganah and we have received recent reports of their intention to stir up strife within Palestine not only in retaliation for the part we played last year in supporting Lebanese and Syrian demands for independence but also, by embarrassing our position in the Mandate, to distract our attention from French activities in Syria and the Lebanon.

'French officials in Beirut have suggested to Paris,' it continued, 'that they should finance the Stern Gang, it being in French interests to back any movement in opposition to the Greater Syria scheme, which, if brought about, would undermine French influence in the Levant.'

With their murder of Lord Moyne and the secret support of the French, the Stern Gang had catapulted themselves into the top league of international terrorists for hire.

A great victory parade through Jerusalem marked the end of the war against Germany in 1945, but it also triggered the resurgence of Jewish terrorism in Palestine. Haganah had held back its militia forces during the war, but in November that year it put a thousand men into the field to wreck the Palestine railway system with a multitude of bombings and armed assaults. This was followed by a wide range of attacks on public buildings. Irgun stepped up their campaign of action by deploying a three-inch mortar that hurled shells at police stations.

'The sound of the exploding projector was unnerving and one then waited for some seconds to see if one's station was going to be hit,' recalled one policeman. 'Then the terrorists took to telephoning half a dozen stations to warn them that a mortar was aimed at the place and would go off in the night. Usually one station got the bomb and the other five had sleepless nights waiting for something that never happened.'

Whereas Haganah did their best to avoid hurting civilians in their attacks, neither Irgun nor the Stern Gang cared how many people they killed during their operations, whether British or native. They were in a horrible race with each other to commit the most headline-worthy outrage.

When the British struck back with Operation Agatha in June 1946, its vehemence took the Jewish community by surprise. The Jewish Authority headquarters was occupied and many of its leading members arrested. This effectively decapitated Haganah and they withdrew from acts of terrorism by the end of the month, saving their strength for the expected war with the Arabs. This left the way clear for Jewish extremists to plan their most destructive assault so far – the King David Hotel bombing. It was Irgun – not the Stern Gang – who took the credit for devising this slaughter. The motive appeared to be the fear that the military intelligence headquarters within the hotel contained incriminating files seized from the Jewish Agency during Operation Agatha – linking prominent Jews to the terrorist war against the British. Indeed, it has since been revealed that it was Haganah who wanted the files destroyed, but left it to Irgun to execute the attack; tragically, this meant they would proceed with a complete disregard for how many lives perished in the attack.

Such was the international revulsion at the vast number of civilian lives lost in the King David Hotel bombing that Irgun immediately tried to distance themselves from the mass murder by claiming they had sent warnings to evacuate the hotel before detonating the explosives. As always with such ludicrous blame-shifting, it seems invidious to accuse the British of not evacuating the hotel when Irgun were renowned for using hoax calls to heighten the terror of their attacks and were engaged in a chaotic firefight with the guards. Haganah put the blame firmly on Irgun by saying they had recommended the operation be carried out at a time when far fewer people would be in the hotel.

That the whole murderous operation enjoyed the tacit approval of many senior Jews later involved in the government of Israel was made clear when, on the 60th anniversary of the bombing, the one-time prime minister, Benjamin Netanyahu, described it not as terrorism but a legitimate act aimed at a military target. An official plaque unveiled at the time blamed the huge loss of life on the British for not evacuating the hotel. This was later modified after protests by the British Ambassador. It remains one of the most deadly terrorist attacks of the twentieth century.

To their credit, the bombing did little to alter the attitude of the British government to finding a solution to the Palestinian problem. Just a few days later, Prime Minister Attlee wrote to the US President, saying, 'I am sure you will agree that the inhuman crime committed in Jerusalem on 22 July calls for the strongest action against terrorism, but having regard to the sufferings of the innocent Jewish victims of Nazism this should not deter us from introducing a policy designed to bring peace to Palestine with the least possible delay.'

Undaunted by the wave of international criticism, Irgun and the Stern Gang continued their acts of terrorism into 1947, culminating in Stern gunmen wrecking a train carrying troops and civilians near Rehovoth and then machine-gunning the survivors. One of their final acts against the British involved kidnapping two army officers. Three Irgun terrorists had been arrested following an attack on a prison camp and were sentenced to death. The day after they were hanged, the two kidnapped officers were found hanging from a eucalyptus tree. When an army engineer went to cut down one of the bodies, a mine exploded in his face.

In parallel with this terrorism ran a sophisticated campaign of illegal immigration, bringing thousands of Jews into Palestine from Europe. British secret intelligence pointed the finger at Haganah as being the main organiser of this human trafficking:

> [Haganah] ensure that batches of immigrants include young people of both sexes in equal proportions as far as possible. Such human material is chosen in order to provide young and vigorous bodies capable of helping, with their labour and their services in the armed forces of Haganah, to establish, develop and defend a Jewish Palestine . . . The principle of selection, which prefers the young and able-bodied to the aged, infirm and destitute, is a negation of the argument that the European refugees should be admitted to Palestine for humanitarian reasons.

Using non-Jewish middlemen to buy up old and half-derelict vessels, Haganah set up false shipping companies to operate them, having them refitted to their specifications and delivered to various Mediterranean ports. On arrival at the port, the original crew were replaced with an entirely new captain and sailors selected by Haganah, preferably from Jewish merchant seamen to ensure tight security for the entire voyage. It was yet another highly effective dimension in their battle to make sure Palestine became Jewish.

In the end, it worked and, with the departure of the last British forces from Haifa, an independent Israel came into being on 14 May 1948. Almost at once, the Jewish state was embroiled in a war with its own Palestinian Arabs and neighbouring Arab states. Both sides turned to organised crime to help them fight on. Palestinian terrorists sold hashish cultivated in Syria and Lebanon to Egypt in exchange for weapons, while the Israelis made the most of their links with organised crime abroad.

Meyer Lansky was a veteran New York Jewish gangster who had worked alongside notorious mafiosi such as Lucky Luciano and Frank Costello. In 1948, Lansky was visited in America by two Israeli representatives.

'They asked me to help Israel,' he recalled. '"What's the problem?" I asked. "I'm at your service."'

The Israelis were fighting the Egyptians in the Gaza Strip and Sinai, and were concerned that American arms dealers were shipping weapons to Egypt via New York ports.

'OK, I'll handle it,' said Lansky, 'and I went over to New Jersey and talked to a few people about how to stop the shipments at the docks. Part of the Pittsburgh consignment fell overboard, and most of another cargo was by mistake loaded onto ships bound for Israel.'

The Israelis were very grateful for the gangster's help, but not grateful enough. In 1970, Lansky decided to emigrate to Israel, but two years later he was kicked out after the Americans put pressure on them.

'I've always served Israel as best I can,' he said philosophically, then considered moving on to South America. 'Perhaps in Paraguay I will carry out a last favour for the Jews. I'll go looking for Mengele [the Nazi war criminal].'

As shown in Palestine, during and after the Second World War, much organised crime within the British Empire was tied into violent independence movements. The line between freedom fighting, terrorism and criminal enterprise was exceptionally fine. This was also true in Africa.

14

THE BESTIAL MR UKU

ON SUNDAY, 12 JANUARY 1947, PC Evan Chima of the Nigeria Police Force was invited to the house of Chief Sunday Udo Ekpo in Calabar province, in the east of Nigeria.

'The constable stayed all the afternoon,' stated Etuk Uku, half-brother to the chief. 'We were entertaining him with palm wine, food and cigarettes.'

When it was nearly dark, Uku and Chief Ekpo offered to escort the police constable part of his way home.

'We left with him,' said Uku. 'When we reached the [house of the] Ndem juju, I spoke in a loud voice and laughed, so that the people in ambush could know we were there. John Uwa then came out of the bush and gripped the constable from behind, whilst Etuk Ekpo hit him on the back of the neck with a heavy stick. Sunday Udo Ekpo and Iwok Ukpong attacked him with machetes and killed him.

'We all helped to drag the body into the bush. Otu Knpo Idem cut off the arm. John Uwa scraped the face. Sunday and I helped scrape the head. Otu Idem scraped the arm after cutting it off.'

The scraping of the policeman's dead body with knives was very important. It gave the impression that he had been attacked by a wild animal – a leopard.

'John Uwa cut out the tongue,' said Uku. 'John Uwa collected all the parts taken from the body and put them in a bag. We then took them to Chief Ukpong at his house. They were given to Chief Ukpong in my presence. Chief Ukpong gave us 100 manillas to be divided amongst the six of us. I received 15 manillas from this.'

This bestial murder was just one of over 80 committed in the British colony of Nigeria from 1945 to 1947. All bore the marks of leopard claws and all were, initially, thought to be the work of wild animals. Such was the climate of concern caused by these savage assaults that the British administration enforced a curfew to stop all movement after dark. What puzzled them was the motive for the killings. Who was organising them and why? It would be up to Senior Assistant Superintendent D.S. Fountain to solve the mystery.

Fountain was an expert on the native customs of Nigeria and the Calabar region and he approached the task as an ethnological exercise. Given a staff of three European officers and 220 armed African policemen, he began to build up a detailed picture of the victims and how they had met their deaths.

'The victim is usually attacked on a bush path bordered by thick farm fallow, affording excellent concealment to the murderer, and the body dragged 30 or 40 yards inside the bush and left in a convenient clearing,' noted Fountain. The attack tended to happen at dusk, about 7 p.m.

'A heavy stick is first used to hit the victim on the back of the neck and render him unconscious,' continued Fountain. 'The actual killing is then done by a yam spike or short stabbing knife, with which wounds are inflicted in the neck and upper part of the body.'

Then followed a series of grotesque mutilations that included cutting off the head with the stripping of the flesh from it, as well as the removal of one arm and the scraping of flesh off that. The arm and head were left near the body to give the impression that it had been savaged and gnawed by a carnivore. To further this illusion, leopard pad prints were made in the earth.

Frequently, a witness was present at the attack but tended to give a confused account of the assault.

'Under first interrogation by the police,' said Fountain, 'the witness says he saw an indescribable "something" attack the victim, or that he saw a genuine leopard making the attack.'

Under further interrogation, this account was modified to describe something more bizarre.

'Sometimes a crude form of raffia mask is worn,' recalled Fountain, but frequently no effort was made at disguise. 'In several cases, witnesses have described the murderers as wearing a certain kind of leaf known locally as "mkpatat" tied round their head. Sometimes the murderer is described as wearing a form of spotted cloth, but this appears to be merely symbolic of the leopard and not used as an actual disguise. In nine cases out of ten, the murderer wears nothing but an ordinary loin cloth. The whole question of disguise – or rather the lack of it – is significant in as much as the leopard man appears to have such supreme confidence in his magic that any precautions of this nature are to him entirely redundant.'

The use of the description 'leopard man' was taken up in the popular press and inflamed the terror created by the murders, but it also made the first important breakthrough in identifying the nature of the criminals. These were not mere thrill killers but part of a wider conspiracy linked to local ritual and belief.

The region haunted by the murderers was 300 square miles in the Abak and Opobo divisions of the Calabar province. The area had benefited from colonialism through the building of roads, schools and hospitals, but despite the presence of many mission churches, the local people had little regular contact with Europeans and clung on to their traditional beliefs.

'The area,' said Fountain, 'remains an oasis of barbarism, with the mental outlook of the people little changed for centuries past. The mind of the local native is full of superstitious fears and hopes. His whole life is bound up with jujus, fetishes, charms and medicines. Witch doctors, sorcerers and diviners abound everywhere and do a lucrative trade. To these people, nothing occurs naturally – the law of cause and effect is practically unknown. At every major or minor crisis in life, witch doctors have to be consulted, certain traditional rituals carried out, sacrifices and invocations made, evil spirits propitiated and so on.'

The Anangs and the Ibibios were the dominant tribes and had a reputation for deadly vendetta. At first, Fountain believed the murders were the result of long-running quarrels between them. Murderers were hired to sort out family disputes over land, dowry or debt. But this didn't explain why many of the victims were not adults but children aged between seven and ten.

The police officer returned to his study of their tribal culture. Leopards were widespread in the country and there was considerable belief in the African version of lycanthropy – werewolves – men turning into animals.

'Certain persons in each village or district would gain the reputation of having the power of changing into leopards,' observed Fountain. 'A reputation which they would do their best to encourage, as it would give them power over other people and add to their prestige and the awe in which they were held. Later they would use their reputed powers to rid themselves of their enemies. Witch doctors would be quick to adopt the idea themselves, or as they so often do now, supply the necessary charms and medicines to people who wished to acquire the power. Armed with his medicines – in which it must be remembered he has the most profound faith – the would-be leopard man waylays his enemy. Possibly he does actually believe that he changes into a leopard at the moment of killing.'

As a result, the mutilations committed at the scene of the crime were intended less to disguise the nature of the killing and were more a ritual demonstration of the animal power acquired by the murderer. Such was the strong conviction of these killers that they had become transformed into wild beasts that their attempts at disguise in front of witnesses was rudimentary and the power of suggestion was such that many witnesses believed they had in fact seen a leopard in action.

'If my hypothesis is correct,' concluded Fountain, 'we are fighting nothing as tangible as an organisation but rather an attitude of mind.'

Every adult male in the region had the potential to be a leopard killer. To combat this, the strength of the local police was more than doubled and armed patrols were carried out between tribal settlements in the dangerous evening hours. Some of the patrols would sleep in the native camps to gain as much intelligence as they could on local characters and disputes.

Individual murders were investigated and sometimes the perpetrators were tracked down, put on trial and hanged. Whole communities were shown the gory remnants of the victims and shamed into giving up information, but still the leopard murders continued. By the beginning of 1947, there was also a new, concerning twist to them: the leopard attacks were being directed at the colonial administrators.

The murder of PC Evan Chima rang alarm bells. This was a political act and Senior Assistant Superintendent Fountain came under extreme pressure to bring the serial murders to an end.

Some academic specialists in African culture have since argued that the witch doctors and their leopard assassins were acting as a local judiciary and police force, carrying out tribal methods of law enforcement on the torn apart victims – that is, in some ways, they all deserved their grisly deaths. If this were the case, because the colonial authorities were meddling in these affairs, the death of one of their policemen was a warning shot to stay out – in effect, a strike against British colonialism. But then how was the killing of children justified?

That this version of events was not exactly true was revealed when the murderers of PC Chima were caught and subjected to interrogation before Fountain. Etuk Uku, the half-brother of Chief Sunday Udo Expo, was especially voluble during his confession. Having described the exact circumstances of the killing of the policeman, he revealed the Idiong cult that surrounded the leopard murders.

'When anyone wishes to kill a person for some personal reason,' explained Uku, 'he will go first to an Idiong member and consult his Idiong. The Idiong will give instructions as to the preparation of certain medicines which will be placed in the bush near a path and which will have the effect of attracting the victim to the spot.'

The medicine could be prepared from Afang leaves and placed in an Afang grove, attracting the victim to the location. But this magic was all part of a commercial service carried out by the Idiong witch doctors.

'At the initial consultation,' said Uku, 'the Idiong member demands a fee, usually of five or ten manillas, but where it is decided to kill somebody, the Idiong instructs that certain parts of the body of the victim be brought back to him. These parts are usually the tongue, hair from the head, flesh from the arm and sometimes the heart and other internal organs.'

The object of scraping the head of the victim was to prevent identification of the body. This flesh was not used by the Idiong.

'The parts of the body taken to the Idiong member,' continued Uku, 'are used to prepare a medicine to give the Idiong juju power and attract people to come for consultations. If these parts were not obtainable, the Idiong would lose power and would not be able to answer questions put to it. Anyone who produces these human parts to an Idiong man will be paid for them. They usually pay from 40 to 60 manillas. All Idiong men will pay for these human parts. It is mostly the bigger Idiong members who do it. Idiong usually advises that murders be committed in the evening, as people will be too frightened to enter the bush after dark to search for the body.'

It seemed, then, that though the choice of victim might at first arise out of personal animosity, many of the bodies were being harvested for organs to be used in tribal magic. This explained the death of so many children, whose body parts were especially valued.

The cult of using parts of children in tribal magic survives into the twenty-first century. In 2001, officers investigating the appearance of a boy's torso in the River Thames linked his death to this practice. Tests on his bones revealed that the unnamed child, later dubbed 'Adam', came from Nigeria. No one has yet been arrested for his murder and ritual dismemberment.

Chief Udo Ekpo, the ringleader of the gang that killed PC Chima, was not an Idiong member, but he did consult Chief Ukpong Eto's Idiong. Chief Ukpong Eto was a practising Idiong member of considerable local renown and lived in the centre of the area plagued by the leopard killings. The two chiefs had quarrelled over money given to them for a previous leopard murder and that was why Chief Ukpong later gave evidence against Chief Udo Ekpo at his trial for the policeman's murder.

As Fountain delved further, he discovered that the Idiong constituted a kind of black magic mafia in the region. An Anang trader proved most helpful in explaining their hold over the land.

'Any person known to be a member of the Idiong Society is honoured by the inhabitants,' said the merchant. 'The influence of Idiong Society in olden days [meant] they usually had a general meeting best known to them where they arranged to sell people as slaves and to kill and make use of some parts of the deceased they needed, such as the skull, tongue, heart, intestines, hairs, eyes, lungs, right or left hand, for the sacrifice to their Idiong gods and for the preparing of charms, known as Nduoho. This Nduoho has power to conceal things which they have done from coming to light. This action of Idiong members and the power of their Nduoho make the inhabitants fear them the most because it is being sacrificed with the human flesh, openly without fear of anybody.'

In the middle of the twentieth century, the Idiong no longer sold slaves but continued to maintain their power through leopard killings, known as 'Ekpe Owo'.

'They are still holding their secret meetings,' said the Anang merchant, 'sometimes in the market places and sometimes in an appointed place by them. This meeting usually consists of notable members. The inhabitants still go to any of the Idiong members they trust for prophecy and advice. The Idiong men prepare them a charm to kill a human being and receive some amount settled. This charm enables them to kill at sunset. The Idiong man will demand parts of the deceased for the sacrifice of their Idiong gods and for further preparation of any protective talisman.

'The Idiong men, in most cases, never take part in the commission of the killing but have power to direct, encourag[ing] the doers to perform the action at the appointed time and place with the power of their charm, which always hypnotises people.'

Finally, in the climax to his investigation, Fountain got a member of the Idiong to explain its hold over the Nigerian people.

'Before the advent of the British government,' said the Idiong insider, 'the Idiong Society was ruling. They had power over everything. They can command to kill anybody they have accused of any thing and there will be no other power to go against their command. They can kill any of their members who reveal their secret and may sell the person as a slave, according to their judgement.'

According to him, the killing of victims by leopard men was a relatively new phenomenon – a variant on more orthodox methods of slaying. Having revealed so much, the informer begged the police to keep the information he had given them secret, otherwise he would suffer the fate of those who spoke out about the Idiong Society.

Fountain now had all the information he needed to reach his own conclusion on the motives behind the leopard-men killings.

'The more the question of Idiong is considered, the more it appears to fit into the general pattern of events,' surmised Fountain. 'It is generally acknowledged to be the most powerful and influential cult in the area, and the oracle is consulted by the people before any decision is made on any matter of major importance. What the oracle says is never questioned and practising Idiong members thrive on their consultations – they are practically all men of considerable substance.

'If parts of the human body are necessary for the practice of this cult, it is certain that Idiong members would have no hesitation in encouraging their clients to murder in order to obtain them. The apparently trivial motives underlying the murders become explainable on this hypothesis, as these would be only secondary, with the sacrificial idea plus the market value of human flesh as the fundamental cause. The leopard cult would have arisen as a natural offshoot of Idiong, fostered by the Idiong priests as their main source of supply of the materials essential to their profession.'

It was perhaps the most bizarre organised crime of all. Its demand for murder came from a commercial need for human body parts, that was its trade: not drugs or arms, but bits of flesh. As to the course of action needed to combat this barbarous business, Fountain was equally clear.

'I now very strongly urge that immediate steps be taken to declare Idiong an unlawful society and that powers be given to the police to destroy all shrines, jujus, and other manifestations of this – at least potentially – evil cult.'

The police came down hard; more locals were arrested and several of those were hanged. 'In the course of time,' said Fountain, 'it will begin to dawn on the people that their medicines are not effective against the police and that murders cannot be disguised as genuine leopard killings.' It was a bold crusade against the rule of ritual.

The crackdown worked, to an extent, but ultimately the colonial police acknowledged that the will of the people was not with them and they could never eradicate these primitive cults and secret societies, which continue to hold influence today.

Earlier in the century, the Ekumeku Society – 'League of the Silent Ones' – had terrorised the Asaba hinterland in Nigeria, directing attacks against colonial courthouses and mission stations. Missionary converts were assaulted, alongside chiefs who were too friendly with the British. The members of the secret society raided prison camps to release their comrades and closed markets, bringing trade to a halt. The British governors declared them an 'Anti-European Club' and sent a military expedition into the interior to root them out. At least 300 members of the Ekumeku Society were arrested and many of them were imprisoned, but it didn't stop the resurgence of their activities a few years later.

Organised crime throughout colonial Africa ebbed and flowed according to how tight a grip the imperial authorities could exert in distant regions. In Uganda, armed gang robbery, known as *bakondo*, in which truckloads of young criminals raided villages and government property, was widespread. When the Uganda police clashed with the bakondo gangs, fierce firefights broke out and several police were killed. This upsurge in violence reached a crescendo in 1954 after Mutesa II, the Kabaka of Buganda, the largest of the kingdoms in Uganda, was arrested by the commissioner of police and sent into exile.

Matiya Kibuka Kiganira, a chief witch doctor, stepped into the power vacuum, calling himself the Buganda god of war, and demanded a return to traditional beliefs. He sold magical objects to his followers, including cowrie shells that ensured the birth of twins or that a wife was a virgin. When the police arrested him for fraud, the head constable in charge of the arresting party was stabbed to death. An enormous crowd that had gathered to protect the witch doctor had to be dispersed with buckshot and tear gas. Kiganira was sentenced to death, but this was later commuted to imprisonment, as the British feared the consequences of his death. This period of anarchy only subsided with the return of the Kabaka.

The unrest in Uganda at this period may also be traced in part to political events in neighbouring countries. As in South-East Asia, the post-war period saw an increase in anti-colonial campaigns. The Special Branch of the Uganda Police was very active in monitoring the movement of Kikuyu rebels from Kenya into Uganda. At least two of these Mau Mau agents were arrested in Kampala in 1954 and one was charged with fund-raising for the uprising.

Such rebellions hastened the end of imperial rule in Africa, but on occasion, and much to the surprise of the establishment, events in that vast continent managed to strike back at the home of empire in Britain.

'Lady Churchill,' said a note dated Monday, 15 March 1954, 'this is a free warning to YOU. I as well as my brave and most ruthless gang will be out to shoot YOU DEAD at any moment in Britain, beginning from today . . . End British atrocities in Kenya now! Then live freely in Britain. I am demanding the withdrawal of all troops from Kenya within 2 months time . . .'

The note was signed, 'Yours most wickedly, Mau Mau Rep, General Stalin, London Branch'.

A postcript carried an additional threat: 'God truly knows that I have taken the oath to fulfil this duty. It must be carried out. We are also sure Mrs Lyttelton's life is at present not so safe too. We will show you both just what we . . .'

It ended abruptly.

Lady Moira Lyttelton was the wife of the Secretary of State for the Colonies.

The death threat note was received at 10 Downing Street, Whitehall, by Jock Colville, Joint Principal Private Secretary to Winston Churchill, then Prime Minister of Great Britain. The Mau Mau uprising in Kenya had begun in 1952 and its murderous events had so far been confined to the African continent. It appeared now, however, that the Kenyan insurgents were trying to bring the war to the streets of London and involve the British leader's wife.

Colville sent the letter on to the Assistant Undersecretary of State at the Home Office. 'I suggested that, although it might well be from a lunatic,' recalled Colville, 'it would obviously be well that the police or MI5 should make an investigation with the least possible delay.'

The note was passed on by the Home Office to the duty officer at Cannon Row Police Station, who made a few telephone calls. 'I then went to Downing Street,' the officer stated, 'and saw the PCs on Numbers 1, 2, 3, 4, 5, 6 and 16 Protection Posts. I informed each one of the threat and directed them to be on the alert to detect anyone acting in a suspicious manner. I also impressed upon them the necessity of keeping the information secret. I did not post any extra men.'

The duty officer ended his shift at 10.15 p.m., having done all he could to protect the Prime Minister and his wife, and making sure the whole process was kept discreet. Unfortunately, this was not to be.

'The first intimation I had that the Press were in possession of the information concerning the threat,' he said, 'was when travelling to duty at about 1.20 p.m. [the next day], I saw at the corner of Bridge Street and Parliament Street a placard which read "Threat to Lady Churchill".'

Colville was furious.

'It was with considerable surprise,' he told the Home Office, 'that the Prime Minister saw in the first editions of Tuesday's evening paper, which arrived here at about 10.00 a.m. on Tuesday morning, that the fact of this threatening letter being received was known. During the course of the morning we received many Press enquiries in this office and it was consequently decided to say that such a letter had indeed been received and that, as is normally the case with threatening letters, it had at once been forwarded to the police.'

As a result of this leak, claimed Colville, a second threatening letter had been received from the Mau Mau's London agent.

'The Prime Minister finds it difficult to understand,' complained Colville in a memo to the Home Office, 'how such a leakage to the Press can have taken place. My letter must have reached you about 6.00 p.m. on Monday evening. Unless the sender of the letter is responsible for the leakage, which seems improbable, the facts must have been divulged to the Press on the Monday evening or in the early hours of Tuesday morning in order to catch the early editions of Tuesday's evening papers. Sir Winston would be obliged if the Home Secretary would enquire into this matter and would be good enough to inform him how he thinks that the Press came to be informed.'

The press thoroughly enjoyed the sensational revelation and a former Metropolitan Commissioner of Police was ambushed with questions, at an unrelated speaking engagement, about how the police planned to protect Lady Churchill.

'Obviously, there is surveillance, and you may give her a detective to accompany her wherever she goes,' he responded. Then, worryingly, added, 'It would be idle to suggest that against any determined criminal you can have protection. All you can do is your best.' This lax answer only inflamed concerns for the safety of the Prime Minister's wife and encouraged other anti-imperialists.

'Lady Churchill will meet a violent death before the end of June,' declared a letter received by a Manchester evening paper. It was signed: 'Freedom for Ireland, Unity is our goal'.

In reality, the threat to Lady Churchill from the Mau Mau was never very serious. Just that month, the Kenyan rebels had suffered serious reverses in their two-year-old campaign when two of their top leaders were captured by the British. Perhaps the letter was a desperate attempt to distract attention from this loss. When Sir Evelyn Baring, Governor of Kenya, sent a telegram to Churchill a week earlier, informing him of the latest developments in his country, he was more worried by the state of the ruling whites than the Mau Mau rebels.

'The political tangle here is baffling,' he wrote candidly. 'Europeans with the low whisky prices and high altitude pressures are both irresponsible and hysterical. This is the worst season of the year and even in normal times tempers are at their most brittle in March.'

The Mau Mau uprising was the most notorious of all African anti-colonial movements of this period. As with the Malayan Emergency, it was the colonial police who were pitched into the brutal conflict, far outnumbering the soldiers involved and taking many of the casualties, but it was also the police who came up with the most ingenious ways of dealing with the terrorist groups.

15

THE BLACKED-UP INSPECTOR DRUMMOND

AS IN MALAYA AND PALESTINE, anti-colonial movements in Africa were viewed initially as matters of law and order. Colonial police forces were tasked with dealing with these 'dirty' campaigns and their adversaries were termed 'terrorists' or more simply 'gangsters'. The same was true in Kenya with the Mau Mau uprising, beginning in 1952. While Kikuyu resentment of colonial rule had been simmering for some time, many of the Kikuyu people were not interested in joining a rebellion. So, in an attempt to terrorise them into joining their cause, the Mau Mau carried out assaults on their own people.

On the outskirts of Nairobi, the huts of Kikuyu who refused to take the Mau Mau oath were set on fire. This set the pattern for a series of horrendous atrocities perpetrated on Africans by the Mau Mau, culminating in the spearing to death of a senior tribal chief who defied their demands.

Like Malaya, a state of emergency was declared and Arthur Young, Commissioner of Police of the City of London, and police trouble-shooter in Malaya, was later flown in to lend his organisational skills to the campaign.

In October 1952, the Kenyan police launched a major operation to arrest the ringleaders of the rebellion. This provoked a series of gruesome murders of colonial families. The Mau Mau spared neither women and children nor old people in their attacks on whites and blacks, often hideously torturing them beforehand. The Kenyan police responded with similar brutality – mutilating and executing suspects.

One night in March 1953, at Lari in the Kenyan Highlands, Mau Mau rebels crept up on a village of Kikuyu while they were sleeping, drenched their thatched huts in petrol and set them on fire. Survivors described what happened next to government investigators:

> Escape was impossible to most, for the doors had been securely fastened outside by the fanatical Mau Mau attackers. Men, women and children, forcing their way out of the windows, were caught and butchered. Some perished terribly in the flames; others were chopped and mutilated by the knives of their enemies – their own fellow tribesmen. Dawn revealed the macabre scene left behind by the bestial wave of Mau Mau; the mangled corpses, human remains literally chopped in pieces, all mingled with the smoking ashes of the burnt homesteads.

As 120 Kikuyu lay dead or dying, the survivors told the police of the horrible assault – 'children being cut up with knives in the sight of their mothers; of others cut down as they tried to run and hide in tall maize'. In the face of this butchery, the British reacted with their own ruthlessness, as one police officer recalled after arresting three Mau Mau:

> I stuck my revolver right in his grinning mouth and I said something, I don't remember what, and I pulled the trigger. His brains went all over the side of the police station. The other two Mickeys [Mau Mau] were standing there looking blank. I said to them that if they didn't tell me where to find the rest of the gang I'd kill them too. They didn't say a word so I shot them both. One wasn't dead so I shot him in the ear. When the sub-inspector drove up, I told him that the Mickeys tried to escape. He didn't believe me but all he said was 'bury them and see the wall is cleared up'.

The Mau Mau killed many more Kikuyu than they did colonial settlers – at least 1,800 to 232 police, soldiers and colonists. As a result, there were many African recruits ready to join the Kenyan police force. One of the most bizarre stories of the uprising involved white police joining with Kikuyu units to form pretend Mau Mau gangs – or pseudo-terrorists, as they became known – to infiltrate the rebel groups. They were bizarre because the white police chose to disguise themselves as black Africans. David Drummond was a key figure in this unusual police operation.

Drummond's Scottish father owned a dairy farm just east of Nairobi, bought with money earned while working for the Kenyan railroad. Over six feet tall and a keen sportsman, David was born in Nairobi and was well versed in the African landscape, speaking Swahili fluently. An expert hunter, he was a fine shot and competed on a national level.

At the age of 20, he joined the Kenyan police force – just one month after the declaration of the state of emergency. Within a few weeks, Drummond had witnessed his first Mau Mau murder: the killing of two white farmers.

It was dark when he entered their house and, not wanting to expose himself to danger, he crawled in on his hands and knees. As he did so, he touched a severed hand. It had been cut from one of the farmers, who had tried to defend himself against a rain of blows from panga knives delivered by a gang of Mau Mau. When the lights went on in the farmhouse, he saw the full horror of their mutilated bodies.

'I went outside and was violently sick,' he recalled. 'It was not so much the fact that two Europeans had been murdered, as the way in which it had been done. I had grown up with Africans. The thought that they could do this to people like me was like a kick in the solar plexus.'

A few weeks later, the news got worse; a young couple were murdered alongside their six-year-old boy, Michael Ruck, who was hacked to pieces. Photographs of his blood-spattered bedroom, with teddy bears and a train set covered in gore, appeared in the national newspapers, enraging white opinion even further.

Drummond went to work in a detention camp at Ol Kalou, screening the local Kikuyu. He got to learn that the main weapon deployed by the Mau Mau was their oath, forced on the local inhabitants, pledging them solemnly to attack Europeans. Fear of the magic surrounding the oaths and the reprisals that would follow if they broke them served as a potent recruiting device. Stories of depraved initiation rites, including the drinking of urine and blood, and sex with animals and children, may well have been the result of interrogations in which suspects told the police what they thought they wanted to hear, but it certainly succeeded in creating a climate of dread and extreme violence.

As part of his intelligence gathering, Drummond recruited informers from among the Kikuyu, who directed him towards Mau Mau terrorists and their suppliers, including gunrunners. One of his best tip-offs concerned General Harun Njeroge, a leader of what were termed 'forest gangsters', based around Molo in western Kenya. The 26-year-old Harun ruled his gang harshly, lashing them for insubordination. He kept his gang small – just 12-strong – strangling any members he considered 'deadwood' or disloyal. Mau Mau insiders passed on to Drummond tantalising information about Harun, but the rebel chief kept one step ahead – until the policeman's fiancée, Mary, noticed some smoke rising from a prohibited area in the Mutamayo forest. Drummond sent Mary to stay with friends and prepared for a dawn raid.

Undermanned, with just three other colleagues to help him, Drummond decided to go ahead with the attack. Armed with an Italian 9 mm Beretta sub-machine gun – a trophy from the Abyssinian War – he set off in the dark before dawn with two police reservists and a Mau Mau informer, armed with Sten guns. Crawling towards the Mau Mau camp, they heard the characteristic sound of Harun beating one of his guards for leaving his post. When the sentry reappeared, Drummond opened fire and the whole camp erupted, bullets slashing through the undergrowth around the police.

'It was then I heard something falling heavily in the bushes above me,' remembered Drummond. 'I looked up to see a grenade caught in a tangle of brambles eight or nine feet just above my head. A second later it went off, blowing the thickets to bits and leaving a throbbing numbness in my ears.'

Miraculously unharmed by the explosion, Drummond ran forward, only to dodge another grenade. Not fully realising the small force pitted against them, the Mau Mau gang bolted into the bush and escaped. One of them had been killed and two were wounded. Drummond later got the two wounded men to disavow the Mau Mau and give him information about Harun. Drummond was determined to hunt him down and, a few days later, a Kikuyu informer told him he was staying on the outskirts of Nakura, a short distance away.

Drummond burst into a hut on the pretext of a routine search and cornered Harun. Relieving him of his gun, the policeman turned him round to search him further. As he did so, the Mau Mau leader slammed his fist into the side of Drummond's face, knocking him down, and ran out. Drummond fired after him, but Harun dashed into the bush and escaped. Now it was personal – and evidence of just how personal the vendetta had become emerged weeks later.

Drummond married Mary and as he carried her over the threshold into their cottage, he noticed a blue envelope on the floor addressed simply to 'Drum'. Ripping it open, he read the message, written in Swahili: 'You have married a nice white girl but you will not enjoy her for very long. I am going to castrate you. It is I, Harun.'

The cottage was isolated in the Kenyan countryside, half a mile from the main road.

Two days later came a second message: 'I wish to tell that when I castrate you I will hang it on a thorn tree for the vultures to take away.'

To protect themselves, Drummond hired a night watchman from a tribe that hated the Kikuyu. One night, the African knocked on his door and told the policeman that he could see men creeping forward among the cows in a nearby field. Drummond grabbed his Beretta and peered into the moonlit pasture, seeing the shadows of the men. To stop them getting close enough to torch his cottage, he fired a long burst into the darkness. Blinded by the flash from his own gun, Drummond waited for what must have been agonising minutes until he heard the sound of his neighbouring farmer's car arriving. The Mau Mau had fled – and a month later Drummond and his wife moved out of the cottage.

Several more letters followed, in which Harun revealed how surprisingly well informed he was about Drummond's movements. The policeman came to the awful realisation that the rebel leader was getting his knowledge from his own informers – one of them was acting as a double agent. When he investigated further, he discovered that the Kikuyu shopkeeper and Mau Mau party secretary was using his position to run a protection racket, extorting money from fellow businessmen in his township.

In order to flush out Harun and banish the rumours that he was untouchable, Drummond decided to take an African approach to his arch-enemy and challenge him to single combat. He posted the messages in cleft-sticks in the forest near Kikuyu camps used by rebels, inviting the Mau Mau chief to a duel. The challenge remained unanswered.

Drummond pursued Harun through the Kenyan landscape, at one point getting within range of him. He fired one shot that blew up dust, just about level with Harun's head. The Mau Mau leader spun round, threw back an insult and sprinted away.

After months of this, Drummond woke up one morning with a rash covering his entire body. He was diagnosed with stress and sent to hospital for two weeks to recover.

It appeared that Harun had finally disappeared from Drummond's patch and, in the lull, the policeman wondered how best he could get close to the Mau Mau gangs in his district. After talking with a second-generation farmer and police reservist called Neville Cooper, the men had the idea of creating their own fake Mau Mau gang. Drummond thought this could be used in reconnaissance, but Cooper went further, saying that the gang should actually infiltrate the Mau Mau and – most remarkable of all – be led by Drummond himself, with a 'blacked-out' face.

Drummond thought the idea was preposterous – simply 'blacking up' wouldn't convince anyone. But Cooper had experience of similar units within the Kenya Regiment, a white settlers' volunteer corps who had captured some hardcore Mau Mau gangsters. Some of these Kikuyu had been turned, and once they had got over the fear of defying their tribal oaths, they had realised that they were being exploited by the terrorists and had come to loathe them as much as the colonialists. It was these men who would be key to the whole operation; they would fight alongside the disguised white men, who would drop into the background as the vengeful Kikuyu took the lead during the missions. For Drummond's unit, Cooper put the word out and several former Kikuyu rebels were recommended.

'The pseudo-gang were an unruly lot,' said Drummond. 'You went down a little path to their shamba, where a group of huts nestled behind a path of maize, and it was always quite startling to come upon a group of bloodthirsty-looking outlaws, with long matted hair and beards that had taken months to grow, dressed in an assortment of skin jackets, caps and raincoats, and armed to the teeth.'

The five ex-Mau Mau, led by a veteran field commander called Thiga, were given training in weapons handling and unarmed combat, while they taught the Europeans about jungle craft. Then came the ticklish question of disguising the white men. Drummond knew he could never replicate the physical features of an African, but if he could just darken himself to pass in a crowd then that would do the job. The usual methods of using polish, stage make-up or burnt cork didn't work because they looked too glossy, came off on clothes and made the whites of the eyes stand out. Having spoken to a chemist, Drummond decided to use a solution of potassium permanganate to tint the skin all over – so even if they had to strip off their clothes, they would be covered. A weaker solution was used as an eye-wash, to colour the whites of the eyes a browny-yellow.

But this was only the beginning. Drummond had spent years noting the everyday habits of the Kikuyu – how they ate their food, blew their noses, smoked a cigarette. He made a wig for himself out of the hair of a dead terrorist, although frequently it was too hot to wear it on patrol and he just used a hat. Clothes worn by rebels were appropriated, as they were impregnated with the smell of months living in the bush. As for his European features, Drummond claimed that some Kikuyu had sharper Caucasian looks. The white men roughened their hands to the texture of a labourer for the moment when the Mau Mau met in a forest and shook hands.

Even so, it seemed a ludicrous notion that Drummond and Jim McNab, a fellow British undercover policeman, could pass close examination by a suspicious rebel commander.

Their most important asset was a Kikuyu 'cover man', who stuck close to them and could think quickly when they came under attention. Then there was Thiga, who had the authority to deal with rival gang chiefs. He would be their leader in the field.

On one of their first operations, the pseudo-gang were sitting around a campfire one night with real Mau Mau gang members. During the conversation, Drummond attracted the interest of a teenage girl follower of the Mau Mau, one of many who liked to serve the rebels.

'After a while she came over and sat close to me, and there was no doubt at all about what she was after,' recalled Drummond. 'I was scared out of my wits. That night I wasn't blacked out further than my face and hands. The next thing I knew she had put a hand on my arm and was cuddling closer. Then she came straight to the point.'

When Drummond refused her sexual advances, the girl got furious and questioned his manhood. At that moment, his 'cover man' came to his rescue.

'He is a man,' he intervened, 'but unfortunately he has VD.'

The girl recoiled and Drummond was saved.

The problem of these fake units being mistaken by white security forces was also a primary concern, bearing in mind the ruthless attitude of many colonial police who were happy to shoot first. This potential hazard was covered by rules of engagement issued by the Kenya Police headquarters:

> No pseudo-gang operation should be carried out during the hours of daylight in settled areas or the Reserves if the object could equally well be achieved by an operation carried out at night . . .
>
> In the event of a pseudo-gang being encountered and being unable to retire, the patrol leader will endeavour to establish his identity by word of mouth or removal of his disguise.

The unconventional nature of this type of police action was summed up in a secret report on the successes and failures of several pseudo-gangs: 'We now have six private armies, each led by a man with highly developed individualistic tendencies.' That certainly applied to Drummond. Then came the warning – these special forces had a 'tendency to succumb to the temptation to "bump off " enemy terrorists encountered rather than to wait patiently for an opportunity to achieve a major success'.

The first major target for Drummond's pseudo-gang was General Jimmy, commander of more than a hundred rebels on Mount Londiani, a forest region in the Rift Valley. Slowly, they built up a picture of the general's movements. As anticipated by the Kenya Police instructions, the biggest danger for them came from British tracker-combat teams who used dogs to hunt down the terrorists and had not been informed of the undercover team.

After long treks into the forest, they met a Mau Mau foraging party, looking for food to take back to the general's mountain hideout. They tagged along, but as they pressed into the jungle, it rained heavily, threatening to wash away Drummond and McNab's make-up.

At one point, Thiga suggested joining the enemy gang, but as part of this process they would take an oath that involved roping themselves together, and General Jimmy's men refused to be tied. They then spoke about their allegiances to senior Mau Mau leaders and it was at this point that one of the pseudo-gang mentioned the wrong name. Immediately, the foragers bolted into the jungle, fearing they had been trapped by a rival faction. It was a frustrating end to weeks of patient work.

In the meantime, word came out that Harun – the rebel who had come closest to unnerving Drummond – was back in the area. The policeman decided to use his pseudo-gang to make contact with him. The plan was that his Kikuyu comrades would suggest joining Harun's gang. This overture was accepted and they were invited to share food with the Mau Mau.

'Harun meant something very special to me,' said Drummond, admitting his nervousness at the meeting. 'I didn't fancy the idea of having supper with somebody who had sworn he was going to castrate me.'

That night, eight of the pseudo-gang arrived at Harun's camp. Drummond had his trademark Beretta and 200 rounds of ammunition. As they pushed through the undergrowth, they were told they would be searched, which meant an examination of the colour of their skin beneath their clothes. Harun had heard rumours of undercover policemen. For a moment, the white men were drenched in a cold sweat. Then Drummond took the initiative, using his knife to silence the sentry sent to check them. Hiding the body in the bush, the pseudo-gang entered Harun's encampment. Each man shook hands with the rebel leader in the Mau Mau manner – a strong clasp, followed by the gripping of right thumbs.

'I looked up and there was his face a foot away,' remembered Drummond. 'His eyes boring into me.'

Supper was rancid meat that smelled terrible. Drummond put it against his mouth, then palmed it, fearing if he ate it he would throw up. Fortunately, the apparent pseudo-gang leader was Thiga, a veteran fighter, and Harun concentrated on talking to him. They spoke deep into the night and then Thiga suggested a drill contest to demonstrate their professionalism. Harun's men stood to attention and presented arms smartly. When it came to the pseudo-gang, they sloped arms with two fine smacks and Harun's men applauded.

'Company! Order arms!'

The police guns were lowered and pointed at the rebels. At that moment, Harun realised something was wrong, but it was too late. The undercover firing squad blasted the Mau Mau. Harun was wounded but dived into the bush. Fearing that his pseudo-gang would be compromised if Harun escaped, Drummond brought in extra police to track him down. A week later, the wounded leader was found.

In prison, Harun demanded to see Drummond. From inside his cell, he congratulated the policeman on winning the duel between them. They spoke for some time, revealing the other side's story, then shook hands Mau Mau-style. It was the last time Drummond would see him. Harun was sentenced to death and hanged.

Despite this success, the situation in Molo deteriorated. Loyalist Kikuyu were murdered along with their families, and white farmers were regularly threatened, their property attacked and animals mutilated. It was the presence of General Jimmy and his gang that encouraged the other Mau Mau assaults and yet they stayed well away from Molo on their mountain-top hideout.

Drummond's luck changed in June 1955. With his pseudo-gang, he picked up the Mau Mau commander's trail. The rebels liked to post scouts to cover their movements and one of them intercepted the pseudo-gang; however, turning it to their advantage, Drummond managed to convince the scout that they wanted to link up with General Jimmy's followers.

A fake oathing ceremony was organised by the pseudo-gang and as some of General Jimmy's Mau Mau crawled beneath an arch of twigs, they were clubbed and bound by the undercover Kikuyu. One of the gang members proved to have a very tough head, as Drummond recalled: 'The clout he got made no impression, he just looked up very surprised and demanded to know why he had been hit like that. He had just got on his feet, and the next moment we found ourselves grappling with this huge African, trying to pull him to the ground. With one heave he threw us off and dashed into the bushes.'

Drummond unsheathed his knife and ran after him. Pulling him down with a rugby tackle, he silenced him. Some of the other Mau

Mau bolted when they heard the brawling, but the captured ones joined the pseudo-gang and helped lead them towards General Jimmy's camp. More operations followed and in the clashes Mau Mau were cut down rather than being captured.

The incessant killing was getting to the 22-year-old Drummond. His Kikuyu comrades marked the notches on the stock of his Beretta and he was horrified when they reached a fifth row.

'I began to wonder if I was getting a kick out of my business,' said the policeman. 'I used to tell myself it was a nasty job that had to be done, that after all I was only doing my duty, and that the important thing was I should do it well. But did all of them have to die?'

Drummond loathed talking to other policemen, who spoke of their victims as 'baboons' and liked shooting them.

Despite these doubts, Drummond and his pseudo-gang had no compunction when they caught a Mau Mau who boasted about killing an elderly couple with pangas. He was executed on the spot. The Kikuyu serving alongside Drummond were happy to act as avengers, believing they were ridding their country of the evil of Mau Mau.

'I was in this thing, this killing machine – and there was no way of getting out. We had a terrible momentum, and nothing, apart from getting eliminated ourselves, could have stopped us going on the way we were.'

On one occasion, they were planning to murder 11 Mau Mau who had joined the pseudo-gang. The plan was to wait until every one of the rebels was sleeping before knifing them, but McNab, the other white policeman, nodded off. As he did so, his boots went into a fire and he woke up, cursing in English. In the pandemonium that followed, some of the Mau Mau escaped, but they were all eventually tracked down and killed before they could inform General Jimmy.

To begin with, Drummond had insisted on removing the bodies of dead Mau Mau to identify them back at police headquarters, but as the headcount mounted, Thiga and his Kikuyu followers refused, resorting to providing only severed hands. The police authorities objected to this, but Drummond said there was little he could do about it. An earlier British Court of Inquiry had looked at the practice:

> In the Prohibited Areas it was an accepted – although not a universal – practice to cut off either one or both hands from a

body where the body could not be brought in . . . The hand was brought back in order that fingerprints could be taken from it.

The need for this was reduced when fingerprinting equipment was issued to all police units and from late 1953 the severing of hands was officially forbidden.

Drummond's search for General Jimmy culminated when they found his camouflaged headquarters deep among the bamboo forest on a mountainside. The camp was surrounded and shot-up in a storm of bullets, but the commander was nowhere to be seen. It would be two weeks before he was found. This time, he was surprised in bed with his mistress. With his pants around his ankles, he was taken into captivity. Later, as Drummond was interrogating his girlfriend, a shot rang out. General Jimmy had been killed while trying to escape – or at least that is what he was told by Jim McNab.

With the death of General Jimmy, by the beginning of 1956 Mau Mau raids had wound down in Molo. It was a victory for the pseudo-gang, but in a final operation, Jim McNab was shot dead. Thiga and the Kikuyu who had fought alongside him were so upset by his death that they shaved off their long beards and cut their hair to attend his funeral. This sign of respect had initially annoyed Drummond, as it destroyed their disguise, but the Africans declared that their enthusiasm for the hunt had gone with McNab's death.

Throughout Kenya, similar ruthless action by British police and soldiers – plus the behind-the-lines action of the pseudo-gangs – brought an end to the Mau Mau uprising in 1957. At least 11,000 rebels had been killed and over 1,000 of them hanged. Drummond received the George Medal in a ceremony at Buckingham Palace, but he was not happy in London.

'When I first got to know him, he was gay and amusing,' said his wife. 'But when we got home he never wanted to go anywhere. He would just sit and gaze into space, day after day.'

The deaths haunted him – as did the thrill of going into action on an operation.

'Now it was all over,' he later admitted, 'and there were no more kicks, just the horror of it all, the regrets, and the loathing I had for myself.'

Thiga and the pseudo-gang were recruited into the regular police force, but it didn't suit their temperament. When directed towards everyday law and order, the Kikuyu overreacted. A bunch of Masai cattle thieves were rounded up and shot. After that, they were disbanded.

Drummond was promoted to chief inspector, the youngest in the Kenya Police, and was happy going back to his police job. His luck finally ran out during a routine mission, when his aircraft crashed. He was badly injured, with his face requiring reconstructive surgery over many operations. The pain he suffered during his long process of recuperation helped him overcome the guilt he had felt at surviving the Mau Mau period. The destruction of his face had obliterated his old self.

More at ease with himself, Drummond eventually returned to work and retired as an assistant superintendent in 1962. Independence came to Kenya in 1963 and, initially, he felt nervous about staying on, but he was encouraged to stay in the new country by his Kikuyu comrades. They wanted him to help build their new country. He developed a whole new career as a security officer for the Kenyan National Parks and a safari tour operator.

By the late 1960s, the British Empire was coming to an end. Almost all its Asian and African colonies had been granted independence; however, one colonial settlement remained a major generator of money and business: Hong Kong. With its wealth and high population concentrated across a small urban landscape, it attracted an array of gangsters determined to turn it into an underworld bonanza – and with that came many temptations, both for its citizens and its police.

16

THE OBLIGING MR LOU

'THE WALLED CITY IN KOWLOON is now neither walled nor a city,' said a Foreign and Commonwealth Office report on the most notorious district of Hong Kong. 'It is a small (6½ acres) area of densely-packed tenement slums near Kai Tak Airport, with an estimated population of some 40,000.'

When a British parliamentary delegate visited it, she was shocked. 'It is a place of real horror, and danger in case of fire. The congestion, lack of sanitation and mixture of living quarters and factory work are really appalling.'

In October 1956, the Walled City was just one part of a district heavily populated with nationalist Chinese refugees, recently fled from communist China. It was a political tinderbox waiting for a spark to set it off and that ignition was provided by a dispute over flags.

'Double Ten Day' – 10 October – is one of celebration for Chinese nationalists, as it commemorates the fall of the Qing Dynasty in 1911, and in Kowloon the nationalist émigré community wanted to party in style. The nationalist organising committee was happy for flags to be displayed on poles or strings but did not want them stuck on walls, as they were difficult to remove afterwards. In one estate in Kowloon, some residents had ignored the ban and pasted two giant Double Ten symbols alongside several other smaller flags on a housing block. When these were torn down, a crowd of residents gathered outside a resettlement office demanding that the flags be replaced.

By 1.15 p.m., the crowd had swollen to 2,000 and at least one agitator was observed to be stirring up the protestors. They wanted 100,000 firecrackers – a traditional sign of apology – plus portraits of Sun Yat-sen and Chiang Kai-shek erected beside a giant nationalist flag. Among the crowd on that day were Triads belonging to the 14K, a notorious drugs-smuggling gang based in Kowloon. They had been busy expanding their membership since arriving in Hong Kong the previous year from southern China and were keen to demonstrate their authority over the population.

Police riot units hurried to the estate near Castle Peak Road and found the crowd had already attacked the resettlement office. As some of the staff had tried to escape, they were set upon and badly beaten. As the police tried to protect them, they were pelted with bottles. Fearing they did not have enough men to carry out a baton charge, police officers fired four tear-gas shells. The mob dispersed back into the estate.

'This incident proved to be a turning point,' noted the official report. Until that moment, the fury of the crowd had been directed at the resettlement staff who had interfered with their nationalist celebrations. The intervention of the police triggered a more general feeling of discontent aimed at the forces of law and order.

Police reinforcements arrived to a storm of stones thrown from the balconies of housing blocks. The resettlement office was looted and set on fire. Using more tear gas, the police managed to quieten the situation and there was a lull in the late afternoon.

By early evening, as workers returned home, there was a revived mood of militancy and it was at this point that the local gangsters took a more active role.

'It is now known that as early as 6.00 p.m.,' said the government report, 'Triad Society members were being mustered to exploit the situation; this undoubtedly had a bearing on the temper of the crowd at this stage.'

Police riot squads marched through the streets, using tear gas to make the crowd disperse, but, knowing their way around the maze of passageways between tenement blocks, the mob quickly reappeared elsewhere, hurling stones at the police. It was then that 14K Triad members, waving nationalist flags, led thousands-strong crowds in an assault on the riot units wherever they found them, taking the opportunity to also loot shops and torch cars. There were serious concerns that the rioting would spread across the island.

The report went on to describe an accident that had occurred as two fire engines arrived to deal with a small fire in a street parallel to the main Castle Peak Road:

> At about 10.00 p.m., the leading fire engine, a Dennis Rolls-Royce machine carrying a 55-foot fire escape ladder, met a heavy fusillade of bricks, pieces of concrete and bottles thrown by crowds of rioters who also attempted to block its passage. The driver was struck on the head by a stone and lost control of the vehicle, which crashed into the crowd, mounted the pavement and pinned several people against a wall at the side of the road. Two people, one a woman, were killed outright and one died in hospital as a result of this accident, while five of the crowd were seriously injured.

While the casualties were being put on stretchers and loaded into ambulances, the rioters continued to throw stones at the emergency services, launching rocks from balconies and rooftops. As one of the wounded was being carried on a stretcher to an ambulance, he was hit by a stone thrown from above.

The fire engine accident and the resulting serious injuries inflamed the crowd, which lashed out at any authority figures caught in its path.

One of these was the wife of the Swiss Consul. Her car was blocked by the mob, stoned and set on fire. The unfortunate woman was engulfed in the flames and later died. Eight Chinese were charged with her murder. An officer of 10th Princess Mary's Own Gurkha Rifles was also trapped in his car. He described the rampaging mob:

> The crowds of several thousand were very mobile, seemingly well organised. The police operated in company sized 'wedges' and soon exhausted their supplies of tear smoke, which was relatively easily 'muzzled' by placing tins and buckets over smoking cartridges and grenades.

In the midst of the chaos, Triad gangsters did not miss a trick in making money out of the mayhem by selling nationalist flags to rioters from the back of their bicycles. They even held up drivers at junctions and forced them to buy flags.

As the rioting entered its second day, barricades were erected and the police had to bring in armoured cars to smash them down. Frequently, the mob lit bonfires to attract fire engines, which were then mercilessly attacked. The police were too thinly spread and had suffered too many casualties to be able to deal with the widespread looting and violence. By the afternoon of 11 October, battalions of heavily armed soldiers had moved into Kowloon. Their presence made all the difference and by the next morning the protests were over.

In the wake of the rioting, serious thought was given to the involvement of organised crime in the violence. Although it was agreed that the initial disturbances were spontaneous and not at all planned, it was felt by the authorities that the continuation of hostilities was directed by criminal elements.

'What is certain,' said Sir Alexander Graham, Governor of Hong Kong, 'is that from a very early stage the disorders were exploited for their own purposes by gangs of criminals, hooligans and Triad Societies. It is significant that nearly half the reported crime in the colony occurs in the northern part of Kowloon, which was the main centre of the rioting.' Explaining this further, he argued that 'it would appear that people of a Nationalist persuasion joined in collaboration with Triad gangs to redress old scores and to attempt to win a dominant position in the Labour world'.

A further report concluded, 'The Triad Societies' capacity for making serious trouble was obviously not appreciated. Up till recently the crime problem in Hong Kong was dealt with almost entirely by deporting criminals and suspects.'

Since January 1955, owing to its strained relations with communist China, this arrangement had stopped. 'The CID [Criminal Investigation Department] now have to gear their machine to the changed conditions, which will include considerably enlarging the branch which suppresses the activities of the Triad Societies.'

This recommendation was taken up, and by 1958 the Hong Kong Police had established its Triad Society Bureau, dedicated to collecting criminal intelligence on Chinese organised crime. It coincided with a boom in the criminal enterprises of the Chinese gangsters.

The 14K were the leading Triad gang in Hong Kong. Since the 1940s, they had been so closely associated with the Kuomintang that nationalist soldiers were conscripted into the society, making their oaths not in the traditional way but before a portrait of Sun Yat-sen, founder of the Chinese Republic. Civilians were keen to show membership of the Triads to prove their anti-communist credentials. With this kind of broad-based support, it is little wonder that the gangsters led the nationalist mobs in 1956.

They were originally known as the '14' after the street number of the address of their headquarters in Canton. When they moved to Hong Kong and won a bloody street battle in 1955 with the local Yuet Tong society – over who could levy protection money – they added 'K' to their name, meaning 'karat' gold, as that gold was considered superior to the local metal. Kot Siu-wong was their leader and continued to organise their establishment in Hong Kong even after he was deported to Taiwan. At one time, he hoped to send a Triad nationalist army back to China when the Kuomintang launched its long-hoped-for counter-invasion, but it never happened. After his death, the sub-branches of the 14K ran their own affairs.

The Hau gang was the most powerful of the 14K sub-branches. With 15,000 members, it ran extortion and protection rackets, and controlled the drugs and prostitution business throughout Kowloon. The Kin gang, closely allied to the Hau, ran illegal operations within the Walled City slum district. Overall, membership of the many sub-branches and splinter groups that made up the 14K amounted to 40–80,000 – a criminal army that completely dominated Kowloon. In the event of an external threat, especially from another Triad force, internal rivalries were quickly forgotten. Their main rival was the Wo group of societies, which had dominated Hong Kong before the arrival of the 14K. Their membership also ran into thousands in Singapore, Macao and other Pacific Chinese communities.

A security intelligence report of 1962 recorded the details of a typical 14K initiation ceremony – one where the recruit didn't have to swear loyalty to a portrait of the nationalist leader:

> The recruit is made to kneel in front of some makeshift altar behind which may be pasted a few pieces of red paper bearing characters for Kwan Ti and a few other deities. Joss sticks and joss paper are burned and often the ashes are mixed into a bowl of wine. An empty bowl is broken and the head of a small

chicken is cut off to show the fate of traitors. Blood from the chicken is mixed into the wine and the middle finger, left hand, of the recruit is pricked and a drop of his blood also mixed into the wine. The recruit then drinks some of this noxious mixture and the ceremony is complete after he has handed over some lucky money to the person conducting the ceremony.

The trafficking of narcotics was a key business for the Triads in Hong Kong. There were three main factors to it. First, Hong Kong acted as a very well-placed distribution point for illegal drugs to the rest of the world, especially Europe and America. Federal Bureau of Narcotics chief Harry J. Anslinger had already drawn attention to this, but had wrongly blamed communist China as the main source when, in fact, most of it came via Thailand from the Golden Triangle in Burma and Laos. Second, raw opium was also being processed in Hong Kong and turned into heroin for export and local consumption. And finally, there was a large, growing internal market for illegal drugs within Hong Kong, which, in 1957, was estimated to number some 30,000 addicts.

It wasn't only the Chinese community that suffered from this addiction. In a drug-rehabilitation centre on Sunshine Island, one anonymous white man told his story. Aged 38, he was born in the colony. At the beginning of the Second World War, he joined the Gloucestershire Regiment and served throughout India and Burma, where his unit were part of the elite Chindit force, fighting the Japanese deep in the jungle.

It was while on leave in India that the soldier acquired the taste for smoking opium from merchant seamen. At first, it was 'just fooling around', as he put it. But then, once he returned to Hong Kong and got a civilian job as a clerk in the War Department, the habit took a grip. Married with two children, he was spending up to $25 on three hits of opium a day. He would travel to the Walled City in Kowloon to buy it.

'The Walled City,' he told an investigator, 'is quite definitely the centre of the drug business, both opium and heroin, in Hong Kong, despite frequent raids by the police.'

Whenever customers first visited its maze of streets, they were given drugs for free, especially heroin. Once it took a hold of them, they were required to pay. Old men came for opium to relieve pain, often stomach trouble. Young men came because they thought it made them look grown-up. Night-shift workers, finding it difficult to get to sleep during the day, took it to keep them going. Triad gangsters encouraged some of their lowly followers to take heroin in order to control them.

'The Walled City provides a virtually secure base for the traffickers' operations,' said the Secretary for Chinese Affairs. 'For although the police do patrol, raid and arrest, the value of their activities is nullified by their inability to prosecute in court and in most cases their only sanction is the seizure and confiscation of such drugs as they find. This is totally inadequate and Kowloon Walled City remains a cancer in the body of Hong Kong. Any plan to deal with drug addiction in the Colony will break down unless this cancer is eliminated or sealed off.'

Although Kowloon was the centre of the drug trade, it was distributed throughout the colony. Most rickshaw coolies sold heroin, while tailor shops in the Wan Chai district were known as the main outlet for drugs to US sailors and other servicemen. Selling drugs provided an income for the addicts themselves and they became key to the entire operation.

One middle-aged man explained that his five-year habit of smoking heroin had cost him $12 a day. He earned $3.70 a day working in a factory, but sold a dozen small packets of heroin daily, netting himself just over $12, thus funding his addiction. As his own cravings increased, he was forced to sell more and more heroin to cover his costs. From the point of view of the main Triad distributor, it was a brilliant self-sustaining and expanding business. An ounce of heroin was purchased wholesale at $250; it was then re-sold at between $375 and $465, making him a profit of between 50 per cent and 86 per cent. It was estimated in 1956 that the value of drugs traded in Hong Kong was worth $100 million.

For the ex-Gloster soldier, he knew he needed help when his habit began to swallow almost all of his $700 monthly income; he confessed all to his commanding officer, who took a sympathetic view of the man's plight and sent him to Sunshine Island for treatment.

Named by a Quaker called Gus Borgeest, the island of Chau Kung To was established as a resettlement centre for Chinese refugees in 1952. Borgeest's method was to get the immigrants farming their own little plot of land, the humble work intending to help addicts get over their opium habit. He was later awarded the Ramon Magsaysay Prize, dubbed Asia's Nobel Prize, for his work on the island. Sunshine Island served as a model for drug-rehabilitation centres elsewhere in Hong Kong.

The smuggling of drugs in and out of Hong Kong was in the hands of the major Triad gangs and police seizures of large deliveries were rare. This was partly because whenever the police received useful inside information, it never came twice from the same source.

'This is due to the fact that the "ring" is so highly organised,' said an investigator. 'The moment a leak develops in a certain section, that section is immediately cut out of the circuit and a substitute provided. All members of the section are dropped and are not used again . . . and there is a great deal of nervousness among informers for fear of reprisals.'

The top traffickers behind each consignment never got involved in the actual smuggling; instead they financed the deals from the background, frequently negotiating payments through the gold market in Macao.

By the late 1950s, 62 per cent of all seizures of raw opium and 100 per cent of all seizures of morphine in Hong Kong originated on ships or aircraft that had passed through Bangkok. By this stage, the importation of raw opium was being superseded by blocks of morphine, as it was less bulky and more suited to smuggling by air. 'The traffic via Bangkok flows so smoothly that it is impossible not to suspect a large measure of official connivance,' said a 1957 official report.

Arthur Maxwell was Commissioner of Police in Hong Kong during this period and had noticed a significant increase in the number of heroin addicts in the city, so much so that eventually they outnumbered the more traditional opium smokers by three to one. Among the shanty towns that had grown up to house Chinese refugees, opium dens had been shut down rigorously, but narcotics dealers had brought in the new, more easily concealable habit of heroin. Clandestine factories sprang up in the colony, some of them operating on an industrial scale, producing heroin both for local consumption and export.

In virtually every one of these factories, the heroin had been manufactured from compressed blocks of morphine imported from

Thailand or neighbouring territories, such as Burma via Bangkok. By importing morphine, the Chinese gangster chemists were able to manufacture heroin directly from it, rather than processing morphine from raw opium, which was slow and gave off giveaway fumes. Each block weighed about eight ounces and was easy to smuggle; its purity meant that just one block could produce ten ounces of heroin, the equivalent of 27,500 doses of the drug – an impressive profit margin.

When it came to re-exporting narcotics from Hong Kong, the primary markets were Europe and America. In 1962, a sensational drugs-bust revealed a surprising mode of transport for these goods: a Royal Navy battleship.

HMS *Belfast* was a light-cruiser armed with 12 six-inch guns and 12 four-inch guns. A veteran of the Second World War, she saw action escorting Arctic convoys and providing covering fire on D-Day. Updated for service in the Korean War, she was coming to the end of her useful life when she set sail from Singapore on 26 March 1962. Her destination was Portsmouth, but she would reach the UK via Hong Kong, Guam, Pearl Harbor, San Francisco, Panama and Trinidad. Someone must have considered this an especially useful itinerary.

On board the *Belfast* were a number of Chinese seamen. Wong Ah Lee was born in Canton, had joined the Royal Navy in 1945 and had served as a Petty Officer Cook in the Captain's galley since 1959. A thirty-eight-year-old married man with four children, Wong Ah Lee lived in Hong Kong. He had been awarded three Good Conduct Badges, a Long Service and Good Conduct Medal and was recommended for advancement. Working alongside him was Kan Ping Kwok, 30 years old, formerly of the NAAFI in Hong Kong, before being transferred to work on board ship. A civilian canteen assistant on the *Belfast* since 1960, he was described as a 'reliable and hard-working man'. He also had a family in Hong Kong.

What happened next is best described by the *Belfast*'s Commander, David Anning Loram:

> Late on the evening of Tuesday, 24th April, 1962, the Master-at-Arms telephoned me and asked me to go to his cabin. There he showed me a suitcase. The case was locked at one end and padlocked that same end but lifting the other corner I saw it contained packages of white powder.

Having got permission to open the case from the Commander-in- Chief Far East, he opened it the next morning in the presence of the Master-at-Arms.

'The case contained 20 bags of a brown substance, and 25 bags of white powder,' said Loram. 'There was also a tin containing ground nuts with eight of the 20 bags packed round the nuts.'

The brown substance was quickly identified as raw opium and the white powder as heroin. Confronted with such a vast amount of narcotics, it was decided to search all the quarters of the Chinese crew. Kan Ping Kwok was identified as the owner of the case and was detained in the ship's cells by the Master-at-Arms.

Later that afternoon, the Commander was called to the ship's laundry and shown a bundle of clothing, two sacks and eight bags of white powder. Enquiries made of the laundry staff at that time failed to trace the owner of the property and it was locked away. That was just the start – further discoveries revealed that the battleship was a floating warehouse for illicit drugs.

Malcom Reed was a Petty Officer on board the *Belfast* and he gives his own account of the drugs-bust.

> We'd left Pearl Harbor and were steaming 2,200 miles for San Francisco. En route information was received from Hong Kong and Singapore that the ship was probably transporting large quantities of heroin and opium for America or England. A few days prior to arrival in America the ship's tannoy system broadcast that all Petty Officers report to the quarterdeck.
>
> On arrival, I and two others we given a situation report and told to search the Chinese-crewed laundry. The Chinese were being held by Royal Marines in the schoolroom. At the laundry I climbed between the large steam presses and with a torch found many dead cockroaches and Chinese newspapers. All were discarded by myself, but I found a fairly large bag of what looked like soap powder. This powder was given to the Commander who dabbed his finger into the substance and stated that it was not soap powder, but could be something that was being sought. I was invited to taste it, which was my initial and final attempt to take heroin.

'The next day,' said Loram, 'I was called by a search team to the Captain's Galley where I saw bags of [a] brown substance being withdrawn from above the strip lights in the Galley. I caused the PO Cook, Wong Ah Lee, who is the man in charge of that Galley, to be detained.'

In the cells, the Commander interviewed the long-serving cook in the presence of the Master-at-Arms and the Chief Petty Officer, who acted as interpreter.

'I told Wong Ah Lee that I knew everything and I wanted him to answer my questions truthfully. I cautioned him before he spoke. I said to him, "I want to know how much opium did you bring on board?" He said, "22¼lbs." This is exactly the weight of the opium found in the Captain's Galley.'

The mystery of the bundle of clothing and bags of heroin in the ship's laundry was solved a few weeks later when the No 1 Laundry Boy stepped forward and informed on his fellow laundryman.

'Lou Yang Hai has told me that the 3 lbs of heroin was given to him on board in Hong Kong by a friend,' he said.

Like the other two Chinese crewmen, forty-three-year-old father-of-four Lou Yang Hai had worked for the Royal Navy since 1950 and had an exemplary record, being described as 'keen, cheerful, obliging' – perhaps too obliging. The No 1 Laundry Boy handed the Commander a piece of paper, 'coloured on one side, blank on the other, which had clearly been scissored in two', observed Loram.

'The blank side had severed portions of three red rubber stamp markings and the paper had been cut across some Chinese markings obviously leaving the remainder of the markings on the part of the paper which had been scissored away,' he continued. 'Even so the name of Wong Lan Chui was decipherable. I was told by Lou Yang Hai that someone would come on board when the ship was in America with the other part of the paper and that if the markings matched up he was to hand over the sack and contents.'

Further investigation revealed letters on board belonging to Kan Ping Kwok, which exposed the Chinese seamen's involvement in a complex trading scheme.

'When I heard that you have decided to put on another package for me without having me pay cash for it, I am very grateful to you,' wrote a Hong Kong businessman to Kwok. 'I think it would be best to chip in another piece, if condition permits, and I will pay you when you return to Hong Kong. I leave everything to you.'

There were cryptic references to colleagues working on other ships travelling between Hong Kong, Singapore and America.

'The itinerary schedule is fine,' said the letter writer. 'I wish you would discuss this with Wong Pak [another potential member of the smuggling gang], and find out whether he would like to have him cooperate or not. If he would, let me know so I can write him a letter recommending him to them for co-operation. At the same time, we can make some spending money on the recommendation.'

Traditionally, would-be dealers had to pay a sum of money to their superiors within the Triad network. 'You can then give him a small gift,' said the letter writer, 'to seal up his friend for what he did.'

The letters also referred to the way that uniformed Chinese members of the *Belfast* crew were more useful to the smuggling operation.

'Because you are in civilian clothes, it is difficult for you to come and go,' Kwok was told. 'It is better to use him [in a uniform]. You can tell him that half of the stuff belongs to you and half of it belongs to the boss. In this way, your return would not be reduced, and at the same time, the danger of our enemy will be greatly reduced.'

When HMS *Belfast* finally arrived at Portsmouth in June 1962, the three Chinese crewmen were escorted to London, where they were charged with being in unlawful possession of opium and heroin. Wong Ah Lee admitted to being in receipt of 22 parcels of opium – 22¼ lb – for which he had paid $4,100 in Hong Kong. Kan Ping Kwok admitted taking on board a suitcase containing 26 packets of heroin – 9¾ lb – and 30 bags of opium – 17½ lb. The laundryman Lou Yang Hai admitted to receiving a sack containing two packets of heroin – 3 lb. The combined illicit value of this cache was estimated at £325,000.

'It is the biggest single haul of illicit drugs that has ever been made,' said the Crown prosecutor. 'It is a quantity far in excess of any illicit market which could be found in this country and there is no doubt that the majority of it, if not all, was destined for either South America or North America.'

For all these men, it meant the end of long and successful careers with the Royal Navy. Whether they were mules, compelled to smuggle drugs for their Triad masters, or were happily complicit in the entire business, we will never know. Perhaps knowing that their naval careers were coming to an end anyway, they wanted to put some extra money aside for their families in Hong Kong. Clearly, it was a complex operation that involved many other Chinese in Hong Kong and on other warships. How much more opium and heroin had the Royal Navy safely transported around the world for the Triads?

All three men pleaded guilty. Kan Ping Kwok was sentenced to five years in prison, Wong Ah Lee to four years, and the obliging Lou Yang Hai got 12 months. 'Quite clearly you were trafficking in this poison and using the cover of one of Her Majesty's ships in which to do it,' said the court recorder.

In August 1963, shortly after its infamous phase as a narcotics transporter, HMS *Belfast* was decommissioned. She is now a popular museum ship anchored in the River Thames opposite the Tower of London.

The massive profit margins of smuggling drugs for the Triads were not the only criminal temptations on offer in Hong Kong. Organised crime gangs exerted an enormous appeal for those figures supposed to be opposing them – the Hong Kong Police Force.

17

THE WHISTLE-BLOWING
INSPECTOR WALLACE

'I FEEL COMPELLED TO WRITE this letter to you, since I have a very heavy weight on my mind,' wrote Probationary Police Inspector Christopher St John Wallace. 'I believe that I can be helped only by a person I can trust completely, and who has the sufficient power to take action – should the case warrant it. The fact is I do not know who to trust in Hong Kong.'

Wallace's letter, dated 16 November 1963, was addressed to the British Prime Minister, Sir Alec Douglas-Home.

Wallace was 24 years old and from Staffordshire. Before coming to Hong Kong, he had worked his way around the world, sailing across the Atlantic with a yacht crew, cutting Christmas trees in Vancouver and working as a trainee manager for the Hudson Bay Company, a Canadian department store.

Having lived in the United States for several months and registered as an immigrant, Wallace received call-up papers for the US Army and served in a Military Police unit on the Panama Canal. From there, he returned to England to work briefly as a sales clerk for a Salford rubber company before qualifying to join the Hong Kong Police. He had been in the colony barely a year when he was shocked by what he saw.

'I feel it is my duty to tell you,' said Wallace to the Prime Minister, 'that this is an extremely corrupt police force – despite everything I've been told to the contrary. I feel so bad about this because it involves dangerous drugs, and all the misery and suffering they bring, not only to the people of Hong Kong but also of many other countries as well. And I feel that if it were not for the fact that this is a corrupt police force, this world menace, if not completely eliminated (where opium and heroin are concerned) could be dealt a very stunning blow.

'But of course,' Wallace continued, 'there is a tremendous amount of money involved, and this means that there is a great deal of power to back it up. I feel that an investigation from the outside would be of no avail. I think that it can only be dealt with from the inside – and it may take a long time to amount sufficient evidence so that the whole rotten system can be dealt with once and for all.'

Wallace had begun his own investigation by chatting to young inspectors like himself, who had also witnessed the corruption around them but felt unable to do anything about it because they were threatened with dismissal. The general feeling was that it was the detective sergeants who wielded the most power in this criminal network, but in most divisions many NCOs were thought to be 'in it up to their necks'.

The corruption began as soon as officers left the police training school. With families to support on low wages, the Chinese officers were most vulnerable. European officers took a little longer to bribe. Corruption among the Europeans would show itself in a more subtle way: when officers proved too effective at cracking down on gambling dens or drug dealers, they would find themselves after a while restricted to deskwork.

In order to discover how the system worked, Wallace himself took bribes.

'I have so far received $300 corruption money (which I sent to the Anti-Tuberculosis Campaign) and anticipate about another $500 at the end of the month,' he told the Prime Minister. 'I can assure you I intended to become involved, as I certainly would not know nearly as much as I do now had I refused to have anything to do with it.'

Wallace could not know the full extent of corruption within the police force, but he suspected that it involved every large station, with the exception of the Narcotics Bureau. He worked in the Kowloon City Division and considered this the most corrupt of them all, with the divisional superintendent and the chief inspector as its ringleaders.

'What I should like to do is to be able to trust my own PCs and NCOs,' he wrote in a later letter. 'And for them in turn to be willing – and able – to do police work as it should be done. The situation does not exist at the present where crime and vice (particularly dangerous drugs and gambling) are concerned.' He was informed by a senior officer in the Anti-Vice Squad that dangerous drugs were controlled by a 'syndicate' of officers and gangsters.

However, as Wallace looked further and further into the endemic corruption around him, the system began to suck him in and he started to see it from the other point of view. In one of his final letters, he expressed doubts that anything could be done about it.

'I am beginning to see that – though it goes against the grain – the advice of more senior officers may hold much wisdom. After all, this is a predominantly Chinese force, with a predominantly Chinese way of getting things done. They appear to be quite effective, though their methods leave much to be desired – which is why I think narcotics will continue to exist on the scale [they do] (as well as illegal gambling etc).'

'I am now of the opinion,' he admitted, 'that a purge on corruption in the HKP may do more harm than good, since it interferes with a traditional Chinese way of doing things, and because it is, by all accounts, a deeply embedded system within the force.'

But, just days later, Wallace changed his mind.

'I was temporarily misled,' he told the Prime Minister, 'into believing that it would be futile to try and fight something which has gone on for so long and has been accepted by so many. I regret having said this. I believe that Hong Kong, more than anywhere else perhaps, needs a good police force – and an honest one particularly.'

He concluded that a thorough investigation needed to be carried out into the integrity and effectiveness of the Anti-Corruption Branch of the Hong Kong Police. Despite the widespread bribery, he believed that other officers would come forward to tell the truth.

'I sometimes feel that it is all rather a bad dream,' Wallace confided in the Prime Minister. 'I have reached a point in my life where I am not too particular what happens to me. Even if I leave this colony penniless and in disgrace, at least I shall take my principles with me – and these are more precious to me than anything else.'

Police Inspector Wallace's heartfelt correspondence was received at 10 Downing Street in London by the Prime Minister's Private Secretary. He passed the letters on to the Commonwealth Relations

Office with a short note, saying the police officer 'is engagingly honest if perhaps impetuous – I shall acknowledge his letters and do no more about it'.

But Wallace had opened a can of worms. By writing to the Prime Minister, his complaints could not be ignored; something had to be done about it. That responsibility lay with Mr J.D. Higham at the Colonial Office, who felt compelled to bat the ball to Sir Robert Brown Black, British Governor of Hong Kong since 1958.

The first point Higham made was that in his letters to the Prime Minister, Wallace had admitted to taking a bribe; therefore, an investigation was required into the circumstances behind it. The implication, perhaps, being that it could be used as leverage against him, if need be. The second point concerned his direct approach to the Prime Minister rather than his going through the proper channels.

'This question of protocol is to some extent an embarrassment to all of us,' said Higham. 'Especially as, without consulting us, the Prime Minister's Private Secretary sent an acknowledgment to the first letter indicating that the Prime Minister would look into Wallace's allegations and saying that "to avoid any embarrassment to you I am sending this letter in a plain envelope". This latter point was no doubt made because Wallace had telegraphed the GPO asking that the first letter be returned – a request with which of course they were unable to comply.'

Higham had then investigated Wallace's background, looking at his Crown Agents recruitment papers.

'The letters show considerable naiveté,' Higham told the Governor of Hong Kong. 'It appears that Wallace is a rather earnest young man without much sense of humour but very keen on police work (at the time of his recruitment desperately anxious to get to Hong Kong). Having left school prematurely for financial reasons, he had studied privately to gain two A levels in order to qualify himself and had started to learn Cantonese.'

'The correspondence,' continued Higham, 'if it can be taken at its face value, confirms the impression given to the recruiters that here is a young man with a strong moral sense who is somewhat out of his depth in the very difficult situation with which we know you have to cope in Hong Kong; he obviously – from the way he keeps changing his mind – is under severe strain and is probably acting in this unorthodox way, not out of "bloody-mindedness" but rather from inexperience.'

Fortunately for Wallace, the Prime Minister's Office had taken a personal interest in the case and wanted to be informed of any investigation. Higham considered the next step was to discuss the matter in person with the Governor when he visited Hong Kong in January 1964.

'We know how deeply concerned you are with this problem of bribery and corruption,' ended Higham. 'Wallace's very amateur investigations are vitiated by the fact that he has been unable, by his own admission, to produce any firm evidence, and it is on this account, we gather, that he asks for a full enquiry.'

But there was still the matter of his admission to accepting a bribe.

'We tend to feel that from what we can judge of him here, from his interviews and these letters, that there are mitigating circumstances in the case which might perhaps mean that it could be disposed of, so far as he personally is concerned, without the imposition of a serious penalty.'

The threat to Wallace remained, but the case was not so easily swept under the carpet. Following a meeting between Higham, the Governor of Hong Kong and a senior police adviser, the following confidential statement was made to the Minister of State of the Colonial Office: 'While it is Hong Kong's view that the allegations grossly exaggerate the extent to which European Police Officers are implicated in corruption, there is no disposition locally to treat them other than seriously.'

And so, Wallace got exactly what he wanted: a thorough investigation of the Hong Kong Police. However, the author of the report was Henry Heath, Commissioner of Police of Hong Kong, and it turned into a ruthless exercise in damage limitation that did much to blacken the reputation of Wallace.

Heath began with a startling admission, appealing to the government's sense of realism. 'Corruption in Hong Kong is a deep-rooted evil,' he said, 'which is traditional in some circles. Few will deny its widespread existence and there is no reason to believe that members of the Police Force indulge in corrupt activities to a lesser extent than officers in other government departments who are confronted with comparable opportunity.'

Heath identified several forms of systemic corruption in Hong Kong. There was extortion, where, for example, a government officer sought out a victim, usually having committed a crime, who was threatened with exposure unless he paid the officer a bribe. Then there was bribery, where a government officer accepted cash on behalf of one party in return for some advantage in a business transaction, or simply to ensure an unspecified favour in the future, or as a gift or commission paid on the successful completion of a deal.

'The police officer is in constant touch with the public,' explained Heath, 'including the criminal elements, and sooner or later he must come into contact with the perpetrators of narcotic offences, gambling, prostitution and general vice. So long as vice and drug addiction continue, the police officer, especially below the rank of Superintendent, will find himself confronted with opportunity and temptation and there will be many who are ready to exploit his slightest weakness in order to obligate him to their own advantage.'

Such dealings, felt Heath, in the overall context of Hong Kong business practice, were more acceptable to the Chinese than they would be in some other communities.

'On the other hand,' said Heath, 'I am happy to state, there is a growing tendency among the criminal elements to resist this form of squeeze and the police officer who systematically indulges in it runs a risk of detection.

'Corruption does exist, and has existed for a long time among members of the Police Force but to no greater extent, I suggest, than elsewhere in Government where similar opportunities arise. Corruption in the Police Force is likely to be of the overt type more readily discernible and police action or inaction, success or failure, in the suppression of vice or in the handling of matters directly affecting the general public such as traffic control and motor vehicle licensing, are factors which easily give rise to allegations of corruption whether justified or not.'

The Police Commissioner believed that the police could also be victims of malicious gossip, in which it was presumed that the mere existence of vice and narcotic addiction was due to corruption.

'Since the liberation of the Colony, anti-corruption measures have been placed high on the list of police priorities,' he assured the British government. 'All senior officers have frequently been directed to give the matter constant and personal attention, especially corruption, which appears to stem from undetected vice and from drug addiction.

Police personnel are frequently lectured on the subject when senior officers, including myself, address large groups.'

He claimed several 'black sheep' had been weeded out and some officers failed to win promotion because of the suspicious manner in which they discharged their duties. Alongside this, measures had been taken to improve the housing, welfare facilities and pay of ordinary policemen, thus lessening the temptation for corruption.

'Working in these conditions,' said Heath, 'it is not difficult to see how a naive and impressionable young officer such as Wallace could leap to the most hasty and unfounded conclusions and become obsessed with the thought that every irregularity and every lost opportunity or the inability on the part of the police to eliminate any unlawful conduct may be due to corruption than to other causes.'

But there was another side to Wallace's short police career that Heath had to bring to the attention of his colonial superiors.

'For some weeks past' – prior to the January 1964 discussions about Wallace – 'rumours had reached Police Headquarters, Kowloon and the Anti-Corruption Branch that one or more European Inspectors in Kowloon had started the practice of conducting police raids against suspected narcotic and gambling establishments without making reports and without following up with official police action, such as prosecutions. The suspected motive was corruption, but it took some time to collect sufficient data for any real conclusions to be drawn.

'Wallace came under suspicion when rumours of his strange behaviour began to circulate. Evidence led to the belief that on occasions, alone, and on other occasions accompanied by police rank and file, he had systematically solicited and corruptly received bribes and on one occasion had demanded and received money in circumstances amounting to the original offence of robbery with violence. His victims were alleged to be persons accused of running opium divans [dens] or heroin stalls.'

According to his divisional superintendent, Wallace had 'gone rogue' – venturing into the Kowloon Walled City to conduct a gambling raid without warrant and without making an official report. On a second occasion, he had taken Chinese police constables away from their usual beats to assist him in raiding suspected vice establishments during his off-duty hours. As Heath saw it, the probationary police inspector was becoming a lone crime-busting machine – but without the sanction of his superiors.

As a result of these unorthodox actions, the divisional superintendent, Kowloon City Division, interviewed Wallace and came to the conclusion that the young man seemed to be distressed and had something on his mind. Shortly afterwards, Wallace revealed to other police officers that he had written to the Prime Minister. There was an immediate panic that the story might leak to the press before a full inquiry could be instituted. In the ensuing rapidly organised investigation, a number of officers serving in the Kowloon District were interviewed.

'It soon became clear that whatever the true facts,' said Heath, 'a fair number of inspectors, especially young officers in their first tour of service, believed in the existence of what they called the "system" which organised corruption in the Police Force. It was also obvious that there had been a great deal of loose talk among young inspectors undergoing their basic training on entering the Force, and undoubtedly some of them passed out of the Police Training School believing that organised corruption was rampant.'

Common gossip among trainee inspectors likened the 'system' to an 'omnibus', in that sooner or later an inspector would be propositioned by someone in the force to join the system and he could either 'get on the bus' or 'run alongside the bus', but in no circumstances, he was advised, 'should he get in front of the bus'.

One of the wilder allegations concerned a divisional superintendent who, it was said, was receiving $HK5 million (over £300,000) in bribes per month. Heath laughed this off as 'canteen gossip'. He did accept there were some lower-level examples of corruption, especially in relation to vice, where money was paid to officers to look the other way. But just one Chinese police constable was found guilty of acting as a go-between, offering payments to prevent action against a narcotics dealer. Charged on account of his irregular association with the keeper of a heroin divan, he pleaded guilty and was dismissed from the police force.

'Regarding the Inspectorate,' said Heath, 'I believe that corruption is not as widespread as the initial stages of this investigation appeared to indicate. Indeed, the inspectors recruited in recent years have a better educational and family background than many of their predecessors and it may well be that the loose talk and gossip on the subject of corruption of recent date is partly because of an increased number of inspectors who are themselves not corrupt.

'Although many have, I believe, acted from the most honest motives, it is unfortunate that they did not exercise a more adult sense of responsibility by reporting their knowledge or suspicions to senior officers instead of indulging in a whispering campaign which has led to an exaggeration of the real facts.'

Having found little to uphold the claims of widespread corruption, the Commissioner of Police turned his attention to Wallace. The probationary police inspector's admission of receiving a bribe meant he should face criminal prosecution, but Heath believed he had acted in good faith and the Deputy Public Prosecutor advised that the matter be dealt with inside the department. In March 1964, Wallace was transferred to the Frontier Division, where the assistant commissioner of his district was instructed to watch his progress.

'So far he shows poor prospects of measuring up to the required standard of conduct and efficiency for confirmation in the rank of Police Inspector,' noted Heath. 'He did reasonably well in his basic training course at the Police Training School, although the Commandant reported that he did not mix well with his fellow officers under training. He is a person who clearly keeps very much to himself and it is doubtful whether he has any real friends in the Force.'

Apparently, Wallace had been warned on several occasions for minor breaches of discipline, such as being late for duty, sub-standard turnout and general neglect of duty.

'He continued to commit minor breaches of discipline,' said Heath, 'and to perform his duties unsatisfactorily after his letters to the Prime Minister and after he was made aware that his allegations (which he said had caused him so much worry) had become the subject of detailed investigation.'

Since his transfer to the Frontier Division, Wallace's performance had shown little improvement. Senior officers continued to reprimand him and reported back that his beliefs concerning the problems of narcotic addiction and corruption seemed to dominate his life. Clearly, Wallace was being subjected to the most subtle of punishments for having spoken out. Mindful, however, of the interest of the Prime Minister's Office, Heath was careful to temper his criticism of the young man:

Mr Wallace is a very complex person and his letter writing to the Prime Minister and actions in Hong Kong and his beliefs have to be viewed against his make up. It is at present, doubtful whether he will turn out to be an efficient inspector of police and his services may, in due course, have to be terminated on those grounds. Meanwhile, however, no legal or disciplinary action is being taken against him. He will also not be disciplined for writing directly to the Prime Minister.

As to the general accusation of corruption within his police force, Heath believed it arose out of a culture clash, as young Britons arrived in Hong Kong and were confronted with Kowloon.

'Some of the European inspectors coming for the first time face to face with "squatter" conditions and vice, including narcotic addiction,' said Heath, 'find it hard to believe that such conditions could continue to exist without official connivance and they tend to draw the wrong conclusions.'

'I am satisfied that, although there is a long way to go,' he concluded, 'the climate of opinion and the attitude of mind of the junior officers of the Force is now moving steadily towards the rejection of corruption. Although there will be setbacks I consider much progress will be made during the coming years.'

With this thorough report, Heath had successfully defused Wallace's accusations and cast just enough doubt on the character of the young man to neutralise him as a figure of reform. The British government were satisfied with the police commissioner's combination of colonial realism and good intentions. Indeed, it was a model of imperial governance: the desire to do the right thing modified by the reality of the situation on the ground. It would take another ten years before the general clamour against police corruption in Hong Kong would reap some practical result.

A decade later, letters bearing allegations of corruption within the Hong Kong Police continued to command the attention of British politicians and civil servants. Winston Churchill MP, son of the great war leader, felt compelled to follow up the claims made by Pun Ting Chau in highly detailed accounts of police misconduct.

'I am a victim,' wrote Pun, 'to what are commonly known in Chinese communities as "Lo Chun Kuk" or "Tin Sin Kuk", swindles and collective corruption on the part of the Royal Hong Kong Police

Force, who have failed to take action on my complaints and orders from the Crown and Hong Kong Government.'

Pun recalled having a meeting in a Kowloon restaurant in June 1973 with a Chinese veteran police informer who spoke openly about Chinese police chiefs accepting kickbacks of 30 per cent of proceeds from gangsters who were happy to pay them 'blind-eye' money to ignore their rackets and swindles.

'Some serving members of the Royal Hong Kong Police Force often associate themselves with Triad society elements in illegal activities,' he alleged, 'and are working together almost as groups.'

Pun's series of letters failed to stimulate any meaningful response from senior officers in the Hong Kong Police, but once they started landing on the desks of British parliamentarians it was a different matter.

A similar series of allegations were made by Elsie Elliott, who had long lived in Kowloon. She wrote to the Foreign and Commonwealth Office in London and was furious at their tortuous response.

'So what actually happens is that I write to you and complain that a policeman has taken part in framing a driver,' she said. 'You ask the Colonial Secretary here, who asks the Commissioner of Police, who asks the Traffic Chief, who asks the Constable accused in the case, who denies that he did anything wrong. The reply then goes back to you and you answer to me: "This case has been investigated thoroughly by Her Majesty's Foreign & Commonwealth Office, and the Minister is satisfied that no framing took place and there is no justification for the allegation." This is the system that has permitted Hong Kong to become the centre of a world-wide drug trade and probably the most corrupt colony that ever was.'

Elliot went further, saying that if there were any future riots in Kowloon, it would be the fault of the British government for ignoring the concerns of its Hong Kong citizens.

'It does not surprise me that Britain has lost an empire,' she concluded. 'The dictatorship of the bureaucracy here does what it likes, with full support from [the] Government.'

This wave of complaints directed at senior figures in Britain finally had a satisfactory response in January 1974, with the launch of an Independent Commission Against Corruption (ICAC). Separate from the police, the commission reported directly to the governor of the colony. It superseded the anti-corruption branch of the police, which itself had been the target of many accusations, including those from Pun, who said they had forwarded his personal address to gangsters, who then visited him.

The immediate cause for the setting up of the ICAC had been the outrageous behaviour of Police Superintendent Peter Godber the previous year. Accused of receiving bribes, he fainted when the suspected crimes were read out to him. A subsequent search of his apartment revealed a large number of documents detailing his complicated financial resources, amounting to over $HK1 million, a figure later revised upwards to $HK4 million. While the investigation continued, Godber fled Hong Kong and returned to his home town in Sussex, where he managed to avoid extradition back to the colony because he had escaped before being formally charged. It confirmed everything so many Hong Kong citizens had suspected.

Spurred on by this incident, the ICAC were given the power to take a much tougher line against such suspects, including freezing their bank accounts and confiscating the travel documents of anyone accused of wrongdoing before they had been charged in a court of law. The very presence of the ICAC forced the Hong Kong Police into cracking down on the Triads and changing its relationship with them: an operation in July 1974 generated more than 3,000 racket-related arrests – double that of the previous year.

In the meantime, ICAC's investigation resulted in several headline-grabbing cases. In February 1975, a retired Chinese police officer told a court in Hong Kong how he had paid $HK25,000 to a chief superintendent to ensure he got the post of divisional superintendent.

'He was flicking his fingers at the time,' said the Chinese police officer. The corrupt chief superintendent raised two fingers, then five, indicating the sum of $HK25,000. He subsequently handed the wad of cash over and a few days later received his promotion.

Peter Godber was eventually extradited back to Hong Kong and in February 1975 was sentenced to four years in prison for corruption. Later that year, the first female Chinese superintendent was accused of holding assets disproportionate to her official income. She had joined the Hong Kong Police as an inspector in 1959, just four years before Christopher Wallace.

Finally, with the establishment of ICAC, the lonely crusade of the probationary police inspector had been vindicated.

18

THE GOLD-FINGERED MR KNOWLES

'THE FAR EAST IS A truly amazing place,' noted Eton-educated Roderic Knowles. 'It seemed to me, from my brief experience, that everybody, in all walks of life, was involved in some kind of racket.'

The revelation had come to him in the Mandarin Hotel in Hong Kong, as he chatted to a beautiful Chinese girl, waiting for a friend to arrive from Macao. Over lunch, he guessed she was a smuggler, taking diamonds into Manila with the assistance of a Filipino minister. It hadn't taken long for Knowles to recognise a fellow villain; he was, after all, engaged in his own racket: smuggling gold into Hong Kong.

For some time, there had been an illicit trade in gold from Hong Kong to India. The demand for gold in India was insatiable, thanks to its cachet as a wedding gift. The bureaucratic government of India in the 1950s had set a high price for it, making it much more expensive in the subcontinent than in the rest of Asia. With a free market for gold in Macao, Chinese criminal syndicates could see a fortune to be made if they shipped the precious metal via Hong Kong to India. The Indian rupee was also highly valued as a currency, so the Asian gold trader would receive payment in rupees in Kuwait, where there was a lively black market in currencies.

There were no export restrictions on gold leaving either Macao or Hong Kong, but there were tough import restrictions in India, where the authorities had to be told of every shipment, so smuggling was the only way to get the gold into India and make a vast profit. In June 1954, 560 bars of gold, valued at about £61,000, were found in the hold of the *Eastern Queen* by Calcutta customs inspectors. Three years later, another hoard of gold was uncovered aboard the *Eastern Saga*, hidden behind panelling in the crew's quarters. The discovery resulted in a massive fine for the Indo-China Steam Navigation Company – they paid up, rather than have the ship confiscated, accepting there was little they could do about it.

'The existence throughout their vessels of panelling,' said a Ministry of Transport investigator, 'made of some light and easily cut material, covering up the steel bulkheads but leaving cavities a few inches wide, provides any dishonest member of the crew with an ideal place for secreting contraband during the voyage. This panelling is erected in the crew's quarters in order to make the vessels comply with the current standards of accommodation of first class ships.'

It was a catch-22 for the ship owners. They had to enforce the international standards of accommodation set in the UK, but to investigate every nook and cranny on board for smuggled gold was an impossible task.

'In order to discover whether or not in any place the panelling has been tampered with,' explained the Ministry of Transport, 'it would be necessary on each voyage virtually to strip the vessel of all the multifarious objects which, of necessity, have to be attached in one way or another to panelling, and to examine with the greatest care the paintwork of the panelling all over its surface in every place. Such a search [would] involve expense and delay, which would [negate] the commercial profitability of the voyage.'

Gold-smuggling fines were thus accepted as another business cost by the shipping company. Besides, stashing the precious metal within the make-up of the ship itself was not the only method of smuggling it abroad:

> Gold has been discovered in the persons of crew members coming through the dock gates after leaving Owner's vessels at Calcutta. The gold ingots which are only a few inches long are invariably concealed in the bodily cavities of the Chinese crew.

A decade later, in 1968, 30-year-old Roderic Knowles decided that smuggling gold into India was too risky. He calculated that a profit could be made instead by buying gold in Belgium and selling it tax-free onto the Hong Kong black market. His margin of profit depended on the volume he could transport from Brussels to Hong Kong and the number of trips that could be achieved in a week.

By reinvesting the profits made on early transfers into larger consignments of gold, Knowles reckoned that, on three flights a week into the colony, he and his public schoolboy couriers could make over a quarter of a million pounds a year. Rather than securing the gold ingots in their body cavities like the Calcutta sailors, they took a more elegant approach, packing the gold in specially designed corsets tightly strapped around their bodies beneath their Savile Row suits or Carnaby Street jackets.

The stepson of Lord Swinfen, Knowles recruited his carriers through the personal column in *The Times*. Interviewing a succession of young men, he was struck by one dressed in the fashionable style of 'swinging' London in the late 1960s. Completely unfazed by the prospect of smuggling gold halfway round the world, the cool young gentleman added just one caveat – 'I'll have to be particularly careful there, as so many of my friends are members of the jet set.'

'First-rate material,' concluded Knowles, happy to employ a man about town similar to himself.

One young man attracted to the personal ad turned out to be an undercover journalist, who exposed the racket in an article for the *Sunday Times*. But Knowles was too media savvy to let that stop him. He immediately put out his own story, saying the gold-smuggling interviews were a hoax, including a photograph of his girlfriend modelling the corsets, with a policeman in the background.

With the *Sunday Times* made to look foolish, Knowles proceeded with the smuggling project, but soon a change in the value of gold meant its price fell and threw out all his calculations. With only a modest profit to be made from smuggling gold into Hong Kong, he turned to another part of the Far East – Korea – where the cost of gold was twice that of the standard world price.

In order to pursue this new venture, Knowles was introduced to the Hong Kong-born manager of a branch of the Bank of America in Seoul, South Korea. The bank manager had contacts in the Korean black market, but it was with a different proposition that he attempted to recruit the young Etonian. The bank insider told Knowles he was willing to sell the secret code for bank money transfers in return for a piece of the action. It seemed too good to be true – vast sums of money shifted around the world with a simple telephone call and a number quoted. This beat all their smuggling missions.

Used to international money deals, Knowles agreed to collaborate with the Bank of America manager. They decided on locations in Europe where the risks of banks double-checking the transactions would be minimal. They settled on a date in August 1968, a Hong Kong bank holiday. With everything in place, the corrupt manager sent two telegrams via Hong Kong, each authorising the transfer of $150,000, one to a bank in Geneva, the other in Amsterdam. As agreed, Knowles and his partners were waiting at the other end in Europe, ready to pick up the money. It worked well in Geneva, as the supervising Swiss bank manager was out at lunch, but in Amsterdam the bank officials became suspicious and decided to check the details with the intermediary Hong Kong bank. From that point on, it all quickly went wrong.

'A white-haired middle-aged gentleman, who looked exceedingly like a cop, walked past,' recalled Knowles of the day of the bank transfer in Amsterdam. He then noticed other men loitering around. '"Hey, Roderic!" one of them yelled, as if he had known me a very long time. Replying or not was of no consequence. The game was up.'

Knowles was arrested and sentenced to a year in prison. One of his partners, based in Hong Kong, got a heavier sentence of four years. In the end, it turned out that the corrupt Bank of America employee was not who he appeared to be. He was, in fact, a CIA agent. According to information later passed on to Knowles, the CIA had set up the English gold-smuggling team, having trailed their activities for some time and found their illicit gold was ending up in communist North Vietnam – helping to finance the war against the Americans.

The CIA agent had fed Knowles and his partners the Bank of America code because the sentence for gold smuggling in Hong Kong was relatively light; for bank fraud, the penalty was a substantial prison term, it being regarded as a much more serious offence in the colony. Thus, the American agents had crushed Knowles's gold-smuggling antics. It was lucky for him that he was caught in Amsterdam; had he been extradited, he would have faced a far longer sentence.

After his spell in a Dutch prison, Knowles returned to business in the Far East, but this time legitimately, as an investment banker.

However, the lure of gold proved too much for him and he re-visited the idea of doing business with India, the world's biggest gold market.

Aside from being smuggled into India from Hong Kong, the precious metal was also supplied via the UK by merchant bankers who lawfully passed it from South African mines to Dubai, then handed it over to Arab fishing dhows equipped with high-powered Rolls-Royce engines, who smuggled it into the subcontinent. Latterly, Swiss banks had taken over the supply of gold but still used the Dubai route.

Having set up a company called Gold Intelligence Services, providing information on gold markets to UK merchant banks, Knowles was flying from Singapore to Bangkok. At 40,000 feet in the air, he was struck by an idea.

He recalled: 'Sri Lanka is about 25 kilometres from the coast of India. If one could persuade the Government of Sri Lanka to allow the setting up and operating of an External Market for Gold in Sri Lanka, the Swiss/Dubai monopoly could be wiped out over night.'

Knowles approached a London merchant bank and they agreed to back him, despite his background in gold smuggling.

'I was quite open about it,' he said. 'I arrived blind in Sri Lanka with no contacts, but by the time I left I knew all the key political players personally, from the Prime Minister downwards. The Finance Minister, a cricket-loving capitalist parading as a Trotskyite, welcomed the project, so long as he could be assured of certain benefits to his party. The only problem was that the Sri Lankan Government was about to abolish its Free Rice to the People programme and it would be political suicide for him to approve my project with the certainty of headlines saying he was taking rice from the poor to give gold to the rich.'

As the Sri Lankan government dithered, Knowles decided to get some competition into the deal and wooed the Prime Minister of the Maldives, another former British colony. He let the information slip to Sri Lanka and within 24 hours the reluctant Finance Minister had agreed to the deal and signed it at Lord's cricket ground in London.

'I was now destined to be Mr 5%,' remembered Knowles excitedly. The great wealth he had been working towards for so long was now within his grasp.

'A week later, after months of flying backwards and forwards to Sri

Lanka, the price of gold, which had always been fixed, was allowed to float on international markets. Gold suddenly became cheaper in India! The contract and project was now worthless.'

After so much investment in time and travel, it was a considerable blow to Knowles. But, just as he wondered what on earth he could do next, another proposal came his way. The CIA had maintained their interest in him as a gentleman who could pull together elaborate schemes.

'I was approached by a guy called Miles Copeland [a senior CIA officer],' said Knowles, and they discussed a number of bizarre ideas. 'One was to sell a dummy nuclear bomb to Colonel Gaddafi of Libya. He was being a pain in the ass to the West at the time and we could embarrass him hugely.

'Miles liked the idea and said he was sure he could get the full cooperation of the CIA, and he was just off to the USA and would discuss it with them. Unknown to me, US policy had changed, and the US government decided on a policy of appeasement with Gaddafi. Instead of informing me of the decision, they decided to blow it . . . in an ungentlemanly way, but quite amusing.'

They leaked the story to the media, saying falsely that Knowles had disappeared to Moscow with the advance payment of £1.5 million he had received from the Libyans for the fake bomb. A girlfriend was later surprised when he turned up in London. But, then again, his friends expected such tall tales from him.

What was it that kept this relatively privileged young man so interested in pursuing gold-plated schemes in the Far East?

'My early youth passion was philosophy,' he admits now. 'Not academically, but authentically as the search for Truth. I chose to see life as a game, and to play, which included many a form of risk-taking and adventuring. I also decided, as part of that playing, to go fortune-hunting, with little interest in money but a great interest in the challenges in acquiring it.

'But one day my understanding of the game of life changed. In seeking help to get the approval of the Indian Prime Minister on a project, I had enlisted the willing support of the acclaimed holy man Swami Muktananda. He said to me the Game of Life is not as you think. It's played on another level and there are rules to the game you have not yet discovered. I resolved to go back on my quest, this time with a difference. There appeared a choice between Wisdom or Wealth.'

One of the last imperial adventurers ultimately turned his back on his elaborate money-making projects and is now a mystic philosopher living happily in Ireland.

As the British Empire entered its twilight period in South-East Asia, narcotics warlords fought over control of the illicit drugs trade. The British Ambassador in Bangkok reported one particular opium battle being fought in August 1967 on the Thai–Laotian–Burmese border between druglord Chan Chi Fu and Kuomintang (KMT) gangsters.

Half-Chinese, half-Burmese Chan was the main opposition to the KMT gangsters, who had muscled into the narcotics business in the region since they had fled from communist China. Chan had hijacked a KMT opium train in Burma, so the Chinese nationalist generals were hungry for revenge.

Chan had brought ten tons of opium into Laos on pack animals from Burma to be delivered to an airstrip on the Laotian side of the Mekong River. As Chan approached the airstrip, the KMT sprang their trap. Some 900 heavily armed KMT troops opened fire on the mule train. But Chan had powerful friends in Laos who resented the intrusion of the nationalists on their territory and Laotian aircraft came screaming in, bombing and strafing the KMT gunmen.

Burmese trucks arrived with ammunition for Chan's men and they fought off the nationalist assault, keeping their opium. Under this intense fire, the KMT lost half their men; the Laotian commander told American agents he would use napalm and fragmentation bombs to drive out 'the invaders'.

'According to the Americans,' said the British Ambassador, 'this particular gang of [KMT] Chinese bandits are ruffians, even by the standards of that area. They have proved so unamenable that even Taiwan will have nothing to do with them.'

Chan Chi Fu kept his grip on the opium trade until he was imprisoned by the Burmese government in 1969 for being too close to the Shan separatist movement. After five years, he came out of jail, taking the Shan name of Khun Sa – under which he became even more infamous – and recruited a new army. Over the next two decades, he manipulated the Shan cause so that he ended up controlling more than half of the opium passing through the Golden Triangle, which amounted to half the world's heroin supply.

'He has delivered as much evil to this world as any Mafia don has done in our history,' said a US Drug Enforcement Administration officer.

Much of this avalanche of opium was destined for Hong Kong.

By 1970, the colony was Britain's last major overseas territory. The increasing influx of narcotics was playing havoc with the British government's efforts to maintain law and order. So much so, that Sir David Trench, Governor of Hong Kong, sent a report to the Foreign and Commonwealth Office in London alerting them to the spiralling crime rates. Murder and robbery were up dramatically and lurid newspaper articles regularly reported Hong Kong citizens being hacked and killed in Triad-related assaults.

'The problems we are facing have no political roots,' said Sir David. 'Indeed, among our critics for permitting the current violence are – not unexpectedly – the Communists, who lose no opportunity of ridiculing our efforts to deal with the situation, while finding our Western ways and our Western pursuit of affluence to be the causes of it.'

The Governor blamed the influence of the Triads, as well as the high population density of the island.

'The really disturbing fact is that the carrying of weapons, chiefly knives, sharpened files and other cutting weapons, is far more prevalent than it was,' continued Sir David. 'There is a very unpleasant tendency towards a far greater readiness on the part of our younger criminals, who are proportionately on the increase, to use them hastily, needlessly and viciously.'

Gang fights had rocketed from 69 in 1968 to 153 in the first half of 1970, as low-level Triad factions fought for domination of the streets. Armed robberies were up, too.

'All this is causing widespread disquiet,' said the Governor. 'There is a marked surge of Chinese opinion in favour of much stronger measures being used against those who perpetrate acts of violence. The recent conviction of three youths on a charge of murder resulting in the imposition of the death sentence was greeted with widespread and undisguised approval.'

In an effort to hold back the crime wave, the Hong Kong Police stepped up its stop-and-search operations, introduced road blocks and raided gang-related premises, resulting in the capture of a large array of dangerous weapons. Despite these measures, Sir David believed the maintenance of law and order was being let down by the introduction of increasingly liberal methods of punishment. Hong Kong criminals had been deterred by the threat of deportation, but neither the Taiwanese nor the Chinese communists were willing to have gangsters dumped on them. As for younger criminals, the courts, under the influence of the UK, were not imprisoning them.

'What is so concerning people here,' concluded Sir David, 'is that they are both unused to violent crime in Hong Kong and aware of how bad it can get amongst their own people when it gets out of control. In the present state of Chinese public opinion, therefore, we need to show we are taking remedial action to the best of our ability. We need to try to meet the criticism that an excessively "progressive" attitude to crime and punishment in the past has brought about this deterioration – which, indeed, may well be true. But at the same time we shall have to take care to keep things in proportion and avoid excessive and unacceptable ways of dealing with offenders.'

When the Governor's alarming report arrived in London, it did not especially upset the Foreign and Commonwealth official who received it.

'We agree that the figures are disturbing,' came the response, 'but the pattern is the same in many other places and is, I am afraid, symptomatic of the times in which we live.'

Crime figures in Birmingham were then dispatched to show that Hong Kong's crime wave was little different from that experienced in several British cities!

Two years later, a new Governor of Hong Kong, Sir Murray MacLehose, alerted the British government to the fact that the colony was a major centre of drugs trafficking. Known affectionately as the 'Jock in the Sock', the Glaswegian governor pulled no punches.

'Our estimate is that the Colony now has not less than 60,000 drug addicts,' he said, 'and probably considerably more, out of a population of four million – proportionally one of the highest, if not the highest, in the world. Its geographical position astride the main communications routes in the area has made it almost inevitable that Hong Kong should also have become a centre of the illicit trade in narcotics.'

The Governor estimated that fifty tons of raw opium and ten tons of morphine were imported illegally into Hong Kong every year. The colony was a major producer of heroin from imported opium, which was exported clandestinely to the United Kingdom, the United States, Canada and Australia. Total turnover of the underworld drugs business in Hong Kong was estimated to amount to $HK1 million a day. The Americans joined in the disapproval of Hong Kong's criminal reputation.

'Its well organised, secretive, criminally oriented groups,' thundered a report to the US House of Representatives in Washington DC, 'provide the brains and banking required to operate a sophisticated narcotics trafficking ring. As a widely-used, international free port, it provides the trafficker an excellent point for trans-shipment of heroin and other opiates to their ultimate destinations, including the United States.'

Vast shipments of narcotics were hitting the streets all across the western world. In June 1972, two Hong Kong Chinese stepped off a BOAC flight at Heathrow airport in London. When the customs officers went through their luggage, they hauled out a bedroll tucked inside a kit bag. Taking a knife, they slit open the bedding and out tumbled 50 packs of heroin. It was part of the biggest haul of heroin smuggled into the UK at that time, worth approximately £350,000 to its distributors. One of the smugglers, a 53-year-old Chinese restaurant owner, was sentenced to nine years in prison; the other received eight years.

Shortly afterwards, the Governor of Hong Kong appointed a Commissioner of Narcotics to deal with the rampant problem. The commissioner got a surprising break in December 1972.

'I was approached in Hong Kong by a Yunnanese gentleman whom I have known on and off for a number of years,' he said. 'He told me that Law Sing-hon, who is the principal trafficker in illicit opium and its derivatives in the region of Burma adjacent to Laos and Thailand and who controls the area, had contacted him in the Colony by courier.'

The courier produced a document in which the 37-year-old Law Sing-hon – more widely known as Lo Hsing Han – detailed his involvement in the trade in Burma and how Kuomintang troops protected it. These irregulars, mostly Yunnanese, formed an army called the Burma Self-Defence Force. At the end of the letter, Law said he wanted to get out of the opium business and wanted the informant to arrange a meeting with the Americans on the Thai–Burmese border to see what could be done to that end.

CIA and US Bureau of Narcotics and Dangerous Drugs officers stationed in Hong Kong flew out with the informant to meet Law

Sing-hon on the Thai side of the border with Burma. He showed them no fewer than 24 opium-refining factories. He then put forward his outline for ending the illicit traffic in Burmese opium.

'The Americans are reported to have made it clear to Law Sing-hon,' said the Commissioner, 'that they could not engage in any programme of crop substitution in Burma without the concurrence of the Burmese Government in Rangoon – a Government for which Law expressed complete contempt, declaring that he was "The Government" in this region.'

Without committing themselves to any further action, the Americans passed his proposal on to their superiors in Washington.

'Why Law should want to get out of the opium business and have made an approach to the Americans at this period in time is not clear,' stated the Commissioner. 'He is only a young man and maybe sees himself becoming an international outlaw and an embarrassment the Burmese Government may feel obliged to liquidate. He has been pilloried in the press recently and is notorious as one of the world's major opium traffickers.

'On the other hand,' considered the Commissioner, 'he may have made so much money that he can well afford to get out of the trade and may hope to redeem his character by lining up with the Americans in a campaign to stamp out opium growing and trafficking. Perhaps a combination of both is somewhere near the truth. But before he goes he is astute enough to realise that provision must be made for the future livelihood of the opium growers and his troops.'

That, as always, was the problem. How could a native population so used to the benefits coming from producing the raw material of the narcotics trade be enabled to swap that for an alternative income? As the Commissioner concluded, it would need agreement between Law and the socialist Burmese government to allow pacification, crop substitution and resettlement in order to stop drug trafficking and heroin manufacture. That seemed unlikely, bearing in mind Law's attitude to the Burmese government and the endless vicious feuding between narcotics warlords in the region.

The Hong Kong Narcotics Commissioner's report was a tantalising account of how even a drugs baron might want to halt the flow of illicit drugs in the Golden Triangle, but it didn't mean anything would really change.

The reason why Law perhaps wanted to get out of the drugs business came later in 1973, when he was arrested by the Thai government for his alliance with the rebel Shan army. Shan commander Khun Sa (the former Chan Chi Fu) took over his business.

Initially sentenced to death, Law was released in 1980 and went back to the narcotics trade, rebuilding his empire. A decade later, he was re-investing his criminal millions in legitimate construction and energy projects in Singapore, and managed also to keep close sanction-busting relations with the Burmese dictatorship. Having blown their links with him in the 1970s, the Americans had long lost their opportunity to deal with him.

Sir Murray MacLehose, Governor of Hong Kong, was equally wary of suggesting a quick fix for the narcotics problems faced by the colony.

'The fact is that the eradication of drug abuse and illicit drug trafficking in Hong Kong lies largely outside our control,' he lamented. 'We shall do what we can, but an effective solution can only be found with the co-operation of other countries in this area.'

The Jock in the Sock understood this would involve persistent negotiations with Thailand, Burma and Laos, and that the Americans, with the United Nations, were the only ones who could exert any kind of pressure on these governments to change their ways.

'I realise that, particularly in Burma, where production is greatest and government control least effective, the difficulties will be enormous and the necessary financial assistance considerable,' he said. 'I recognise that the action I have proposed in the international field will be delicate, laborious and probably expensive. But something must be done, and be done soon, if we are to make real headway against this problem, which is as serious for its social effects on the Colony as it is for the international reputation of its British administration.'

The irony was that 70 years after the British had hoped to wipe their hands of the opium trade, it was causing their imperial administrators an even greater headache. Indeed, it might well have been better for all concerned if the British Empire had kept its monopoly on the opium trade and policed it more effectively. Instead, it was now run by Asian opium barons whose activities were far beyond its reach.

The Walled City of Kowloon remained the dark symbol of uncontrolled crime in Hong Kong in the 1970s. Its fetid, enclosed alleyways haunted by emaciated addicts, gaunt prostitutes and Triad gangsters continued to dissuade police from entering. Christian missionary Jackie Pullinger famously ventured into its shadowy labyrinth, describing a grotesque world comprising illegal dog restaurants and child prostitutes. Everything was stolen from the outside world, including the electricity, tapped from the public supplies by a tangle of wires.

> But you cannot steal sanitation, so excrement must be emptied into the stinking alleys below. At street level there are two toilets for all thirty thousand people; the 'toilets' consist of two holes over overflowing cesspools, one for women, one for men.

Yet, within this hell, Pullinger found a certain kind of order. There were schools, and she even managed to make Christian converts among the Triad gangsters.

'Despite its reputation, the Walled City is relatively crime-free compared with the neighbouring parts of Kowloon,' noted a government official. The reason for this was that organised criminals abhorred disorganised crime and thieves were regularly disciplined by Triad gangsters. Most of the poor people within the Walled City were employed by drug dealers. It was only when anti-vice campaigns began to have some impact on the slum that its inhabitants were compelled to turn to robbery. The worst danger was from fire. It was impossible for the emergency services to negotiate the maze of alleyways and when a building was weakened by fire, it simply collapsed.

Whenever the Hong Kong government tried to do something about the Walled City, they came up against the problem that it fell within disputed territory. Under the original agreement with Peking in 1898 – by which the New Territories of Hong Kong were leased for 99 years – Chinese officials had been allowed to exercise jurisdiction within Kowloon, so long as it did not clash with British interests. For 20 years after the Second World War, the Chinese communists had ignored the growing slum, but when the British tried to clear and resettle some of its inhabitants, local communists kicked up a fuss.

Despite this political mischief-making, the British slowly but surely began to clear up the Walled City. It began with successfully opposing the building of illegally constructed tower blocks on the edge of the slum. Then, when a building fell down or there was an outbreak of disease, the

Hong Kong government would help to re-house the inhabitants. All of this was done without force, as the communists knew they could not be seen to oppose the humanitarian action of the British.

In 1984, the British government under Prime Minister Margaret Thatcher signed the Sino-British Joint Declaration in which the ending of the lease of 99 years over the New Territories was extended to include Hong Kong Island and Kowloon. Britain agreed to hand over its last major overseas territory to the Chinese in 1997.

Buoyed by her successful resistance to Argentine tyranny in the Falklands War of 1982, Thatcher had initially hoped to turn the prosperous colony into a democratic self-governing state like Singapore, but unrelenting communist Chinese opposition and the subsequent damage political uncertainty might do to the Hong Kong business community frustrated that. Instead, the 'one country, two systems' concept was agreed by both sides – an approach originally designed by the communists to deal with the nationalist enclave of Taiwan.

With this agreement, the Walled City was no longer a political hot potato for the Hong Kong government and both communist Chinese and British agreed to its demolition. A series of successful police raids had broken the power of the Triads within the slum and, when the time came, there were no major demonstrations against its destruction. More than $HK2 billion was spent on compensating the residents and those businessmen who ran factories in the teeming slum. By 1993, the Walled City was ready to be knocked down. A year later, work had begun on transforming the site into the Kowloon Walled City Park. Remnants of the old Walled City, including its inscribed stone South Gate, are dotted around the greenery.

If the handing over of Hong Kong to China in 1997 signified the end of the British Empire at the close of the twentieth century, the demolition of its Walled City marked the conclusion of its fight against organised crime throughout that dominion. It had been a long and highly determined crusade against the dark forces unleashed by its own frequently well-meaning policies. But nothing changed overnight and, although it is now no longer the responsibility of its colonial police, the trade routes established by that imperial global trading network will continue to be hijacked by crooks, gangsters, smugglers and narcotics warlords for many years to come – and in that battle the British still have a part to play.

NOTES ON SOURCES

MUCH OF THE MATERIAL FOR this book has been uncovered from government papers in the British National Archives, Kew. The abbreviations of the principal collections are:

CO – Records of the Colonial Office
FO – Records of the Foreign Office
FCO – Records of the Foreign and Commonwealth Office
WO – Records of the War Office & Armed Forces
KV – Records of the Security Service
MEPO – Records of the Metropolitan Police Office
CRIM – Records of the Central Criminal Court
HO – Records of the Home Office
CAB – Records of the Cabinet Office
PREM – Records of the Prime Minister's Office

CHAPTER 1

The case of Mr Hartley, his trials and tribulations, is chronicled in several documents within the British National Archives, File FO 46/669, principally 'In Her Britannic Majesty's Court for Japan', a signed statement by Hartley, dated 17 April 1890; Hartley's 'Claims against the Japanese Government', 5 May 1890; and Hartley's letter to the Marquess of Salisbury, 31 July 1897. Mr Bryce's comments in the House of Commons report in *The Times*, 25 June 1886; see also 'Importation of Opium into Japan', *The Times*, 7 February 1879. *Economist* quote from James, *The Rise and Fall of the British Empire* (London: Little, Brown, 1994).

Early Gladstone quote from Hansard record of House of Commons

Debate on 8 April 1840, volume 53, cc749-837. *The Times* editorial quote, 3 December 1842. Lawson, Duff and later Gladstone quotes from Hansard record of House of Commons Debate on 10 May 1870, volume 201, cc480-524.

Indian Royal Commission quote from lecture by John Richards, 'Opium and the British Indian Empire: The Royal Commission of 1895', Cambridge, 23 May 2001. See also Hanes and Sanello, *The Opium Wars* (London: Robson Books, 2003).

CHAPTER 2

Roos-Keppel's four-page report of clash with Hakim Khan and his gang at Tarnab, dated 2 March 1911, from Liddel Hart Centre for Military Archives, King's College London, File PP Donlea, Item 1. See also 'Indian Frontier: 23 Outlaws Killed', *The Times*, 2 March 1911, and Caroe, *The Pathans* (London: Macmillan, 1958). For gang raid on train, see 'Train Attacked by Pathan Outlaws', *The Times*, 22 December 1913.

Two quotes on illicit arms trade quoted from T.R. Moreman, 'The Arms Trade on the NW Frontier of India 1890–1914', *Journal of Imperial and Commonwealth History*, Volume 22, Issue 2, 1994. Basra shipping robbery recounted in letter of 28 May 1912 to British Consul in British National Archives, File FO 602/27. MacFarlane's tale told in 'Draper's Adventures Among the Turks', *The Times*, 7 December 1912. Further accounts in 'Gun-Running in the Persian Gulf', *The Times*, 30 December 1910, and 'British Interests in the Persian Gulf', *The Times*, 8 July 1911.

Roos-Keppel's letter to Secretary to the Government of India, from Camp Simla, 3 August 1909, including 'Note on the Adam Khel Gun-Runners' by J.L. Maffey, political agent, Khyber, contained in India Office Library & Records, File L/PS/7/230. Translation of Roos-Keppel's notification to the Maliks, greybeards and men of the Para Chamkanni, 9 March 1899, in India Office Library & Records, File L/PS/7/113. Caroe quotes on Roos-Keppel in *The Pathans* (London: Macmillan, 1958). Keppel quotes on fighting gunrunners on Makran Coast from Keppel, *Gun-Running and the Indian North-West Frontier* (London: John Murray, 1911). Critical comments on expeditions against gunrunners, including that of Colonel Holdich, who served on the North-West Frontier, in Fraser, L., 'Gun-Running in the Persian

Gulf', proceedings of the Central Asian Society, London, read on 17 May 1911. Roos-Keppel's obituary in *The Times*, 12 December 1921.

CHAPTER 3

'Shipping Merchant's Death', *The Times*, 24 August 1918; 'Miss Carleton's Death,' *The Times*, 13 December 1918; 'Chinatown Opium Traffic', *The Times*, 14 December 1918; 'Carleton Inquest', *The Times*, 24 January 1919; and several other articles covering the de Veulle trial, including 'De Veulle Sent to Prison', *The Times*, 8 April 1919. See also 'West End Dope Parties', *News of the World*, 15 December 1918; 'Cocaine from East Africa', *The Times*, 19 May 1919; 'An Overdose of Heroin', *The Times*, 27 January 1922. Delevingne quote from the chapter he wrote for Linstead, *Poison's Law* (London: The Pharmaceutical Press, 1936).

The criminal career of Won Tip is contained in several letters and documents in a Metropolitan Police File at the British National Archives, MEPO 3/430, including letter from Special Branch, dated 9 April 1927; Central Police Office Liverpool, 8 June 1927; Special Branch, 20 June 1927; Liverpool City Police, 14 July 1927; and the report by Chief Inspector H. Burgess, 8 December 1924.

Chang quotes from *News of the World*, 30 April 1922, and British National Archives, File MEPO 3/469. For more details on Brilliant Chang and Chinatown drugs world, see Morton, *East End Gangland* (London: Little, Brown, 2000), Kohn, *Dope Girls* (London: Granta, 2001) and Berridge, V., 'The Origin of the English Drug "Scene" 1890–1930', *Medical History*, 32:51–64 (London: UCL, 1988). George Sims's account of a London opium den reproduced in the *Ashburton Guardian*, Canterbury, New Zealand, 14 March 1919; see also Chrysler, *White Slavery* (Chicago: Alice Shellbarger Hall, 1911). Fu Manchu quote from Rohmer, *The Mystery of Dr Fu Manchu* (London: Methuen, 1913).

Chinese accusation of British opium corruption, 1 May 1920, in British National Archives, File CO 873/301. Chinese imperial decree criticising Chinese governors, 27 September 1910, in British National Archives, File FO 233/133, and Foreign Office report coming to similar conclusion in FO 881/8725.

CHAPTER 4

Russell Pasha quotes and details of life from his memoirs, *Egyptian Service 1902–1946* (London: John Murray, 1949), Seth, *Russell Pasha* (London: William Kimber, 1966) and his obituary in *The Times*, 12 April 1954.

Ministry of the Interior report on Cypriot drug dealers in Alexandria, 28 November 1928, in British National Archives, File FO 141/471/1, also contains case of Melissaratos and Loverdos, memorandum from Sir Malcolm Delevingne, 3 July 1928, and letter from Egypt's supreme judge, Sir Wasey Sterry, 12 November 1928. Oriental Products Company smuggling case described in Cairo Residency Paper, 15 December 1928, British National Archives, File FO 141/471/2.

CHAPTER 5

Quotes from Anslinger and details of his life and career from Anslinger and Oursler, *The Murderers – the Story of the Narcotics Gangs* (London: Arthur Barker Ltd, 1962) and McWilliams, *The Protectors – Harry J. Anslinger and the Federal Bureau of Narcotics 1930–1962* (Newark: University of Delaware Press, 1990).

Clash between British and Americans over opium smuggling from North Borneo to the Philippines described in several documents in the British National Archives, File CO 874/914, including letter from American chargé d'affaires to Lord Curzon; statement from US Secretary of War, 9 March 1921; letter from Sir J. West Ridgeway, Secretary of North Borneo Company, to Colonial Office, 13 April 1921; and letter from Governor of North Borneo, 9 April 1921.

Tong description from Ashbury, *The Gangs of New York* (New York: Garden City Publishing, 1927). Canadian police reports on narcotics smuggling into Canada and US by Howe and Deleglise in early 1920s contained in British National Archives, File MEPO 3/425. FBI memorandum quoting Federal Bureau of Narcotics information on Diamond and Luciano visiting Germany in FBI files 39-2141 section 1. Reference to Del Grazio in 'Seized in Germany on Narcotic Charge', *New York Times*, 6 December 1931. For full details, see Newark, *Lucky Luciano* (St Martin's Press: New York, 2010).

CHAPTER 6

Delevingne letter to Prince Charoon, 12 January 1927; Paskin's letter to British North Borneo Company, 12 August 1927; Sir Edward Cook's response, 'Opium: Namazie and others', 10 September 1927: all in British National Archives, File CO 129/502/9. Clementi's telegram, outlining Hong Kong experiment, 12 December 1927; Cabinet meeting notes and Delevingne memorandum opposing Hong Kong Governor, 22 November 1927; Paskin notes on 'loophole', 11 October 1927: all in British National Archives, File CO 129/506/3. Delevingne and Clementi notes on opium to Macao in British National Archives, File CO 129/502/10.

Clementi-Smith and Chinese Secret Society details in 'Death of Sir Cecil Clementi-Smith', *The Times*, 7 February 1916; 'Secret Societies in the Malay Peninsula', *The Times*, 28 July 1909; 'Chinese Secret Societies', *The Times*, 24 May 1889 and *The Times*, 11 June 1888; 'Secret Societies in Sarawak', *Straits Times*, 17 August 1889; and mention of Triads in *The Times*, 24 September 1889.

CHAPTER 7

Maurice Springfield quotes come from his privately published memoirs, *Hunting Opium and Other Scents* (Halesworth: Norfolk & Suffolk Publicity, 1966). Howard Humphrey case details, including his letter of 31 January 1923 to Chin See Mei in Osaka, Japan, and a Metropolitan Police CID report of 26 March 1923, are contained in British National Archives, File MEPO 3/1044; see also report in London *Pall Mall Gazette*, 15 March 1923. For an excellent recent study of the Shanghai Municipal Police, see Bickers, *Empire Made Me* (London: Allen Lane, 2003).

Report on prostitutes and other vice contained in 'Memorandum on moral situation which confronted Shanghai Defence Force during period of February–April 1927' in British National Archives, File WO 32/2526. Early pornographic film description from Lee, *The Underworld of the East* (London: Sampson Low & Co., 1935). Reference to illicit drugs stored in French Concession in Shanghai Intelligence report April–September 1926, prepared in British Consulate-General, in British National Archives, File FO 228/3291. 'Great World' quotes from Sternberg, *Fun in a Chinese Laundry* (London: Secker & Warburg, 1965).

Details of life of Fairbairn in Robins, *Gentleman & Warrior* (Harlow: CQB Publications, 2005). Fairbairn quotes from Shanghai Municipal

Police, *Manual of Self-Defence* (Shanghai: Chinese Publishing & Printing, 1915) and Fairbairn and Sykes, *Shooting to Live with the One-Hand Gun* (Edinburgh: Oliver & Boyd, 1942). Secret General Staff Intelligence report, Shanghai, entitled 'Chinese Secret Societies and Political Organisations', 18 March 1937, in British National Archives, File WO 106/5375. Description of Du from Auden and Isherwood, *Journey to a War* (New York: Random House, 1939). See also Martin, *The Shanghai Green Gang* (Berkeley: University of California Press, 1996) and Fenby, *Generalissimo* (London: The Free Press, 2003).

CHAPTER 8

Accounts of assaults on Shanghai Municipal Police by Japanese in British National Archives, File FO 371/22075. Letter from Consulate-General, Mukden, 27 January 1939, describing Japanese drug smuggling in British National Archives, File FO 371/23584. Russell Pasha quotes on Japanese from his *Egyptian Service 1902–1946* (London: John Murray, 1949). Quotes from Miner Searle Bates and American Consul on Japanese opium dealing in China from Brackman, *The Other Nuremberg* (London: Collins, 1989). Letter from British Egg Packing & Cold Storage Co., Shanghai, 24 October 1939, in British National Archives, File FO 371/24662; see also 'Shipments Said "Hijacked" by Japanese Firm', *China Press*, 28 October 1939.

Account of SMP clashes with Japanese police in 'Shanghai Despatch', 7 November 1939, and assassinations in Shanghai, 'Shanghai Summary', 28 July 1941, British National Archives, File WO 208/246A. Harbin report on Chinese bandits/partisan raid on Noho, 28 November 1939, British National Archives, File FO 371/24697. Kedrolivansky case contained in secret memorandum, 28 May 1948, British National Archives, File KV2/2306. Shanghai intelligence report on crime and gambling in Shanghai, October 1940 – March 1941, British National Archives, File WO 208/246B. Fairbairn knife quote in his *Get Tough!* (Boulder: Paladin Press, 1974 [originally *c.*1942]). Details of Inspector Hutton's torture and death in statement given by E.H. Aiers, personal assistant to the Commissioner of Police, Shanghai, to Major Stephen, Royal Marines, 2 October 1945, and other documents in British National Archives, File WO 325/58.

Chinese gangs as part of anti-Japanese resistance in Malaya described in SOE Force 136 Memorandum, 14 August 1945, File WO

203/2545, and 'Kuomintang Guerrillas in Malaya', 18 June 1945, plus 'Communist Guerrillas in North Malaya' intelligence report, 23 July 1945, File WO 203/5553, both British National Archives. Information on Peter Dobree from his obituary in *The Times*, 19 November 2004. For an account of Force 136 and British wartime behind-the-lines activities, see Trenowden, *Operations Most Secret* (Manchester: Crecy Books, 1994).

CHAPTER 9

Gangoo's story is told in the anonymously authored *She Wasn't Ashamed: Autobiography of an Indian Prostitute* (Lahore: International Publishers, 1942). See also Banerjee, *Dangerous Outcast* (Calcutta: Seagull Books, 1998) and Peers, D.M., 'Imperial vice: sex, drink and the health of British troops in North Indian cantonments, 1800–1858' in Killingray, D. and Omissi, D. *Guardians of Empire* (Manchester: Manchester University Press, 1999).

Government report on prostitution in India and Burma in 'Extent, Distribution and Regulation of the "Social Evil' in the Cities of Calcutta, Madras, Bombay and in Rangoon Town' by E.C.S. Shuttleworth, District Superintendent of Police, Rangoon, November 1919, in British National Archives, File HO 291/122. Lieutenant Colonel Osmond's letter to War Office, 6 November 1941, with supporting extract from letter describing prostitution in Singapore, in British National Archives, File CO 273/667/13. Report on enforced prostitution by Japanese Navy in Western Borneo by Captain J.N. Heijbroek, Dutch Intelligence Officer, 5 July 1946, in British National Archives, File WO 325/170.

CHAPTER 10

Accounts of Ang Bin Hoey in 'General Review of the International Situation in Malaya', HQ Malaya Command, Weekly Intelligence Review No. 27, based on information received up to 10 May 1946; telegram about attack on informant's family, based on police report, 17 January 1947; 'Secret Report on Triad, Ang Bin Hoey and Kuomintang in Malaya', 22 January 1947, all in British National Archives, File CO 537/2139. See also 'Chinese Gangsters in Malaya', *The Times*, 15 September 1947 and Comber, *The Triads* (Singapore: Talisman Publishing & Singapore Heritage Society, 2009).

Chin Peng quotes are from his memoirs in Ward, *My Side of History* (Singapore: Media Masters Pte Ltd, 2003). For story of Lai Te, see also Comber, *Malaya's Secret Police 1945–60* (Singapore: Institute of Southeast Asian Studies, 2008) and Mackay, *The Malayan Emergency 1948–60* (London: Brassey's, 1997). Onraet quotes from his memoirs, *Singapore – A Police Background* (London: Dorothy Crisp & Co., 1947); see also his obituary, *The Times*, 10 May 1952. Federation of Malaya Police quote in report of October 1957, includes also description of ranks inside Ang Bin Hoey, now in British National Archives, File FO 370/2504.

CHAPTER 11

Jack Morton quotes from his lecture 'The Co-ordination of Intelligence in the Malayan Emergency', copy in British National Archives, File KV4/408. Young's publicity gaff covered in a series of telegrams, 31 January – 1 February 1952, in British National Archives, File CO 1022/105. Physical description of Young quoted in Comber, *Malaya's Secret Police 1945–60* (Singapore: Institute of Southeast Asian Studies, 2008).

Reports of attacks on communist agent and Chinese detective from Special Branch Pan-Malayan Review of Security Intelligence, January 1953, in British National Archives, File CO 1022/210. Secret signals used in resettlement camps recorded in Malayan CID Secret Abstract of Intelligence for the period 16–31 January 1952, and captured MCP document on terrorism in Secret Abstract for 1–15 December 1951, both in British National Archives, File CO 1022/202.

Re-designation of communist bandits as terrorists in Secretary of Defence memorandum, British National Archives, File CO 1022/48. Headhunter quote from article by P.J. Dixon in *The Spectator*, 5 September 1952, and further information on Iban in radio broadcast in Kuala Lumpur, 15 March 1952, both in British National Archives, File CO 1022/57. Jack Moran quotes from his memoirs, *Spearhead in Malaya* (London: Peter Davies, 1959). Peter Guest quotes from his journals, extracts of which are published in Stewart, *Smashing Terrorism in the Malayan Emergency* (Subang Jaya: Pelanduk Publications, 2004). Roy Follows quotes from his memoirs, *The Jungle Beat* (Bridgnorth: TravellersEye Ltd, 1999).

CHAPTER 12

'Remarks of the Honourable Harry J. Anslinger, United States Representative on the United Nations Commissions on Narcotic Drugs, Eighth Session, 15 April 1953 – the Illicit Narcotic Traffic in the Far East' and subsequent British Embassy in Washington DC comments, 15 January 1954, 13 April 1954 and 29 April 1954, all in British National Archives, File FO 371/112506. For comment that British police officers in Hong Kong colluded with FBN to lie about communist Chinese opium seizures, see McWilliams, *The Protectors* (Newark: University of Delaware Press, 1990); see also Meyer and Parssinen, *Webs of Smoke* (Lanham: Rowmen & Littlefield, 1998). CIA report in Intelligence Memorandum, 'An Examination of the Charges of Chinese Communist Involvement in the Illicit Opium Trade', 9 November 1956, CIA/RR IM-438.

Report by political agent in Kuwait of incidents involving smuggling of narcotics, to Foreign Office, 19 May 1954, in British National Archives, File FO 371/112506; memorandum on drug smuggling in Kuwait, prepared by Eastern Department of the Foreign Office, 15 April 1957, in British National Archives, File FO 371/129979. Letter from Royal Afghan Embassy, London, to Foreign Office, 18 April 1957, and report from Sir John Russell, senior diplomat at British Embassy in Tehran, 21 February 1957, both in British National Archives, File FO 371/129979. Later Anslinger quotes from his *The Murderers* (London: Arthur Barker Ltd, 1962); Russell Pasha quote from *Egyptian Service 1902–1946* (London: John Murray, 1949). Excerpts from Central Narcotics Intelligence Bureau report quoted in 'Intensified Drug Traffic', *The Times*, 30 March 1948.

CHAPTER 13

Description of King David Hotel bombing in '39 Killed in Jerusalem Headquarters', *The Times*, 23 July 1946 and 'Action to Cope with Terrorists', *The Times*, 24 July 1946. Police Sergeant S.W. Mills quote and further police quotes from Horne, *A Job Well Done* (Lewes: The Book Guild, 2003). For a thorough investigation of bombing, see Clarke, T., *By Flood and Fire* (New York: GP Putnam's, 1981).

British General Staff quotes from 'History of the disturbances in Palestine 1936–1939', Jerusalem, December 1939, and description of cordon system used against Arab gangs, December 1937 to March

1938, both in British National Archives, File WO 191/88. Description of Palestine Police gendarmerie from memorandum by General Haining, 14 February 1939, and note on recruiting Sudanese by Major G.S., 16 February 1939, both in British National Archives, File WO 106/5720. Extract from British secret intelligence report on Zionism, Irgun and Stern Gang (especially their Axis link), 28 October 1941; Jewish Agency views on Irgun dissension, 28 January 1945; and A.J. Kellar's report on the Stern Gang, following his Middle Eastern visit, February 1945, all in British National Archives, File KV 5/29. 'Lord Moyne Shot', *The Times*, 7 November 1944. See also Bell, *Terror Out of Zion* (New York: St Martin's Press, 1977) and Heller, *The Stern Gang* (Ilford: Frank Cass, 1994).

Secret British intelligence report on Jewish illegal immigration, 18 July 1947, in British National Archives, File KV 3/56. Lansky quotes from Eisenberg, Dan, and Landau, *Meyer Lansky* (New York & London: Paddington Press, 1979).

CHAPTER 14

Description of the murder of PC Evan Chima and the confessions of Etuk Uku, Paul Nwaka, an Anang trader, and Udem Edem Ebo, an Idiong member, are all contained in 'The Leopard Murders and the Idiong Society', a police report written by Senior Assistant Superintendent D.S. Fountain, 3 February 1947, sent by the Governor of Nigeria to the Secretary of State for the Colonies, now in the British National Archives, File CO 583/294/4. This file also contains the British Curfew Ordinance for the Abak and Opobo Divisions of the Calabar Region, 7 December 1946.

Fountain's earlier report, 'The Leopard Murders – Review of Situation', sent by the Governor of Nigeria to the Secretary of State, 16 October 1946, is in British National Archives, File CO 583/294/4. Some of this material found its way into a newspaper article by Graham Stanford, 'The Leopard Men Strike at Dusk', London *Daily Mail*, 30 June 1947. See also '10 Leopard Men Hanged', *The Times*, 23 September 1946; Ahire, *Imperial Policing* (Milton Keynes: Open University Press, 1991); Clayton and Killingray, *Khaki and Blue* (Ohio University: Monographs in International Studies, Africa Series, No. 51, 1989).

Copy of the Mau Mau letter, threatening Lady Churchill, 15 March 1954; Colville letter to Guppy, 18 March 1954; statement of Inspector

Amey, 19 March 1954, all in British National Archives, File MEPO 2/9602. Telegram from Baring to Churchill, 7 March 1954, British National Archives, File PREM 11/696. See also 'Police Protection of Ministers', *The Times*, 19 March 1954.

CHAPTER 15

Lari and 'Mickeys' atrocity quotes from Anderson, *Histories of the Hanged* (New York & London: W W Norton & Co., 2005). Drummond quotes from Holman, *Bwana Drum* (London: WH Allen, 1964); see also Drummond's obituary in *Daily Telegraph*, 12 June 2007. For greatly contrasting accounts of Kenya Emergency, see Stoneham, *Mau Mau* (London: Museum Press, 1953) and Alao, *Mau-Mau Warrior* (Oxford: Osprey, 2006).

Rules of engagement for pseudo-gangs, Kenya Police Headquarters, 27 October 1955, and secret military report on 'Future Use of Special Forces' in Kenya, 24 November 1955, both in British National Archives, File WO 276/431. Court of Inquiry report regarding allegations of brutality against Mau Mau, including the severing of hands from dead bodies, December 1953, in British National Archives, File PREM 11/696.

CHAPTER 16

Hong Kong government 'Report on the Riots in Kowloon and Tsuen Wan, October 10th to 12th, 1956'; Sir Alexander Grantham's draft report, 6 December 1956; and further comments by A.M. MacDonald, 17 January 1957, and W.A. Muller, 18 January 1957, all in British National Archives, File CO 1030/389. Gurkha quote from McAlister, *Bugle and Kukri* (Ryde: Regimental Trust 10th Princess Mary's Own Gurkha Rifles, 1984). Descriptions of Walled City by P.H. Grattan, Private Secretary, 20 December 1973, and Dame Joan Vickers in letter to Prime Minister Edward Heath, 6 December 1973, both in British National Archives, File FCO 21/1139.

Description of 14K in security intelligence report 'Triad Societies in Hong Kong', 1962, in British National Archives, File WO 208/5183. See also Traver, H. 'Controlling Triads and organized crime in Hong Kong', *Hong Kong Journal*, 4 January 2009, and Booth, *The Dragon Syndicates* (London: Bantam Books, 2000). Secretary for Chinese Affairs report on 'The Drug Problem in Hong Kong', 7 May 1957, in

British National Archives, File CO 1030/899. Report by Arthur Maxwell, Commissioner of Police in Hong Kong, 'The traffic in narcotics between Bangkok and Hong Kong', sent to the Foreign Office, 4 April 1957, in British National Archives, File FO 371/129979.

Metropolitan Police documents regarding smuggling of drugs aboard HMS *Belfast* in 1962, including statement of ship's commander, David Anning Loram, New Scotland Yard descriptions of perpetrators and translations of incriminating letters, all contained in British National Archives, File CRIM 1/3955. See also 'Chinese from Ship on Drug Charges', *The Times*, 20 June 1962, and 'Gaol for Drug Traffickers', *The Times*, 26 July 1962.

The account by Malcolm Reed was given to the author following correspondence with Mr Reed as son.

CHAPTER 17

Copies and extracts from Probationary Police Inspector Wallace 's six letters to the Prime Minister, from 16 November 1963; letter from Prime Minister's Private Secretary, 9 December 1963; J.D. Higham's letter to Sir Robert Brown Black, Governor of Hong Kong, 31 December 1963; note for the Minister of State, 12 March 1964; and memo entitled 'Corruption in the Hong Kong Police Force ' by Hong Kong Commissioner of Police Henry Heath, 12 August 1964, all contained in British National Archives, File CO 1037/250. Thanks to Keith Lomas of the Royal Hong Kong Police Association.

Letter of complaint about Hong Kong Police corruption by Pun Ting Chau, 3 January 1974, and response of Winston Churchill MP, all contained in British National Archives, File FCO 40/555. Letters from Elsie Elliott, 30 January 1974 and 17 March 1974, plus account of ICAC in British National Archives, File FCO 40/554. Documents regarding case of Peter Godber, including Report of Commission of Inquiry, 13 June 1973, in British National Archives, File FCO 40/451. See also 'Hong Kong Court Told of Bribe for Promotion', *The Times*, 18 February 1975 and 'Chinese Woman Police Officer is Accused', *The Times*, 20 June 1975.

CHAPTER 18

Roderic Knowles's quotes from his book, How to Rob Banks Without Violence (London: Michael Joseph, 1972), and about his later life, from author interview with him. Regarding the CIA interest in his gold smuggling, Knowles claims this information came from a journalist's brother who worked for British Intelligence: 'He assured me (on several occasions) that what his brother had confided in him was absolutely true.' See also Knowles, R. *What the Hell Am I Doing on Planet Earth?* (Drogheda: Choice Publishing, 2005). Quotes on gold smuggling by ship come from Ministry of Trade and Civil Aviation report by D.G. Fagan, sent to Colonial Office, 30 May 1958, in British National Archives, File CO 1030/753.

Account of Chan Chi Fu opium battle from British Consulate in Chiang Mai, 11 August 1967, and related documents in British National Archives, File FCO 15/145. Letter from Sir David Trench on Hong Kong crime wave, 6 August 1970, and response from Sir Leslie Monson, 7 January 1971, both in British National Archives, File FCO 40/299. Report from his successor Governor of Hong Kong, Sir Murray MacLehose, entitled 'International aspects of the narcotics trade as they affect Hong Kong', addressed to British Foreign Secretary, Sir Alec Douglas-Home, 19 February 1973, accompanied by statement from Hong Kong Commissioner for Narcotics, N.G. Rolph, describing covert approach of Law Sing-hon, 23 January 1973, in British National Archives, File FCO 40/460. See also *The US Heroin Problem and Southeast Asia – Report of a Staff Survey Team of the Committee on Foreign Affairs, House of Representatives* (Washington: US Government Printing Office, 1973) and 'Chinese Jailed after Biggest Heroin Haul', *Daily Telegraph*, 19 January 1973.

Jackie Pullinger quote from her book, *Chasing the Dragon* (London: Hodder & Stoughton, 1980). Crime-free Walled City quote from 'Descriptions of Walled City' report by P.H. Grattan, 20 December 1973, British National Archives, File FCO 21/1139.

BIBLIOGRAPHY

For precise archival references to unpublished sources, newspaper and journal articles, see Notes on Sources.

Ahire, P.T. *Imperial Policing: The Emergence and Role of the Police in Colonial Nigeria* (Milton Keynes: Open University Press, 1991)

Alao, A. *Mau-Mau Warrior* (Oxford: Osprey, 2006)

Andersen-Rosendal, J. *Moon of Beauty: Women and Love in the East* (London: Museum Press Ltd, 1975)

Anderson, D. *Histories of the Hanged: The Dirty War in Kenya and the End of Empire* (New York & London: WW Norton & Co., 2005)

Anderson, D. and Killingray, D. *Policing the Empire – Government, Authority and Control, 1830–1940* (Manchester: Manchester University Press, 1999)

Anslinger, H.J. and Oursler, W. *The Murderers – the Story of the Narcotics Gangs* (London: Arthur Barker Ltd, 1962)

Ashbury, H. *The Gangs of New York* (New York: Garden City Publishing, 1927)

Auden, W.H. and Isherwood, C. *Journey to a War* (New York: Random House, 1939)

Banerjee, S. *Dangerous Outcast: The Prostitute in 19th Century Bengal* (Calcutta: Seagull Books, 1998)

Barber, N. *The War of the Running Dogs* (London: Cassell, 2004)

Bell, J.B. *Terror Out of Zion: Irgun Zvai Leumi, LEHI, and the Palestine Underground, 1929–1949* (New York: St Martin's Press, 1977)

Berridge, V. 'The Origin of the English Drug "Scene" 1890–1930', *Medical History*, 32:51–64 (London: UCL, 1988)

Bickers, R. *Empire Made Me* (London: Allen Lane, 2003)

Bishop, R. and Robinson, L.S. *Night Market: Sexual Cultures and the Thai Economic Miracle* (New York: Routledge, 1998)

Booth, M. *The Dragon Syndicates* (London: Bantam Books, 2000)

Brackman, A.C. *The Other Nuremberg – the Untold Story of the Tokyo War Crime Trials* (London: Collins, 1989)

Brown, E.A. *Indiscreet Memories: 1901 Singapore Through the Eyes of a Colonial Englishman* (Singapore: Monsoon Books, 2007)

Caroe, O. *The Pathans 550 BC–AD 1957* (London: Macmillan, 1958)

Chrysler, C.B. *White Slavery* (Chicago: Alice Shellbarger Hall, 1911)

Clarke, T., *By Flood and Fire* (New York: GP Putnam's, 1981)

Clayton, A. and Killingray, D. *Khaki and Blue: Military and Police in Colonial Africa* (Ohio University: Monographs in International Studies, Africa Series, No. 51, 1989)

Cloake, J. *Templer: Tiger of Malaya* (London: Harrap, 1985)

Comber, L. *Malaya's Secret Police 1945–60* (Singapore: Institute of Southeast Asian Studies, 2008)

Comber, L. *The Triads: Chinese Secret Societies in 1950s Malaya and Singapore* (Singapore: Talisman Publishing & Singapore Heritage Society, 2009)

Eisenberg, D., Dan, U. and Landau, E. *Meyer Lansky – Mogul of the Mob* (New York & London: Paddington Press, 1979)

Fairbairn, W.E. *Get Tough!* (Boulder: Paladin Press, 1974 [originally *c.*1942])

Fairbairn, W.E. and Sykes, E.A. *Shooting to Live with the One-Hand Gun* (Edinburgh: Oliver & Boyd, 1942)

Fenby, J. *Generalissimo: Chiang Kai-shek and the China he Lost* (London: The Free Press, 2003)

Follows, R. *The Jungle Beat* (Bridgnorth: TravellersEye Ltd, 1999)

Glenny, M. *McMafia: Seriously Organised Crime* (London: Vintage Books, 2009)

Hanes III, W.T. and Sanello, F. *The Opium Wars* (London: Robson Books, 2003)

Heller, J. *The Stern Gang* (Ilford: Frank Cass, 1994)

Holman, D. *Bwana Drum* (London: WH Allen, 1964)

Horne, E. *A Job Well Done: Being a History of the Palestine Police Force 1920–1948* (Lewes: The Book Guild, 2003)

James, L. *The Rise and Fall of the British Empire* (London: Little, Brown, 1994)

Keppel, A. *Gun-Running and the Indian North-West Frontier* (London: John Murray, 1911)

Killingray, D. and Omissi, D. *Guardians of Empire* (Manchester: Manchester University Press, 1999)

Knowles, R. *How to Rob Banks Without Violence* (London: Michael Joseph, 1972)

Kohn, M. *Dope Girls* (London: Granta, 2001)

Lee, J.S. *The Underworld of the East* (London: Sampson Low & Co., 1935)

Linstead, H.N. *Poison's Law* (London: The Pharmaceutical Press, 1936)

Mackay, D. *Eastern Customs: The Customs Service in British Malaya and the Opium Trade* (London: The Radcliffe Press, 2005)

Mackay, D. *The Malayan Emergency 1948–60* (London: Brassey's, 1997)

McAlister, Maj. Gen. R.W.L. *Bugle and Kukri* (Ryde: Regimental Trust 10th Princess Mary's Own Gurkha Rifles, 1984)

McWilliams, J.C. *The Protectors – Harry J. Anslinger and the Federal Bureau of Narcotics 1930–1962* (Newark: University of Delaware Press, 1990)

Martin, B.G. *The Shanghai Green Gang: Politics and Organised Crime 1919–1937* (Berkeley: University of California Press, 1996)

Meyer, K. and Parssinen, T. *Webs of Smoke* (Lanham: Rowmen & Littlefield, 1998)

Moran, J. *Spearhead in Malaya* (London: Peter Davies, 1959)

Morton, J. *East End Gangland* (London: Little, Brown, 2000)

Newark, T. *Lucky Luciano* (St Martin's Press: New York, 2010)

Onraet, R. *Singapore – A Police Background* (London: Dorothy Crisp & Co., 1947)

Pasha, Sir R.T. *Egyptian Service 1902–1946* (London: John Murray, 1949)

Pullinger, J. *Chasing the Dragon* (London: Hodder & Stoughton, 1980)

Robins, P. *Gentleman & Warrior: The Legend of WE Fairbairn* (Harlow: CQB Publications, 2005)

Rohmer, S. *The Mystery of Dr Fu Manchu* (London: Methuen, 1913)

Seth, R. *Russell Pasha* (London: William Kimber, 1966)

Shanghai Municipal Police, *Manual of Self-Defence* (Shanghai: Chinese

Publishing & Printing, 1915)

Sinclair, G. *At the End of the Line: Colonial Policing and the Imperial Endgame 1945–80* (Manchester: Manchester University Press, 2006)

Springfield, M. *Hunting Opium and Other Scents* (Halesworth: Norfolk & Suffolk Publicity, 1966)

Sternberg, J. *Fun in a Chinese Laundry* (London: Secker & Warburg, 1965)

Stewart, B. *Smashing Terrorism in the Malayan Emergency* (Subang Jaya: Pelanduk Publications, 2004)

Stoneham, C.T. *Mau Mau* (London: Museum Press, 1953)

Trenowden, I. *Operations Most Secret – SOE: The Malayan Theatre* (Manchester: Crecy Books, 1994)

Ward, I. *My Side of History* (Singapore: Media Masters Pte Ld, 2003)

INDEX